EXISTENTIALISM AND THE
MODERN PREDICAMENT

EXISTENTIALISM
AND THE
MODERN PREDICAMENT

F. H. HEINEMANN

GREENWOOD PRESS, PUBLISHERS
WESTPORT, CONNECTICUT

Library of Congress Cataloging in Publication Data

Heinemann, Frederick Henry, 1889-1970.
   Existentialism and the modern predicament.

   Reprint of the ed. published by Harper, New York,
which was issued as no. TB28 of Harper torchbooks.
   Bibliography: p.
   Includes index.
   1. Existentialism. I. Title.
[B819.H4 1979]   142'.7   78-14042
ISBN 0-313-21103-5

Reprinted with the permission of A & C Black Limited

Reprinted in 1979 by Greenwood Press, Inc.
51 Riverside Avenue, Westport, CT 06880

Printed in the United States of America

10 9 8 7 6 5 4 3 2 1

To the memory of
José Ortega y Gasset

PREFACE

THIS book arose from a paper entitled "What is Alive and What is Dead in Existentialism?" It was first published in the issue *L'Existentialisme devant l'Opinion Philosophique* of the *Revue Internationale de Philosophie*, July 1949, and reappeared in an enlarged German edition in the *Zeitschrift für Philosophische Forschung* (1950–51) and in Spanish in *Sur*, Buenos Aires, 1952. In its present form it is based on lectures delivered in the University of Oxford.

It is hoped that this book may be helpful to all those who, dissatisfied with a merely linguistic approach to philosophical problems, are looking for an alternative. If there is a message in these essays, it is that there are alternative modes of philosophizing, and that it does not make sense to exclude them by dogmatically adhering to a narrow and arbitrary definition of philosophy. All those who have still eyes to see for themselves will recognize that, even if one rejects the proposed solutions, the problems here discussed are real and most urgent. Though they are not eternal, they are recurrent, because their source is the condition of man. They cannot be eliminated as pseudo-problems, for they arise from life and their verification consists in being lived. A philosopher who has something to say must have lived his problems if they are existential, and he must have first-hand knowledge of them if they originate in scientific research. To-day we are faced with the central problem of finding a new mode of philosophical expression adequate to the present condition of man, and therefore a new starting-point. If this book should prove to clear the ground for this great purpose, it has not been written in vain.

My thanks are due to the editors of the above-named journals, to those of *The Hibbert Journal* and of *Philosophy*, for their permission to use the material of some of my papers published by them, and especially to Mr Christopher Baynes and to my wife for their great help in the revision of the text.

Oxford
8th February 1953

PREFACE TO THE SECOND EDITION

THIS edition has given a welcome opportunity for revising the text and bibliography. An addition has been made to Chapter XII which, I hope, will clear up certain misinterpretations concerning the alleged death of Existentialism. A paper referring to Sartre's latest development is included in an Appendix, together with new material concerning Heidegger and Marcel.

OXFORD
8th March 1954

PREFACE TO THE TORCHBOOK EDITION

The prospective reader of this new edition may well ask the following questions:

(1) What may I expect from this book?

(2) What is the relation of this edition to former editions?

(3) What is the standpoint of the author?

(4) Has the thesis of the book withstood the test of time?

(5) Where does this book lead and how are we to go on from there?

I shall attempt to answer these questions as briefly and precisely as possible.

As to the first question, it was not my intention to write one more book *about* existentialism. The book has sprung *from within* the movement. I was myself involved in it from its very beginning. It was my fate to assist at its birth, to predict its end, and to be co-actor in the drama which unfolds in these pages. This book arose out of these experiences, out of personal existential suffering, and out of acquaintance with the authors discussed. Existentialism became one of the dominant European philosophies of our century and therefore would seem to deserve attention. Moreover, its history offers an instructive example of the manner in which individuals become mere organs of their generation and have to play a specific role, sometimes against their own will. Having been implicated in this movement, I hope to be able to reveal its inner springs and central problems. Unlike most other books on the subject, however, this one is not only an introduction and report, but also a *criticism from within*. This critique is provided by the authors themselves, i.e., by their failure to base comprehensive philosophies on the principle of existence and by their final abandonment of it.

As to the second question, this book is identical with the second English edition, except for the correction of misprints and some new bibliographical notes. It is, however, not quite identical with the German and Spanish editions. These contain both more, in the historical chapters, and less, in the discussion of general problems. These differences which concern minor points but not the central thesis, arose from an adaptation of the text to the climate of thought on the continent of Europe which differs considerably from that in the Anglo-Saxon world. Both in England and in America, where positivistic, pragmatic and anti-metaphysical attitudes prevail, the utterances of existentialists are often regarded as meaningless. It is therefore by no means easy to make a philosophy derived from experiences of one continent intelligible to citizens of another continent.

For this reason I have chosen a standpoint beyond the conflicting parties. My view may be called *post-existentialist* and *meta-analytical*. I have attempted to go beyond the philosophies of existence which still predominate in Western Europe and beyond the different schools of philosophical analysis which are so influential in the Anglo-American world. The precise meaning of the term "post-existentialism" will, I hope, emerge from the final chapters of this work and from a second book, *Beyond Existentialism*, which has recently been published in German (Stuttgart: Kohlhammer 1957). As to the meaning of the term "meta-analysis," I may be allowed to refer to the papers of the same title in the *Proceedings of the XIth International Congress of Philosophy*, Vol. V (Résumé) and in the *Archivio di Filosofia* (Rome, 1955). I trust that this perspective makes it possible to see the predicaments common to the schools both of the Continent and of England and America—and, indeed, to modern man.

This book is written from the point of view of the Western world. For me, in contradistinction to Toynbee, the West is *the* World, for the simple reason that it is the free world. My perspective is, if this oversimplification be allowed, *the World* and *the East*. By "the East" in this context I do not mean "Asia." I refer to the confederation of the ideologically, socially, and economically related communist states. For years I have been haunted by one question: Does the West still possess the power of spiritual leadership to counteract the dictatorial menace of the East? For me this is not a political question—as it has been, of necessity, misunderstood by an East Berlin critic who attacks me as a "bourgeois" defender of imperialist interests and denounces the existentialists as the spearhead of a new fascist counter-revolution. This catalogue of charges may sound fantastic to Western ears, but it is a not unusual instance of decay of clear thinking in the East. My chief concern remains the battle of the minds.

For this reason I have asked: Are the existentialists the spiritual leaders of our time? My answer that they are not has meanwhile been confirmed by Sartre. In his autobiography, now in progress, of which only a brief fragment has been published in English translation, Sartre proclaims himself a Marxist and declares that "Marxism is an all-inclusive whole reflecting our age" and that "no one can go beyond it." [1] This is a capitulation to the East and confirms the dissolution of his own version of existentialism.

I do not wish to anticipate here my answer to the fifth question: Where does this book lead and how are we to go on from there? The three closing chapters are reserved for that purpose. I would like only to express my conviction that the answer is of importance to religion and theology. Even if the "principle of existence" as currently formulated should prove inadequate as a basis for existentialist systems, it may continue to play a considerable role as a regulative principle. The present discussion of existentialism and religion confirms this.

As to the principle of *inner* response which I have proposed as an alternative to that of existence, I beg the

[1] Cf. *The Listener*, London, 1957, p. 915.

reader not to misinterpret it in a naturalistic manner. Such a misunderstanding will, I trust, be made impossible by my book *Beyond Existentialism*.

I have always admired C. S. Peirce for his humble attitude of "fallibilism," in his own words, "the doctrine that our knowledge is never absolute but always swims, as it were, in a continuum of uncertainty and of indeterminacy," although I would not have made a "doctrine" out of it. We are all fallible and I am bound to have made mistakes which the reader is asked to correct. But mistakes may be fruitful and therefore in the pragmatist sense of Peirce and James, "true." If it was a mistake to call Heidegger an existentialist, it was almost providential, extremely fruitful and of great consequence.

In order not to misunderstand the tendency of the book the reader should persevere to the end. Then he will understand my intention to find a way out of the existentialist crisis and a secure foundation for a new philosophy. All those, however, who bemoan this constant rise and fall of philosophies and are inclined to draw pessimistic conclusions from it, should remember Hegel's words: "It is of the essence of the Spirit to suffer death and, nevertheless, to remain alive."

October, 1957   F.H.H.

ACKNOWLEDGMENTS

FOR permission to print in this book extracts from works still in copyright the author thanks Geoffrey Bles for N. Berdyaev's *Dream and Reality*; Dennis Dobson for Solovyev's *Lectures on Godmanhood*; Victor Gollancz for K. Jaspers's *Way to Wisdom*; G. Marcel's *Homo Viator*; The Harvill Press for G. Marcel's *The Philosophy of Existence* and *The Mystery of Being*; Harcourt Brace & Company Inc. for *The Republic of Silence* (copyright 1947 by A. J. Liebling); Routledge & Kegan Paul Ltd. for K. Jaspers's *The Perennial Scope of Philosophy* and L. Wittgenstein's *Tractatus Logico-Philosophicus*; Vision Press Ltd. for M. Heidegger's *Existence and Being*; Oxford University Press for S. Kierkegaard's *Concluding Unscientific Postscript*, translated by D. F. Swenson, *The Present Age*, translated by Alexander Dru and Walter Lowrie, and *The Journals of Sören Kierkegaard*, edited and translated by Alexander Dru. If not otherwise indicated, the translations are those of the author.

CONTENTS

I. THE PROBLEM

So many books and papers on Existentialism are published nowadays, that anyone who takes part in the discussion has first of all to present his credentials and to specify the point of view from which he wishes to discuss this topic.

I write as someone who has experienced at first hand the rise of this movement in Germany, its transplantation to France, and its recent reception in the Anglo-Saxon world. In 1929 I published a book, *Neue Wege der Philosophie*, in which I introduced the term *Existenzphilosophie*; and to my knowledge I was the first to describe this phenomenon. I interpreted the whole modern philosophy from Descartes to the present time as being based on the antithetical principles of discursive reason (*ratio*) and life. I understood "existence" as a new principle which aims at overcoming the onesidedness of the rationalist as well as irrationalist philosophies, and which, instead of starting with Descartes' *cogito*, in its double meaning as consciousness and thought, begins with the subject standing in a threefold relationship with man, the Universe and God. "The person responding to or being interdependent with man, the Universe and God, is the key for the interpretation of the human world, of History, and of the Universe itself." This starting with man as a being-within-the-world seemed and still seems to me sound. It allows us to avoid the fallacy of isolation, which takes elements as isolated although they have meaning only in interrelation with other elements. Instead of cutting off consciousness and its elements from an external world, this new philosophy starts with man as a responding being. This enables us to eliminate pseudo-problems arising from the faulty isolation of consciousness, such as the problem of the existence of the external world. It is not only logically impossible to *prove*, with Descartes, or to *disprove*, with Berkeley, the existence of material objects, the problem is meaningless; it simply does not arise except on faulty assumptions. I do not for a moment pretend that this interpretation has been accepted as valid by those existentialists who published their books after 1929. But it still stands, and it seems to be, if not the *terminus a quo*, the *terminus ad quem* of this whole movement.

I can say this, because existentialism has meanwhile turned full circle; a fact which makes its reinterpretation attractive. Kierkegaard protested against Hegel's all-comprehensive World-Mind in which the individual disappeared like a wave in the sea. He introduced existence as a specifically religious category, meaning by it the single, finite, responsible, simple, suffering and guilty creature, who has to make a decision in face of God and who consequently is more interested in ethical questions and in salvation than in abstract speculations. "Existence" here refers, in a religious sense, to the Self of man who grasps eternity in an instant (*Augenblick*) and falls into utter despair if he loses eternity and overrates the temporal. It opens a new way to the Transcendent; man stands again before God; but he remains the single one, the person who is separated from his fellow-men and from the Universe. Jaspers and Heidegger translated these religious terms into philosophical concepts and secularized them. Heidegger arrived at an agnostic position, whereas Sartre and Camus are openly atheistic. But these terms have now been retranslated into religious language by Gabriel Marcel, Nicolas Berdyaev and Martin Buber. Jaspers, in his latest publications, moves in the same direction. The Personalist Emmanuel Mounier, in his spirited account of *Existentialist Philosophies*, defends the thesis that every type of Existentialism develops a dialectic of conversion, swinging between the poles of existence lost and existence regained, and that therefore, whether Christian or Atheistic, Existentialism marks a return of the religious element into the world. This is doubtless an overstatement; but it is true that the way of existentialism has led from religion through agnosticism and atheism back to religion. It seems as if the chief possibilities of this standpoint have been explored, and that therefore the time for its reassessment has come. This reconsideration is imperative, because existentialism has become fashionable and is in danger of being dismissed before its deeper motives are understood. We have therefore to ask: What is alive and what is dead in existentialism?

But what is existentialism? Its representative or expressive value cannot be doubted. It represents one of the essential forms of West European philosophy in the age of European collapse. German *Existenzphilosophie*, French *Existentialisme* and Italian *Esistenzialismo*, though profoundly differing in form and content, have this in common —that they arise in the wake of national catastrophes. But what are they? Are they, as the Marxists say, last desperate attempts of a declining bourgeoisie, which just before its definite submergence clings to an overemphasized individualism as to a life-belt? Or are they, on the contrary, an expression of genuine philosophizing, a protest, a movement of spiritual resistance against the pseudo-philosophies of the totalitarian world-views of the bolshevists and the fascists? Or are they attempts which, however, have already failed in that part of Europe which has been submerged by the floods of the Russian Eurasia, and whose fate in Western Europe depends on the political developments of the next decades? And if there is something genuine in these attempts, shall we in the Western hemisphere allow it to wither away, only because this movement has become the fashion of the day?

2

"But," someone may object, "is not the very question with which you start ambiguous? What do you mean by 'alive' and 'dead'? If we call a plant or an animal 'alive' we know where we are. It is a descriptive term which may be very difficult to define; and in some cases, which lie on the borderline of organic and inorganic matter, *e.g.* of a virus, it may not be easy to decide whether

to call it 'alive' or not.   But if you call a thought 'living'
and a problem a 'life issue', do you not simply mean that
it has some relevance to our present position, *i.e.* to our
interests, needs and wants; that is to say, are you not
using the term, I would not say, with an emotive meaning,
but in any case implying some sort of evaluation?"   To
this I venture to reply: It is quite true that the term
"alive" has different meanings.   First, a descriptive meaning.   If we call a body alive which shows activity, organization, and a more or less stable form which remains the
same in spite of continuous renewal of matter, we may, in
an analogous manner, call a thought alive which is able to
produce activity and to organize certain forms of behaviour,
i.e. to move people either to feel, or to think, or to act in a
specific manner.   The mediæval problem whether angels
are male or female no longer moves us in any way because
we no longer believe in angels.   This issue is dead because
it has no meaning for us.   And this is the second meaning
of the term.   A problem or a theory is alive if it is felt as
meaningful or significant.

Some Logical Positivists are inclined to maintain that
existentialism is dead because its problems and utterances
are meaningless.   Exactly this is said by Professor Ayer
concerning Heidegger's and Sartre's metaphysics.   With
reference to Heidegger's statement, *das Nichts nichtet*, and
Sartre's proposition, *le Néant est néantisé*, he remarks:
"Whatever may be the affective value of these statements,
I cannot but think that they are literally nonsensical!"
"What is called existentialist philosophy," he concludes,
"has become very largely an exercise in the art of mis-
using the verb 'to be'." [1]   It is evident (1) that not all the
statements of these people can be meaningless, and (2)
even if some of their statements were meaningless, this
would by no means imply that their problems are meaningless.   Moreover, the contention of the Logical Positivists that all metaphysical propositions are meaningless
is itself meaningless, for it is based on a faulty classification
of genuine propositions into empirical and *a priori* proposi-

[1] "Novelist-Philosophers V, Jean-Paul Sartre," *Horizon*, vol. **xii**,
no. 67, 1945.

tions. This classification is arbitrary and by no means exhaustive.[1] On the other hand, I agree with the Logical Positivists that it has to be our task to cut out the meaningless propositions as dead wood.

I further agree that there is a third meaning of the term "alive", which implies a reference to an act of evaluation or to a judgment of value. "Alive" is here equivalent to "deserving of interest", "fruitful", "leading on to new problems or methods", or "likely to be of some help either in the elucidation of our position or in the practical solution of our problems". This indeed is the most important sense of the word, and in this sense we shall attempt to find out whether there is anything alive in Existentialism. It may be that it is based on a specific experience, and that it appears alive to those who share it and dead to those who do not. Therefore it may be difficult to reach agreement concerning our issue in any one of the three senses of the word "alive".

For this reason we have to move on to a higher level which transcends Logical Positivism. We appeal to a tribunal before which the competing schools of our time, including Logical Positivism, Marxism and Neothomism, have to defend themselves. Certainly the existentialists would be enormously alive if they were the spiritual leaders of our time. For in this case they would not only move us to certain actions, but point the way out of our darkness, and they would make a new form of life possible. Therefore we formulate a second question which in a corresponding form has to be addressed also to the other schools: "Are the existentialists spiritual leaders of our time?"

3

If we wish to answer this question we have first of all to define what we mean by a spiritual leader. I regard the problem of spiritual leadership in an age of disbelief as one

---

[1] Cf. my papers, "Truths of Reason and Truths of Fact," *The Philosophical Review*, September 1948; "Vérités de Raison et Vérités de Fait," *Proceedings Tenth International Congress of Philosophy*, Amsterdam, 1949; "Verdades de Razon y Verdades de Hecho," *Notas y Estudios de Filosofía*, I, 2, 1949.

of the most important of the moment. It arises because those who should lead the younger generation have either lost the gift for leadership or do not see that it matters. This is true of ministers, philosophers, poets and artists. One example may illustrate this fact. When I recently published a paper on this topic,[1] a Vicar of the Church of England wrote me a four-page letter, but only to tell me that no leader was necessary at the moment, "that the one increasing need for man is to *hope* for the spiritual leader to come. When we see man prepared to stake his life on faith in God through Christ, the Kingdom of Heaven will be just round the corner—where as a matter of fact it has always been, if we could but turn the corner". I wonder how these good tidings will be received by the millions of displaced and persecuted persons for whom in fact hell has been just round the corner. The Universities by no means fill the gap. On the contrary, the still prevailing positivistic and linguistic mood of the philosophers and the mass of unco-ordinated knowledge of the special sciences leaves the souls of the students empty, who naturally turn elsewhere for guidance. Otherwise Sartre could never have gained his enormous influence in France and in the whole world. If we now want to know whether his leadership is genuine or spurious, we have to know what a spiritual leader is. Everything depends here on our asking the right questions.[1] We may ask: What are the essential qualities required of a leader? This is the traditional approach which may be called individualistic, aristocratic and isolating, because it concentrates on the "great man" in isolation from the field in which he acts. The "hero", however, does not exist in this isolation. We have therefore to go on to a deeper level by asking: What is the *function* of a leader in human society? And what is his relation to the field in which he acts? In fact, he has always to fulfil specific functions in relation to the members of the group. He has to bring light into their darkness, order into the chaos of their experience, to discover meaning, to make them feel and understand what was incom-

---

[1] *Cf.* my paper, "Spiritual Leadership in an Age of Disbelief," *Hibbert Journal*, October 1951. I use a few passages of that paper.

prehensible to them, to distinguish the essential from the inessential, the valuable from the valueless, and to show them the direction in which they should walk and what they should do. He must have the capacity for imparting his vision of truth to others and for inducing them to choose a specific way of life.

All this becomes rather complicated and beset with difficulties in an age of disbelief in spirit and spiritual values. Spiritual leadership is based on a response of spirit to spirit; but what happens if there is no response, or if there is no spirit to respond? Indeed, people no longer believe that there is spirit, or that they have a mind, or that there is objective truth. Does not any attempt at spiritual leadership break down because it cannot be exercised *in vacuo*? In fact, the leader is dependent on the concrete historical conditions of his specific society, which we may call his "field"; and if we want to answer the question, we have to introduce a new hypothesis, *i.e.* that leadership is a field-phenomenon, and a new theory, the field-theory of leadership. Leadership arises in a specific field and therefore varies from field to field. A leader does not exist in isolation as a "great man", but depends on the field in which he operates. Just as a magnet in an electro-magnetic field attracts, on the one hand, the iron-filings, and, on the other hand, is determined in its direction by the forces of the electro-magnetic field, so the leader attracts his followers and is nevertheless determined by their unconscious or conscious desires to a higher degree than he himself realizes. In certain cases he may even be said to represent an integration of the forces of the field. Surely his position is far more complicated than that of a magnet; he is not a mere physical object which is forced by the field into a specific direction. To a certain degree he remains free to choose his way, and in so doing he transcends the field. He is determined by the field, just as the latter is influenced by him. The manner of this interdependence, however, changes from field to field. His dependence on the field may increase or decrease, and *vice versa*. Every disturbance of the forces, and every ensuing deformation of the structure of the field, is accompanied by a corresponding disturbance and deformation in the behaviour of the "leader". It is our fate to pass through an epoch of field-deformation, which is unmistakably expressed in contemporary art, and our dictators are "deformed leaders". The "age of disbelief" is therefore an age of "disturbed or deformed belief".

On the basis of this hypothesis we may distinguish the following possible types of spiritual leaders. First, the field-influencing leader; secondly, the field-dependent leader, according to which of these two factors prevail. True leadership, we feel, will be more recognized in the first than in the second case. The field-dependent leader is essentially immanent in it, whereas the field-determining leader transcends the limits of the present situation. This transcendence may be merely tentative. Someone may clear the ground and explore the possibilities which still remain open without making an exclusive decision for one of them. He represents the third type, the field-exploring or scouting leader. He is more of a potential than a real leader, because the latter really shows the way out of the dilemma. Further, there may be a man who cashes in on the contemporary bewilderment and who uses all the means at his disposal, such as suggestive power, mystification and propaganda, apparently in order to advertise his new way of life, in fact, however, in order to acquire power or to extract money from his pupils. He claims to possess knowledge which he has not got, and to lay the foundation of a new science which is no science. He is the representative of the fourth type, the situation-exploiting pseudo-leader. Sartre's *bon mot: L'existentialisme—c'est ce qui me procure l'existence,* brings him dangerously near to this type. There is a fifth type, the founder of a sect. He influences the field by narrowing it and by concentrating on specific points. Acclaimed by his followers as the Messiah, he will be rejected by the majority. He succeeds only when his endeavour does not lead into a blind alley.

4

If we want to give a precise answer to the question whether or not the existentialists are spiritual leaders of our time, we have to know whence and whither they attempt to lead us. Their point of departure is the fact and problem of alienation, their aim the liberation from estrangement. This rather complicated problem of central importance points to facts, but also to their interpretation. Alienation is a fact. There exists a feeling of estrangement in modern man which has considerably increased during the last hundred years. It is connected with certain changes in human society, with the agglomeration of millions of people in great cities cut off from Nature, with the Industrial Revolution, and with the collectivizing trend bound up with machine production. The prophets of woe, like the American R. Seidenberg, tell us that this trend must lead in any society, whether democratic, fascist or socialist, inexorably to a condition of total crystallization in its structural edifice and to a final depersonalization of man.[1] The facts to which the term "alienation" refers are, objectively, different kinds of dissociation, break or rupture between human beings and their objects, whether the latter be other persons, or the natural world, or their own creations in art, science and society; and subjectively, the corresponding states of disequilibrium, disturbance, strangeness and anxiety. We should, however, be clear about the fact that, whenever we talk of alienation, a specific interpretation is implied which is based on certain assumptions varying from person to person and, as we shall see presently, from thinker to thinker. But there is one point common to all of them, *i.e.* the belief that a preceding unity and harmony has been transformed into disunity and disharmony.

In fact, alienation is a multi-dimensional phenomenon, psychological, psychopathological and sociological, for it concerns the individual as well as the group. The rôle it plays in psychopathology may be gathered from the fact

[1] *Post-historic Man*, Oxford, 1951.

that the French term *aliénation* generally denotes profound mental disturbances. Alienation from God is a religious problem, and estrangement from Nature a metaphysical one.

Hegel was the first of the great philosophers to treat this problem seriously. He coined the terms *Entäusserung* (externalization), *Entfremdung* (alienation), *Selbstentfremdung* (self-estrangement) and *Vergegenständlichung* (objectification), and gave them a specifically philosophic connotation. He has two different discussions of the problem. Within the *Phenomenology of Mind* he devotes a whole chapter to "Spirit in Self-estrangement: Culture". I cannot enter into a detailed analysis of this chapter, but the following points must be mentioned. Hegel starts with the assumption that reality is essentially spiritual, and he therefore refers estrangement primarily to the mind. Man as a spiritual being, or in Hegel's language, the mind produces what we call culture and civilization. His own creations, works of art, religions, philosophies, science, law and the state become members of new realms of the objective or of the absolute mind. In creating these worlds man loses his soul and lives in imaginary realms. His creations, embodiments of his own mind, are in a certain sense outside him, and yet they form somehow part of his own self. Shakespeare's Hamlet, *e.g.*, has acquired an existence independent of the poet, and nevertheless Hamlet is Shakespeare. This alienation, Hegel maintains, pervades the whole sphere of culture. He has a special sub-chapter on "Language as the Actuality of Alienation or of Culture". He refers here in the first place to spoken language, to the Self which expresses itself in words; these words acquire a sort of alien existence, independent of the Self, and this is true also of written language. Language is our creation, but our words, propositions, statements, exclamations or imperatives somehow form a realm of their own, cut off from the speaker or writer. They belong, and do not belong, to him. This is a point of topical interest. If Hegel is right, if Language represents a specific mode of self-estrangement, then we have to ask ourselves whether the preoccupation with language as language, so prevalent in our time, is not an expression of the very estrangement which we are discussing.

So far Hegel dealt merely with human creation, but surprisingly he encounters the same fact in every sort of creation, in that exercised by Nature as well, as in the creation of Nature by God or by the Mind. Here alienation becomes of central importance and reaches metaphysical dignity. Seeing that the Absolute in Hegel's system is Spirit or Reason (*Vernunft*), Nature itself is defined as "self-estranged spirit". *Die Natur ist der sich-entfremdete Geist.* If God, as Mind, has created Nature, he has created it as something alien to himself. In other words, Nature is Mind or the "Idea" in the form of other-ness (*Anderssein*). This is a most interesting speculation. One might argue that Hegel puts everything upside down. We human beings have reached the stage of estrangement from Nature in the enormous capitals of the West; but Hegel, instead of interpreting the fact of our estrangement from Nature, transforms it into a metaphysical estrange-ment of Nature from Mind. Everything seems thus turned upside down. If, however, one concedes Hegel the right to make his own assumptions and to start with the priority of the Mind, one sees that he points to a specific phenomenon which one could call "creative alienation", namely to the fact that in every act of creation an element of estrangement is implied. It is bound to emerge in the parent-child relationship as well as in any sort of spiritual and intellectual creation.

This fact of estrangement is so central in Hegel's thought that his whole system is based on it. The Mind has to return from the stage of self-alienation to itself, *i.e.* to an absolute knowledge of itself. The absolute Idea or Reason enters the stage of self-alienation in Nature and returns from this estrangement to itself as Mind. Its self-development begins with the abstract element of thought, goes on to Nature, and returns to itself as Mind. In a dialectical movement the Logic forms the thesis, the Philosophy of Nature the antithesis, and the Philosophy of Mind the synthesis. In this circular movement the liberation from alienation, which later on became a central motive in Existentialism, forms an important element.

Karl Marx was quick in grasping the central rôle of alienation. In his early writings, *e.g.* in *Nationalökonomie und Philosophie* (1844), he accepted Hegel's conception, but transformed it at once from an "alienation of creativity" into an "alienation of productivity", corresponding to his replacement of idealism by materialism. Now it is not the Mind, but man who becomes alienated. In the process of alienation and in the return to himself man becomes man, and not, as in Hegel's case, mind becomes mind. Marx interpreted Hegel as if he meant that labour forms the essence of creativity, and that man is the result of his labour, albeit of his intellectual labour. He replaced this by manual labour and translated Hegel into the language of political economy. The division of labour now becomes the basis of alienation and the worker himself self-estranged, a commodity which he has to sell on the labour market. The aim is therefore the return of the worker or of the proletarian to himself from this self-estrangement; this, however, is only possible through revolution. The "alienation of productivity" is transformed into the "alienation of labour", and therefore into the "alienation of classes" or into the class struggle. On the basis of these assumptions, Marx interpreted the history of his time and, in a broader sense, the history of capitalism as the history of the self-alienation of man which had to be overcome by the proletarian revolution.

Existentialism arose because the solutions proposed by Hegel and Marx proved ineffective for overcoming the fact of alienation. On the contrary, they rather seemed to aggravate the process of estrangement. Hegel's all-embracing world-mind seemed to absorb the individual, his personality and self. On the other hand, Marx' proletarian revolution brought about the dictatorship of the proletariat and the totalitarian state which crushed the liberty of the individual and endangered the integrity of the person. The two world wars have brought about the danger of European self-destruction, and the atom bomb threatens the very existence of man. The fact that Existentialism arose as a reaction to Hegelianism and Marxism implies that it has something in common with them, namely the desire to overcome the alienation of man. All three of them want to liberate man from his self-estrangement. Though fundamentally different in particulars, their ways are similar. Since, however, existentialism responds to a different challenge, its starting-point is different. It is neither Hegel's Mind nor Marx' material production, but the fact of alienation itself.[1] And the existentialists are by no means as sure as Hegel and Marx were of their ability to overcome it.

[1] The reality of alienation may be strikingly illustrated by the most interesting case of George Santayana, the Spaniard who grew up in America. He experienced it as a personal fate. The feeling of being *a stranger by nature* as well as by accident grew upon him in a world which he saw moving towards chaos and universal triviality. He felt, however, his personal experience to be only a special case of the alienation suffered by the spirit on this earth. He knew that it is "the fate of all spirit to live in a special body and a special age, and yet, for its vocation and proper life to be addressed from that centre to all life and to all being". Cf. *The Philosophy of Santayana*, edited by I. Edman (Constable, 1953), p. 895.

II. BEYOND TECHNOLOGY?

I

"THE century of technological revolution" would seem to be a title more adequate to the present age than "the century of the common man". For the first time in history technology has acquired a central and dominant position in human life. That this was not always the case may be illustrated by the fact that the historians of the past, with very few exceptions, neglected technology, and that a history of technology does not yet exist. The joint editor of a future "History of Technology," Charles Singer, reminds us that the articulation of five hundred thousand years of such a history would by no means coincide with the traditional scheme of our general history which covers merely five thousand years. Five events would divide such a history into six periods, namely "the rise of the Neolithic culture about 10,000 B.C.; the Urban Revolution round about 3500 B.C.; the rise of the Ancient Empires about 3000 B.C. and the introduction of metals and of writing soon after 3000 B.C.; the decline of the Ancient Empires (and the rise of the Far East) about 500 B.C.; and the rise of Experimental Science round about A.D. 1500".[1] It would seem, however, as if a sixth event, *i.e.* the technological revolution of our time, marked the beginning of a new epoch of no lesser significance than the Urban Revolution. Whereas Europe's predominance since about 1500 was based on the development of her science, the technological revolution of the twentieth century coincides with the rise of America and Eurasia. We witness, in fact, a world-wide technological revolution, for the technological progress in our age has been greater and quicker than that in the last two thousand years. We have mastered the air; we have reduced distance on this planet to insignificance; we have discovered new "island universes" and extra-galactic systems; we have penetrated

[1] *Technology and History* (Oxford, 1952), p. 15.

the world of the atom, released its enormous energies and constructed the atom bomb. These facts have simultaneously revolutionized the life of human societies. The social and political revolutions of our time differ from all preceding revolutions, in that they arise from the change in economic conditions brought about by the development of technics and industry, and that they owe their inauguration, their efficiency and, alas, their cruelty to the application of technological knowledge. In those societies which were lucky enough to escape these revolutions the impact of technics on their life was no less profound.

Suddenly we find ourselves face to face with the machines which we have created. They are our children; on the one hand similar to us, like the electronic brain which competes with us in calculating; on the other more foreign to us than a work of art or the products of manual labour. As automata they seem to move according to their own laws, helpful as long as we control them, but menacing as soon as they get out of hand. Here therefore a new phenomenon arises which I should like to call *technological alienation*. Hegel, as we saw, stressed the fact of *creative alienation* which arises out of the creative work of any mind. It referred to the creations of man in art, philosophy, science, law, and politics, but also to Nature as a creature of the Divine Mind. In all these cases, Hegel held, an estrangement arises between the creative mind and its creations. Marx understood Hegel's thought very well, but translated Hegel's idealistic creative alienation into a materialistic *productive alienation* or into the alienation of labour. He wanted to overcome this alienation with the help of the proletarian revolution. Technological alienation is, as we shall see, of a somewhat different type. It is determined by the characteristics of technics.

2

Technology derives its enormous power from its double origin in practice and theory. Practice came first. Originally therefore the term "technics" meant "the totality of well-defined manipulations and procedures by which certain results are achieved". Here it is almost identical with skill, which was able to reach a surprisingly high standard with hardly any scientific foundations. At a second stage, rules were abstracted from these activities, formulated and handed on to others. Here therefore the term "technics" was applied to "a body of rules which govern such a production". At a third stage, scientific reflection and calculation precede action; and correspondingly the term "technics" now means "a body of scientific methods applied to work or to the production of goods and of tools". Singer holds that in our own time *Technology* has become almost synonymous with *Applied Science*, but, as in all cases of "almost synonymous terms", they remain different. In the nineteenth century technology became an instrument for dominating and exploiting Nature, together with its forces and products, in the interest of human needs. Even to-day it is defined as such in most German books. It is, however, characteristic of the twentieth century that the same methods are applied to the exploitation of human forces in the interests of the State and of the ruling class. In so far as it arose from practice, technology has proved to be amazingly stable, and has rightly been called one of the oldest and most conservative of human institutions. On the other hand, as based on scientific calculation, it is full of unlimited possibilities and is potentially revolutionary. Its revolutionary potentialities increase the more the techniques for the production of goods are supplemented by those for the production of tools, and further by the production of machines which again may be tool-producing. The machines demand a specific type of knowledge, the *know how*, and a specific type of organization to handle them.

The production of tools became so important in the modern era that Franklin defined man as the tool-making animal. Marx accepted this definition and added:

> The use and creation of tools characterizes the human mode of work (*Arbeitsprozess*). . . . The epochs of economic production are differentiated, not in terms of *what* is made, but in terms of *how* it is made, *i.e.* with what tools. . . .

> Tools are not only the measuring rod of the development of human capacity for work, but also indicate the social conditions under which work is done. . . . They are, so to say, new organs added to those of the body.[1]

We should, however, never forget that tools are means to an end. If tool-making becomes the primary end, the means prevail over the end. Singer adds that man is a maker of words and of tools, and that "he did not greatly improve his tools until he had advanced sufficiently in constructing a language, that is in the technology of making symbols".[2] This remark is not strictly correct, because most words grow and are not made, but it is nevertheless interesting because in our time words, which are a means for expressing and communicating feelings, thoughts, etc., are discussed as if they were the primary end.

Words, tools and machines have the natural tendency to become independent of their creator and to appear as foreign to him. Thence it follows that technological alienation as such is not novel. It comes into prominence to-day because of the all-pervasive influence of technology. No one can evade it. Aeroplane, car, radio and press disturb even the solitude of the hermit. A new attitude, *i.e.* a technological approach, takes possession of every man, and school children are likely to know more about motor-cars and aeroplanes than their teachers. The progressive mechanization of life is, however, self-stultifying. It leads to frustration, which may be experienced any day in the endless delays in the world capitals during rush hours, caused by the number of cars and by the mechanical traffic controls.

3

The important point is that both the spirit of technology and its frustration penetrate our behaviour whether we notice it or not. Thereby the arts, architecture, painting, music, literature, and also philosophy are profoundly

[1] *Das Kapital* (2nd ed., 1872), vol. i, pp. 165–166.
[2] *L.c.*, p. 9.

transformed. This brings about a simplification of their problems, but at the same time a loss in substance. My thesis is that, with some notable exceptions, most contemporary artists and philosophers have become, partially or totally, technicians, and that we are all in danger of suffering the same fate. What then is the difference between art and technics? The artist uses techniques and technical skills as a means to an end, whereas a technician adores them as ends in themselves. The artist uses his material in order to create a whole. He gives new life to it, inspires and animates it. The technician, on the other hand, is satisfied if he arranges his tones or his colour-patches according to specific rules. He has pleasure in constructing as such without taking into account whether or not a meaningful whole arises to be enjoyed by ordinary people. He may even use his technical rules as a criterion for right and wrong in his craft, despising or rejecting whatever does not comply with them. Of course, these differences are not absolute. No one is always merely a technician or merely an artist, but in certain periods and works the technician dominates the artist. Moreover, we must be very careful in order to avoid injustice. An artist is bound to be a technician. Skill and craftsmanship are of the utmost importance to him. If Stravinsky endorses Tschaikovski's saying: "I wanted to be an artisan, just as a shoemaker is", he is on the right track. Natural craftsmanship in the service of art is indispensable, but as soon as artificial techniques claim the place of art, the end of art proper is near.

Among the musicians Arnold Schoenberg perhaps offers the clearest example of a great and original musician who profoundly influenced the music of his time, in whom in the end the technician got the better of the artist. He knew quite well that there is no technique without invention, and that invention must create its own technique. He even believed that "music conveys a prophetic message revealing a higher form of life towards which mankind evolves". Nevertheless, experimenting with the atonal system and using his twelve-tone technique, in his last period he consciously constructed his music on the principle of the emancipation of the dissonance. This gave to dissonances a status equal to that of the consonances in classical music. He claimed to have laid the foundation "for a new procedure in musical construction which seemed fitted to replace those structural differentiations provided formerly by tonal harmonies". According to this method a special set of twelve tones has to be invented for every new composition. He succeeded in basing a whole opera, *Moses and Aaron*, solely on one set. "Nothing is given by this method", he confessed, "but much is taken away." We cannot help asking, Is not art proper taken away? Has not the technician, constructor, mathematician and engineer frustrated the artist? In any case, his work offers an excellent example of technological alienation. After all, his music is of our time, and nevertheless these last creations remain alien to the majority of people. The same is true of some works of the second great contemporary musical reformer, Igor Stravinsky, though his case is far more complicated. In search of a style he experiments, like his friend Picasso, with different styles. An enormously gifted born composer, for whom composition is a daily function which he feels compelled to discharge, he is an excellent craftsman who sometimes becomes an artificial technician. As an anti-Romantic he shuns ideas and emotions and believes in absolute music; therefore he disregards the literary significance of words and sentences and is merely interested in the metrical or rhythmical structure they serve.

This offers a striking parallel to the experimental writing of Gertrude Stein, who was also a friend of Picasso. Possessed by a passion for exactitude in the description of outer and inner reality, she produced a simplification of language combined with the destruction of associational emotion in poetry and prose. She hated sentences, and her words became intellectual constructions disengaged from their conventional groupings. One example from her *Tender Buttons* may suffice:

> The care with which the rain is wrong and the green is wrong and the white is wrong, the care with which there is a chair and plenty of breathing. The care with which there

is incredible justice and likeness, all this makes a magnificent asparagus, and also a fountain.

Could one wish for a more striking example of technological alienation? The technician has here frustrated the artist to such a degree that the natural meaning of words and sentences is lost. Donald Sutherland attempts to persuade us that the pattern of words may be significant apart from their actual meaning. The point is, however, that these utterances are a true mirror of the twentieth century where, as she says, everything cracks, everything is destroyed, and everything isolates itself. Gertrude Stein once said that the difference between her writing and that of the insane was that you could go on reading her. But what an age! Intellectuals write like lunatics and lunatics claim to reveal profound wisdom!

4

Within philosophy the same problem presents itself in a somewhat different form. Thinking needs certain techniques. Otherwise it would remain "a train of thought unguided" (Hobbes). It is well known that Descartes and the inaugurators of Modern Philosophy began with a search for a method. Descartes believed that there was truth worth searching for, that it was to be found in the sciences, that it was indubitable, and that certain rules could be formulated for finding it. He abstracted these rules from his own mathematical work and adopted them in his philosophy. To-day this science of methodology is replaced by a kind of technology, *i.e.* a doctrine of the tools of thought and of the machinery of thought, which should enable us to achieve our results quicker and with greater certainty.

"We may look at thinking, as we may", says Vaihinger, "we may compare it with calculation or with the performance of a machine, we cannot uphold the ordinary view that thought is an end in itself; thought serves something else, and all its particular functions are to be regarded from the point of view of mechanical means of thought." [1]

---

[1] *Die Philosophie des Als Ob*, p. 181.

In this vein his *Philosophy of "As If"* stresses the importance of fictions as tools of our thought.

Within contemporary empiricist schools, whether they are called Logical Positivists, Logical Empiricists, Scientific Empiricists, or Analysts, the trend towards establishing the pre-eminence of the technician is paramount. Bertrand Russell claims that the new empiricism surpasses the old one in that it has "a special method of construction, namely, mathematical logic". "Mathematical Logic makes it possible, as it never was before, to see what is the outcome, for philosophy, of a given body of scientific doctrine, what entities must be assumed, and what relations between them." Russell is such a rich personality, indeed one of the richest and most all-embracing philosophers of our time, that it would be preposterous to call him a mere technician. It is nevertheless true that his lasting contributions to philosophy rest on his logical engineering in the *Principles of Mathematics* and the *Principia Mathematica.* His technical improvements of Symbolic Logic are of the first order—*e.g.* the construction of a new symbolism, the introduction of propositional functions, his theory of description, his theory of types and his application of Ockham's razor—but they cannot be discussed here. They are far more important than his untenable identification of logic and mathematics. As a philosopher, Russell is essentially a logician, and once expressed the opinion that all philosophical problems were at bottom of a logical nature or no problems at all. His influence among philosophers is based on his logical technology. Those, however, who expected a reform of philosophy and the solution of all philosophical problems with the help of the new logic, have been disappointed. The leaders of the contemporary empiricist schools seem to be chiefly, though not exclusively, technicians. This appears to be true of Rudolf Carnap, the leader of the formalist school. He devotes himself to a logical analysis of language, and especially to the construction of symbolic systems and of artificial languages. He is the technician of artificial languages. In his book *Meaning and Necessity, e.g.*, he wants to develop a "new method for the semantical analysis of meaning, that is a new method for analysing and describing the meanings of linguistic expressions". These methods may be of great importance for the advancement of logic.

Carnap's formalization and his identification of language with a calculus are rejected by a second group of contemporary linguistic philosophers. They could be called the *ordinary-usage-school*, for following Moore and Wittgenstein they take the ordinary usage of language as their standard and hold that metaphysical theories are based on misinterpretations of ordinary usage. With Moore they believe that philosophers should always start with asking: "What do we mean when we say that . . . ?" With Wittgenstein they are inclined to transform this question into the other one: "What would you do to recognize an instance of *x*?" Although it is impossible to make any definite statements about Wittgenstein's teaching before his lectures are published, I think it is fair to say that, at the moment, he is most influential as a technician of colloquial language. From the start his chief concern was method:

> The object of philosophy is the logical clarification of thoughts. Philosophy is not a doctrine, but an activity. A philosophical work consists essentially of elucidations. The result of philosophy is not a number of "philosophical propositions", but to make propositions clear.[1]

The logical clarification of thoughts later became a logical clarification of language, and as such more and more complicated and sophisticated. For he, as a linguistic intuitionist, stressed the importance of the specific circumstances in which the questions arise and the answers are formulated, and the corresponding different usage of language. There is no longer *one* logic of language nor *one* method applicable to all problems, but there are many logics and many methods. In the end it may be found that every subject-matter and perhaps even every word has its own logic. All he could teach, therefore, was procedure or techniques, exemplified by specific examples.

[1] *Tractatus*, 4. 112.

This again favours the pre-eminence of technology and of techniques in this school.

One example may suffice. John Wisdom, Wittgenstein's pupil, writes in his Presidential Address on *Metaphysics*, discussing the knights in a game of chess:

> One who says it is of the essence of a knight that he should leap over other pieces and that therefore these knights are not knights isn't wrong. . . . For he's quite right—a knight which can't jump isn't a horse without the usual trappings, but a horse on wheels in a plough, Hamlet without the Prince of Denmark, wealth which none can buy, a predicate which like existence nothing can lose nor gain, reason which like a feeling one can't give nor yet retain.[1]

This colloquial style is the delight of young philosophers in this country; but one concerned about the future of philosophy cannot help asking: Are these techniques really adequate to a discussion of metaphysics? Do they really contribute to an elucidation of metaphysical thought? It is most interesting to compare this quotation with that from Gertrude Stein. One cannot help feeling that in both cases a mannerism of language and thought arises.

Even someone who emphatically denies that in these schools the technician prevails, cannot close his eyes to the dangers of a merely technological approach to philosophical problems. These dangers are the following. First, loss in substance. One may achieve technical perfection, either of formal precision or of sophistication in argument, and nevertheless lose substance. One goes on talking and talking, and in the end one talks about nothing. Husserl had sometimes the feeling that he had been sharpening his knife all the time until in the end nothing was left to be sharpened. The second danger is problem-blindness. The technician looks through his technical glasses. If they are green, he is unable to see anything that is not green. If his opponent has used red colours, he tells him that this is falsification and that he should have painted everything in green. If an adherent of Schoenberg should claim that the whole Classical Music is worthless because

[1] *Proc. Arist. Soc.*, vol. li (1951), p. 14.

it is not written in the twelve-tone technique, he would not be taken seriously. In philosophy, however, a similar absurdity concerning Classical Metaphysics would be hailed as a great discovery. The abusive and much abused term "senseless" shamefully covers the death of living issues.

> "Most propositions and questions", Wittgenstein writes, "that have been written about philosophical matters, are not false, but senseless. We cannot therefore answer questions of this kind at all, but only state their senselessness. Most questions and propositions of the philosophers result from the fact that we do not understand the logic of our language.
>
> "And so it is not to be wondered at that the deepest problems are really *no* problems." (4.003.)

Les problèmes sont morts, vivent les pseudo-problèmes! Indeed the third danger is the substitution of pseudo-problems for real problems. If, *e.g.*, the technician is of the opinion that philosophical problems are merely verbal, then he is inclined to demand of his opponent that he should re-formulate all his problems as linguistic ones. The great philosophers of the past, Locke, Berkeley and Hume, who attempted to analyse the acts of thinking, are told that

> they needed to discuss instead the functions of terms connectives, propositions and arguments, the numerals algebraic signs and formulæ out of which the statements of our theories are built.[1]

But do we not all experience acts of thinking? Did not the author of this quotation have to think before he wrote the review of George Humphrey's *Thinking*? How is he to persuade us that his problems, instead of the traditional ones, are the real problems?

In short, if a technician achieves a complete formaliza-tion of language, his formalism may be excellent, but philosophy vanishes. If, on the other hand, he relapses into common sense, this may be most entertaining, and we may learn much from him about the use of ordinary language, but again philosophy disappears. Nietzsche once said:

---

[1] *Times Literary Supplement*, 25.4.52.

Why does a philosopher so rarely succeed?   He needs qualities which usually ruin men, namely

(1) an immense variety of qualities; he must epitomize man, all his high and low desires; danger of inner contradiction and of feelings of self-disgust;

(2) he must possess curiosity, *i.e.* a desire to know the most diverse subjects: danger of fragmentation;

(3) he must be just and fair in the highest sense, but also deeply committed in love, hate (and injustice);

(4) he must not only be an onlooker, but also a law-giver: judge and judged;

(5) unusually versatile, and nevertheless firm and hard; flexible.[1]

Here technological abilities have no place.   In fact, mere technics are not enough.   A technique as such is not a philosophy, though it may be, *pace* Nietzsche, an indispensable tool.   A tool or a method is necessarily limited in its scope, and its limits may easily be mistaken for the limits of the subject-matter.

5

Here is the point where the concrete problems of our time arise.   That human activities, whether in philosophy or in the arts, have become technical in this sense, points to the fact that they have lost their ground in human existence.   They themselves, and with them men, are uprooted.   How can they regain their ground?   How can they be replanted in human existence?   How can human beings find their roots again?   It is clear that we cannot do without techniques, but the question is: How can we return from artificial techniques to natural techniques? How can we achieve what the *Gestalt*-psychologists call a figure-ground transformation?   How can we again transform technology into a means to an end, instead of regarding it as an end in itself?   How can we subordinate it to spiritual values?   How can we dominate the machine without being dominated by it?   These are some of the concrete problems which arise out of our present predicament and which we cannot escape.   They are

[1] *Werke* (Kröner), vol. xvi, p. 350.

existential, and indeed existentialism may be interpreted
as a reaction to the all-embracing powerful influence of
technology.   On this point I am in agreement with Paul
Tillich, who writes:

> What all philosophers of Existence oppose is the *irrational*
> system of thought and life developed by Western industrial
> society and its philosophic representatives.   During the last
> hundred years the implications of this system have become
> increasingly clear: a logical or naturalistic mechanism
> which seemed to destroy individual freedom, personal
> decision and organic community;   an analytic rationalism
> which spans the vital forces of life and transforms everything,
> including man himself, into an object of calculation and
> control;   a secularized humanism which cuts man off from
> the creative source and the ultimate mystery of existence.[1]

John MacPartland, who quotes these words in his booklet
The March Towards Matter, in which he attacks the
materialistic trend of the modern mind, adds: "This is
about as clear a statement as one could hope to find of the
object of the Existentialist Revolt." [2]   I do not adopt this
or any other definition as a starting-point.   Rather, I ask:
What is the function of existentialism in present circumstances?   If the existentialist philosopher reminds us of
the dangers inherent in a technological civilization and
of the necessity of having roots, he may fulfil a function
vital for the survival of man.

6

The existentialists have seen the problem, but so far
have failed to solve it.   The truly existential question therefore remains: How can we free ourselves from the bondage
of technology from which East and West suffer?   We must
be clear that we cannot go beyond technology in the sense
of getting rid of it.   We cannot smash the machines,
motor-cars, aeroplanes and radio stations, and go back to
a pre-technological age.   To disregard techniques would

[1] P. Tillich, "Existential Philosophy," *Journal of the History of Ideas*,
vol. v, no. 1, pp. 44–70.
[2] The Philosophical Library, New York, p. 78.

not only be impossible, but foolish and harmful. Neither Nature nor we can do without them. Nor can we get rid of philosophical techniques. If I have postulated meta-analysis,[1] this should not be misinterpreted, as if I wanted to discard analysis; by no means. What should be avoided is, first, the artificial isolation of analysis from its correlative synthesis, and secondly, the blind application of a special form of analysis appropriate to mathematics to a field not suited to it. We should in every case search for the specific kind of analysis adequate to the subject-matter in question. Psychology, for instance, demands specific methods of analysis. It is not possible to break up, in Locke's terminology, all complex ideas into alleged simple ideas, but it may be possible to analyse complex functions into simpler partial functions; that is to say, functional analysis is one of these methods.[2]

In short, we cannot go beyond technology, but we can go beyond technological alienation, *i.e.* beyond that stage where technology dominates us instead of our dominating it. It is as easy to see the problem as it is difficult to solve it. In fact, there is no general solution to it, but every one, the artist, musician, painter, writer, philosopher and the man in the street, has to find his own solution. All one can do, therefore, is to indicate directions in which solutions may be found.

A return to facts, to concrete experience and to reality, would seem to be the first requirement. The disregard of facts, their distortion and completely arbitrary transformation by the propaganda machines of dictatorial states, is one of the most distressing phenomena of our time. If, for instance, it suits communist tactics, American germ warfare in Korea is a "fact", of course not verifiable by an impartial observer. A lie repeated day by day will soon become an established truth. But are we not also in danger of shunning facts if we concentrate our attention exclusively on technological problems of musical composition, of painting, or of the logical syntax of language?

---

[1] *Hibbert Journal*, July 1952, p. 396.
[2] *Cf.* my paper, "The Analysis of 'Experience'," in *Philos. Review*, vol. L (November 1941), pp. 561 ff.

A return to facts implies for the philosopher a return to facts as established by science. Philosophy cannot be fruitfully pursued without a thorough first-hand knowledge of at least one special science, be it mathematics, physics, biology, psychology or history. A study of the language of science is not enough. A philosopher needs factual knowledge. Plato, Aristotle, Descartes, Leibniz, Kant, Hegel, Dilthey and Collingwood achieved mastery in special sciences, and this fact was the basis of their philosophical pre-eminence. Facts, established by science, remain, however, second-hand as long as we ourselves do not observe and experience them. A philosophy adequate to the needs of the time cannot be produced on the writing-desk. There is no substitute for primary experience of what we call external and internal reality. Responding to the challenge of the external world and of a society which wants to suppress him, man discovers himself as "reality", *i.e.* as a free agent, able to resist and to defy external threats. Unless he regains the ability to control himself and subordinate machines to moral and spiritual ends, he will never be able to escape the destructive influence of the technological era.

There are, however, formidable obstacles to be overcome before he can hope to reach this goal. The technological revolution has by no means reached its end, it is just gathering momentum, and the second half of our century may well be dominated by its second stage. Its first stage implied, as Norbert Wiener [1] rightly remarked, the devaluation of the human arm and generally of man and animal as a source of physical power; its second stage, which we are just entering, threatens to devalue the human brain "at least in its simpler and more routine decisions". The new science of Cybernetics and the machines based on it, such as the ultra-rapid computing machine, herald an automatic era compared with which the first half of our century was mere child's play. The automatically controlled machine is already with us. A unified system of automatic control machines is in sight. A completely

[1] *Cybernetics*, Cambridge, Mass., 1949; *The Human Use of Human Beings*, London, 1950.

automatic factory working without any manual labour, a chess-playing machine (Wiener), and lastly a *machine à gouverner*, *i.e.* a machine controlling all the decisions and actions of the members of a whole state and, potentially, of a world-state (Père Dubarle), are already on the books of the scientists. The "reasoning machines", we are advised, will take ten to twenty years to be fully developed, but perhaps only two years under the pressure of war. May heaven save us from these blessings. The alternative with which we are faced is: *either* atrophy of our brain power; degeneration of man; decline of his intellectual and spiritual activities which become more and more mechanical; and in the end slavery in new totalitarian régimes with over-centralized control; *or* a spiritual revolution; an awakening of man to the fact that he, after all, is a spiritual being with inexhaustible spiritual powers; and a stern determination to defend his liberty and to subordinate the so-called progress of science and technology to the moral and spiritual ends of humanity within a democratic order. Courage, faith and heroic defiance may be the only means for mastering a dangerous development which we are unable to stop.

The problem how to master technology will therefore remain with us for decades and perhaps for centuries to come. It is existential in the true sense of the word, for the age of technology endangers the existence of the human person more than ever.[1]

---

[1] That the long history of American ideas culminates in John Dewey's instrumentalism as a technological theory both of knowledge and value, is the interesting thesis of Richard D. Mosier's book *The American Temperament*, University of California Press and C.U.P., 1952. He writes: "Ideas are definitions of operations, plans of action, not the mere flow of phenomena in the subjective consciousness; and this development, known as the instrumental theory of knowledge, is in fact a theory of technology as well. The quest for certainty with which the age began is thus brought to a new stage by the answer that secure values can only be realized by perfecting methods of inquiry and action . . ., it is the answer that the knowledge of most worth is the knowledge of technique by which values can be reached or restored" (p. 300).

III. THE EXISTENTIAL CHRISTIAN

I

The Kierkegaard-Renaissance is one of the strangest phenomena of our time. A lonely thinker of nineteenth-century Denmark (1813–55), who made no mark on his own age and died in misery in a Copenhagen hospital, has become a central figure of the contemporary scene, the originator of two schools—the philosophical school of the Existentialists, and that of Karl Barth's and Emil Brunner's Dialectical Theology. His influence, growing from decade to decade, was based on the translation of his works, first into German, since 1909, then into Italian, since 1910, into French, since 1929, and lastly into English, since 1938. How is this strange fact to be explained? He was a proleptic man who, as a single individual, experienced in the middle of the last century something which has become common experience in our own day, and who had the power of expressing it in a most interesting, paradoxical and challenging manner. The literary representation of his thought is, moreover, so enigmatic, obscure and sometimes mysterious, that his writings make the impression of great profundity and offer an occasion for indefinite new interpretations. Unable to find a direct expression of his thought, he chose the way of indirect communication, he used in the manner of the Romanticists pseudonymity and anonymity, and wrote as "Victor Eremita", "Johannes de Silentio", "Constantine Constantius", "William Afham", "Johannes Climacus", etc. He did his utmost to mystify everybody by saying: "In the pseudonymous books is not a single word of mine." In fact, however, every word is his own, and to resolve this contradiction is left to the reader, who consequently never knows exactly where he is. Invited to a sometimes amusing, and sometimes exasperating game of hide-and-seek, he is entitled to any psychological or psychopathological explanation of this strange phenomenon, but in the end he cannot do much more than distinguish Kierkegaard[1], Kierkegaard[2] . . . Kierkegaard[n], without being able to forget that these *n* Kierkegaards are emanations of one and the same person.

One is completely lost among the multitude of his forty-three æsthetic, philosophical and religious publications, if one does not choose the right starting-point. The best advice I can give is to begin with the *Concluding Unscientific Postscript* (1846) and *The Point of View for my Work as an Author* (1848). The first book marks the turning-point in his spiritual life, the end of his æsthetic production and the transition to his religious works; it is, at the same time, of philosophical interest because of his criticism of Hegel and because it formulates as "An Existential Contribution" the transition to "Existential Pathos". The second is an extremely interesting interpretation of his writings. He sees his providential mission in exposing Christendom as a prodigious illusion and in calling its followers back to an existential Christian life.

If one wants to understand Kierkegaard, one has to know a few biographical details. He was born on May 5, 1813, in Copenhagen, as the youngest of seven children. His parents were of peasant stock. His father was a melancholic man. When a child he had one day, as a shepherd within the loneliness of the Jutland Downs, cursed God for his miserable life. Shortly before his death, in his eighty-second year, he confessed this fact to Sören, who was shaken by it as by an earthquake, and who understood it to mean that henceforth the curse of God was to rest on the family. Under a very strict orthodox Lutheran education of a somewhat sombre and depressing kind, Sören could not really enjoy his childhood. He tells us that he was never a child, never young, never a man, that he had never really lived, and that he enjoyed no "immediacy", no direct *joie de vivre* and no immediate contact with other people. "I did not have 'immediacy', and have therefore, humanly understood, not lived; I have started with reflection . . .; I am in fact reflection from beginning to end." He lived the imaginary life of his pseudonyms. An outsider during his school and university days, very gifted, witty, but polemical and himself the object of mockery, he imbibed at the University of Copenhagen, which he entered in 1830, the then prevailing Hegelianism.   In 1840 he passed the theological examination, entered the pastoral seminary, and delivered his first sermon in a Copenhagen church in 1841.   The year 1840 saw also his engagement with Regina Olsen, which he broke off in 1841, an event of great consequence for his literary and spiritual life.   It marked the beginning of a very prolific literary activity.   His polemical nature brought him into conflict with the Danish *Punch*, the *Corsair*, and with the official Church.   He regarded it as his mission to defend true Christian life against its distortion by the Church. These polemics broke his health. On October 2, 1855, walking in the streets of Copenhagen he collapsed, and was brought unconscious to the Frederiks Hospital, where he died on November 11.

2

Who then was Kierkegaard, and why is it necessary to start with him in a discussion of existentialism?   In the present meaning of the term he was neither an existentialist nor a philosopher of existence.   Nevertheless, he is the originator and the most original mind of this whole movement.   He it was who introduced the term "existence" with a new meaning into European thought. He was an *existential theologian-philosopher, an existential religious philosopher, or rather an existential Christian.*

Why should he be considered by philosophers, although he has not yet found his place in the textbooks of philosophy?   His challenge to traditional thought should not be overlooked.   He represents a reaction against, and a break with, the whole of modern philosophy from Descartes to Hegel.   In 1842 he started a polemic against the followers of Descartes under the title *Johannes Climacus; or, De omnibus est disputandum.*   On this point he is in agreement with Karl Marx.   Both reject Descartes' *Cogito ergo sum*; both replace it by the *Sum ergo cogito.*   But the two give a diametrically opposed interpretation to the *Sum*

(I am). Marx interprets it in a materialistic sense, as material being, as an action which produces not only the economic and social conditions of our life, but our existence itself; he rejects consciousness and mind as mere superstructure and ideological reflection. Kierkegaard, on the other hand, does not reject them, though objecting to Descartes', and especially to Hegel's, interpretation of consciousness and mind. He does not protest in the name of material existence and of the proletariat, but in the name of the individual and his soul. His attitude to the philosophy of consciousness is paradoxical. He rejects abstract consciousness and abstract thought for the sake of the concrete spiritual individual, with his "inwardness" and "subjectivity". He is opposed to Hegel, although as a pupil of the Hegelians he has some admiration for him, especially for his *Phenomenology of Mind*. "I cherish", he said, "a respect for Hegel which is sometimes an enigma to me; I have learnt much from him, and I know that on returning again to him I could still learn much more. . . . His philosophical knowledge, his astonishing learning, the sharpsightedness of his genius . . . I am as ready as any disciple to concede. . . . But for all that, one who is thoroughly tried in life's vicissitudes and has recourse in his need to the aid of thoughts will find him comic—in spite of the great qualities which are no less certain." [1] He protests against Hegel's abstract thought, his stress on the Universal, against his pantheism and his dissolution of all differences in the all-embracing unity of the Logos, against his idea of "mediation" and his elimination of all risks. He rejects his speculation and speculative philosophy in general in which the philosopher does not *commit* himself [2] or in which, as Sartre would say, he is not engaged. He rejects passionately his speculative talk about religion, and especially about Christianity. This kind of speculative interpretation seems to him a chimera and a sheer impossibility, based on a total ignorance of what religion and Christianity are. They are not something to be talked about, but something to be lived; religion is subjectivity, an inner transformation.

[1] *Concluding Unscientific Postscript*, p. 558.   [2] *L.C.*, p. 50.

The problem is not to speculate about Christianity, but to be a Christian.

Kierkegaard defends the Particular against the Universal. This point is noteworthy, partly because it will reappear in some of the existentialists, especially in Sartre, and partly because it is near to those intuitionists who stress the particularity of every situation in which we act, either politically (Burke) or morally (Bradley, Prichard and Carritt). One could call this standpoint the intuitionism of particular situations. Kierkegaard is, however, more concerned about the human condition as such and about the singularity of the individual. His protest is specifically religious and Christian. The suffering guilty creature protests against the dissolution of its substance either through speculation or through objectivity or through so-called social progress. He protests against the objective age and against objective thought which is indifferent to the thinking subject and his existence and which translates everything into results. "It is only systematists and objective philosophers", he writes, "who have ceased to be human beings, and have become speculative philosophy in the abstract, an entity which belongs in the realm of pure being." [1]

3

In 1846 Kierkegaard wrote a review of a novel. Its second most interesting part is republished under the title *The Present Age*. Here he protests against the levelling brought about by the phantom of public opinion, the ascendancy of the mass and of mass-man, socialism, the demon of collectivism and the collective as an artefact. With rare sharpsightedness he describes, in a masterly manner, a process which we all have to witness with a growing sense of frustration.

"The levelling process", he writes, "is not the action of an individual but the work of reflection in the hands of an

---

[1] *L.c.*, p. 85.

abstract power. It is therefore possible to calculate the law governing it in the same way that one calculates the diagonal in a parallelogram of forces. The individual who levels down is himself engulfed in the process and so on, and while he seems to know selfishly what he is doing one can only say of people *en masse* that they know not what they do; for just as collective enthusiasm produces a surplus which does not come from the individual, there is also a surplus in this case. A demon is called up over whom no individual has any power, and though the very abstraction of levelling gives the individual a momentary, selfish kind of enjoyment he is at the same time signing the warrant for his own doom. Enthusiasm *may* end in disaster, but levelling is *eo ipso* the destruction of the individual. No age, and therefore not the present age, can bring the scepticism of that process to a stop, for as soon as it tries to stop it, the law of the levelling process is again called into action.

"It can therefore only be stopped by the individual attaining in his loneliness the courage and dauntlessness of a religious man answerable to God." [1]

Levelling destroys the singularity and qualitative difference of the Self, and therefore the order of value and of status. A sort of external alienation arises; the individual disappears in the mass. "To battle against princes and popes is easy compared with struggling against the masses, the tyranny of equality, against the grin of shallowness, nonsense, baseness and bestiality." [2] He speaks in the name of the "exception", the *extraordinarius—i.e.* people singled out for an exceptional burden and for an extraordinary mission—but also in the name of every religious person, who alone, he thinks, can stop a levelling process arising from his elimination.

This implies a new interpretation of alienation. The disappearance of the Self in the mass is external alienation. Kierkegaard would go a certain way with Hegel. He would agree that alienation is a self-estrangement of the mind, not, however, of the abstract or universal, but of the individual mind or of the Self. He would further admit that man's intellectual culture represents a realm of estrangement, yet would interpret this fact in a com-

[1] *The Present Age* (trans. A. Dru) (Oxford, 1940), p. 30. I have altered the translation of the last sentence.
[2] *The Journals* (ed. A. Dru), § 1317.

pletely different manner. It now means: Man has lost his self, has ceased to be man, has suffered dehumanization. Having become "objective", he fails to be a subject. He has become an abstract phantom and has lost his concrete life. He has ceased to exist and is, in fact, non-existent. He is no longer a Christian, though externally he may be a member of a church.

Self-estrangement is to him primarily a process going on in one's own self, not an external, but an internal relation, based on one's own attitude to oneself. Kierkegaard therefore becomes the psychologist or rather the psycho-pathologist of self-estrangement. He heralds the Age of Anxiety by describing the state of alienation as anxiety. There is no precise equivalent in English for the Danish *Angest* and for the German and modern Danish *Angst*. Unfortunately Dr Lowrie translates it as dread, and Kierkegaard's book as *The Concept of Dread*. But anxiety, or French *angoisse*, seems to be better, for it is opposed to fear. Fear refers to something definite, as in "I fear him" or "I am afraid of the operation". Anxiety, however, refers to something indefinite. It is the uncanny apprehension of some impending evil, of something not present, but to come, of something not within us, but of an alien power. He describes it as a "sympathetic antipathy and an antipathetic sympathy", as "a desire for what one dreads . . . an alien power, which captivates . . . with a sweet apprehension". He compares it to a dizziness "in which freedom succumbs". Here he anticipates on the one hand Sartre, who goes on to pathological forms of this sympathetic antipathy, namely to sadism and masochism, and on the other hand Heidegger, by saying that "anxiety and nothing regularly correspond to each other". In *The Concept of Dread* (1844) this sort of alienation finds a most profound and penetrating psychological analysis as "being dominated in a state of anxiety by an alien power which threatens our dissolution".

He goes, however, one step further in his analysis of alienation as an internal happening within oneself in his *The Sickness unto Death* (1849). Anxiety is now transformed into despair, and despair is "the sickness unto death". This is one of the most important of his publications; it implies a phenomenology of despair and of its forms and, at the same time, a sort of existentialist psychology of despair. It marks simultaneously an important stage in the spiritual history of modern man, namely the point where modern doubt and scepticism turns inward, focuses on one's own self and therefore leads to despair. Despair, says Kierkegaard, is the misproportion in the relation of the self to itself, or every disturbance in the process of becoming a Self, a sort of self-consumption, a specific illness of man as a spiritual being, arising from his attempt to separate himself from the power which created him, or from the fact that he neglects what is eternal in him and forgets his spiritual nature. Whoever has no God has no Self, and who has no Self is in despair. There are different forms of this despair. If one is unconscious of having a Self, the despairing subject remains unconscious of the fact that he is despairing. If, however, the despairing man is conscious of his state, then he is either in despair at not willing to be himself, or in despair at willing to be himself. The despair at not willing to be oneself is the despair of weakness; the despair of willing desperately to be oneself is defiance. Here one has lost selfhood and one attempts desperately to become again oneself. These are a few of the forms of despair discussed by Kierkegaard which may be supplemented by others.

His interest in this subject is, however, by no means chiefly psychological, but existential, religious and metaphysical. "I believe", he says, "the time is not far off, when one will experience, perhaps dearly enough, that one has to start, if one wants to find the Absolute, not with doubt, but with despair." This is exactly what he did. Starting with despair, his problem became how again to become oneself. His solution was *redintegratio in statum pristinum*. He coined for it the term "repetition", and he meant by it "becoming again oneself before God". He wrote a most interesting book, *Repetition*. Here he shows that his hero, after his entanglement in the world, regains himself; that the split in his personality is healed; and that he reunites all forces; that is what he means by repetition. Or, on a higher plane, that Job, after having lost everything, after having passed through all possible tribulations, becomes again himself, blessed with double his former possessions; it is this that Kierkegaard calls repetition, becoming again oneself before God. Repetition is and remains for him a religious category.[1]

4

Kierkegaard acts as a provocation to thought, calling upon his reader to question old established opinions and to rethink his whole position. He achieves this by formulating apparently very simple questions. How to become a Christian? To ask this seems to be paradoxical, because his contemporaries were Christians; but, in his opinion, they were only nominally, not actually so. There have never been real Christians, he would say, and the 1806 years of their history should be brushed out, as if they had never existed. "At the present time the difficulty of becoming a Christian involves actively transforming an initial being-a-Christian into a possibility, in order to become a Christian in reality."[2] He reminds his readers that it is easier to become a Christian if one is not a Christian, than to become a Christian if one is one. It is not only difficult to leap into the air and to come down again on the same spot. It is still more difficult to make a decision if there was an earlier decision (*i.e.* to be baptized) which is not the individual's own decision and which hinders him from becoming aware of the fact that he has still to make his *own* decision.

Do not pretend! is Kierkegaard's message to our age, which is filled with pretence. Do not pretend to be a Christian if you are not! Do not pretend to be a man if you are not human! Do not pretend to be religious if you are not! Do not pretend to be a philosopher if you are not! These variations of Kierkegaard's theme

---

[1] *Cf.* my paper, "Origin and Repetition," in *The Review of Metaphysics,* December 1950.
[2] *Concluding Unscientific Postscript,* p. 326.

are of topical importance. The mere fact that we are born as men does not imply that we are human. On the contrary, it lulls us into pretence. We are in constant danger of becoming inhuman, partly because our position between beasts and angels is somewhat uncertain, and partly because every sort of domination implies the temptation to inhumanity, especially in an age of technology, which invests the master with almost unlimited power. To be human is not a fact, but a task. We should therefore ask: What does it mean to be human? What is man? What should he be? What is the meaning of humanism in our time? Likewise the mere fact that one has read philosophy or that one does belong to a philosophical school does not imply that one is a philosopher. Here again it is easier to become a philosopher if one is not, than to become a philosopher if one believes that one is, but is not. Therefore we are forced to formulate the following questions. What does it mean to be a philosopher? Is genuine philosophizing possible which does not take into account its existential implications? What should the function of philosophy be in present circumstances?

There is no room here for elaborating the far-reaching and most provocative implications of these questions. It is, moreover, unnecessary, because Kierkegaard concentrates on the problem, how to become a Christian. The other problems are only potentially implied in it. Nevertheless, they are there. All these questions are merely special cases of the general problem, how to go on from unauthentic being to authentic being.

5

But what is his proposed philosophical solution to the general problem? It may be summarized in the following propositions from his *Concluding Unscientific Postscript.*

1. All essential knowledge concerns existence, or only such knowledge which has an essential relationship to existence is essential knowledge.

2. All knowledge which does not relate itself to existence, in the reflection of inwardness, is essentially viewed contingent and inessential knowledge; its degree and scope is indifferent.

3. Objective reflection and knowledge has to be distinguished from subjective reflection and knowledge. The way of objective reflection leads away from the subject to abstract objective truth (mathematics, metaphysics and historical knowledge of different kinds). In this sphere the existing subject may be disregarded; its existence or non-existence becomes infinitely indifferent.

4. The objective way of reflection leads to objective truth, and while the subject and his subjectivity becomes indifferent, the truth also becomes indifferent, and this indifference is precisely its objective value; its objectivity is either a hypothesis or an approximation.

5. Subjective knowledge requires personal appropriation. In subjective reflection truth becomes appropriation, inwardness or subjectivity. In fact, the only reality which an existing being can know otherwise than through some abstract knowledge is his own existence. Here it is necessary that the existing subject should plunge itself into its own subjectivity.

6. Only ethical and religious knowledge are therefore essential knowledge; they alone are essentially related to the fact that the knowing subject exists; they alone are in contact with reality. In them alone truth and existence coincide.

7. The essential truth is subjective or internal; or "truth is subjectivity".

What do these theses amount to? They imply a complete revaluation of human knowledge. They represent a reaction not only against Hegel, but against modern science in general, in so far as it becomes more and more abstract. Kierkegaard rejects the senseless accumulation of knowledge. He wants to discard the superfluity of knowledge, in order that we may again learn what it means to live as a human being. He discards the old distinction between truths of reason and truths of fact; both of them are of little avail to him because they neglect what is essential to him, true existence, *i.e.* existence in the face of God. He substitutes for it the distinction of objective or inessential, and subjective or essential truth. He wishes to return from abstract inessential knowledge to concrete essential knowledge, from the exterior to the interior, from the objective to the subjective, from possibilities to reality. It is as if he said: "What shall it profit a man, if he gain all possible knowledge of the world and lose his own soul?" It is easy to see that Heidegger's and Sartre's distinction between unauthentic and authentic being, Jaspers's and Berdyaev's opposition to objectification, and Mounier's distinction between existence lost and existence regained, are either derived from, or internally connected with, Kierkegaard's discrimination between inessential and essential knowledge.

Subjective knowledge refers to existence. But what does he mean by existence? Not existence in the traditional sense of "being there" in its opposition to essence; it does therefore by no means imply the priority of existence before essence (Sartre). It points to *human* existence, but not to man as a finite being, as Heidegger would have it, but to him as a synthesis of the finite and the infinite, the temporal and the eternal. Like Plato's Eros, "existence is the child that is born of the infinite and the finite, and is therefore a constant striving".[1] It concerns man's spiritual being in its interconnection with passion and will, the self that reflects, chooses, decides, and may become sinful and guilty, and therefore man in the process of coming to be. It would, however, be a complete misunderstanding if one interpreted existential thought as thought whose subject-matter is existence. No, it refers to the mode in which the subject is *engaged* in his thought. Mathematical and scientific knowledge may be reduced to a manipulation of symbols which anybody may understand and handle in a quasi-mechanical manner without being himself internally concerned about them. In philosophy and religion, however, it is different. A true philosopher and a truly religious man are not interested in their thought only. Thought alone is here not enough.

[1] *Concluding Unscientific Postscript*, p. 85.

It is not enough to know philosophical doctrines or religious dogmas; one has to be, or rather, as Kierkegaard would say, to become, a philosopher and a religious man. Here one cannot be indifferent to one's thinking; one has to exist in one's thought; one has to assimilate and to appropriate one's own ideas which belong to the thinking subject and to no one else. While in objective thought the results matter, "subjective thought puts everything in process and omits the result".[1]   Kierkegaard's existential thought becomes, therefore, dialectical. "Since the existing subject is occupied in existing, it follows that he is in process of becoming. And just as the form of his communication ought to be in essential conformity with his mode of existence, so his thought must correspond to the structure of existence."[2]   Therefore it must be dialectical. Here is the source of Jaspers's dialectic.

"The objective accent falls on *what* is said, the subjective accent on *how* it is said."[3]   A modern reader is at once reminded of the difference of knowledge *that* and knowledge *how*; the first referring to something that is the case, the second to the manner in which something has to be done. This American knowledge *how* is external, it can be verified; a man proves that he has the knowledge *how* to plant a tree by planting it. Kierkegaard's knowledge *how* is internal and cannot be verified in an external manner. "At its maximum this inward 'how' is the passion of the infinite, and the passion of the infinite is the truth."[3]   In this manner subjectivity and the subjective "how" constitute the truth. But what does that mean? How can passion, subjectivity and the "how" constitute truth? Evidently, this cannot refer to logical, mathematical or scientific truth. On the contrary, objective truth, discovered by the intellect, is either certain or approaches certainty. Subjective truth however, we are told, becomes a paradox; and this fact "is rooted precisely in its having a relationship to an existing subject".[4]   Far from being certain, it is an objective uncertainty held fast in an appropriation-process of the most passionate inwardness, the highest truth attainable for an existing individual.

[1] *L.c.*, p. 68.   [2] *L.c.*, p. 74.   [3] *L.c.*, p. 181.   [4] *L.c.*, p. 177.

Subjectively, something is true because the person passionately believes in it, has appropriated and assimilated it with his whole existence, even if, or rather because, the object of his belief is a paradox and an absurdity. This is a most interesting point. Absurdity is here experienced by modern man, but not yet as later on by Sartre, as a quality belonging to the world and pervading his whole experience, but as a quality belonging to the highest truth. "What now is the absurd? The absurd is —that the eternal truth has come into being in time, that God has come into being, has been born, has grown up, and so forth, precisely like any other individual human being, quite indistinguishable from other individuals." [1] The definition of truth has become an equivalent expression for faith, and the Christian faith appears as a paradox and an absurdity.

In face of these statements, the following questions reappear with still greater urgency. What did Kierkegaard mean by truth? Is his thesis that truth is subjectivity not meaningless? It must be remembered that the terms "true" and "truth" are by no means univocal. We are accustomed to restrict them logically to propositions; for us, propositions only are true and false. But this is not the case in common usage. We may say that someone is true to his word, to his friend and to himself, and here "true" has the meaning of "loyal, constant, faithful or adhering faithfully"; it corresponds to the German term *treu*. In Shakespeare's *Cymbeline* this meaning of the term "true" prevails to such a degree that the whole play may be called "an experiment in truth", or, like Beethoven's *Fidelio*, "in praise of fidelity"; for the real hero of the drama is Imogen; she alone passes the test of faithfulness; she alone remains true to herself and to her husband. In Kierkegaard's case "true" means likewise "true to oneself", but with a difference, *i.e.* "to one's eternal self" and therefore "true to God" or "faithful". Truth is no longer a quality of propositions, but of human beings. It means the same as to "exist truly", viz. in the face of God, to partake in Divine Truth, or to choose

[1] *L.c.*, p. 188.

one's eternal destiny. Faithfulness does not refer to the finite, but to the infinite in its relation to the finite.

6

It should now be time for a "concluding unscientific postscript" to Kierkegaard. What then is alive and what is dead in his thought? His longing for the concrete; his search for reality; his dissatisfaction with abstract science which moves in mere possibilities without ever reaching reality; and his knowledge that choice and decision transcend the relativity of knowledge and introduce something unconditional;—all this is very much alive. The symbolic tendency of scientific development is so relevant and the danger of the abstract sciences becoming transformed into a mere play with symbols so great, that one of the most important German post-war novels, Hermann Hesse's *Glasperlenspiel*, centres in the Kierkegaardian problem of the transition from abstract play to concrete existence as one of the most essential of our time. The revaluation of the person in his relation to the Transcendent is likewise topical. The pressure of the group, class, party and the state, threatening the liberty of the individual, has considerably increased since Kierkegaard's days. For this reason his stress on human existence is valuable. He has shown that it is man who matters; that knowledge and philosophy have existential implications, and that philosophy, in its most essential parts, must be existential. But as so often happens, he was right in what he affirmed and wrong in what he denied. Overrating subjective reflection he underrated objective reflection. His devaluation of objective knowledge is dead, for it is a purely personal affair. It is understandable for a religious person to say that all worldly knowledge is foolishness before God; but from the point of view of knowledge it does not make sense to reject objective reflection, for subjective and objective reflection are strictly interdependent. If one desires knowledge of the subject, one wants it in an objective manner. His over-emphasis on subjectivity and his thesis that truth is subjectivity are provocative. It is true that abstract science does not contain, as some positivists assume, all true propositions. There is truth outside science, *e.g.* in great works of art and in the wisdom of the sages. There is further "personal truth", truth in which I believe with all my heart, which I accept as the basis of my existence and for which I am prepared to die. Religious truth is of this kind; it is *sui generis*; it cannot be verified by sense experience; its "justification" resides in the fact that it is able to provide a spiritual centre not only for individuals, but for a whole community. Religion is the "personal truth of a community" and cannot therefore remain purely subjective; it must acquire some degree of objectivity; and in fact every religion claims a specific objectivity. A protest against the abstract objective truth of science may have its merits, because it makes room for extra-scientific, personal and religious truth, but to go to the other extreme by saying "subjectivity is truth" is an overstatement. It is bound to lead, and it has led, on the one hand, to the mistaken assumption that an existentialist logic is possible, and on the other, to relativism and irrationalism, *i.e.* to the fatal assumption that the individual has arbitrarily to decide what is true or false, right or wrong. The anti-intellectualism and irrationalism which are implied in Kierkegaard's transition to choice and decision can hardly be counted as positive assets. The opening up of a way from the individual to the Transcendent is valuable; but here the interrelations with other persons and with the world, so vital for the life of the person, are neglected.

Was Kierkegaard then a spiritual leader and shall we accept him as such? He is doubtless of outstanding importance through the originality of his views, the seriousness with which he accepted what he regarded as his mission, and the courage with which he attacked those powers and institutions which, in his view, endangered the existence of the *homo religiosus*, the Christian, and of man in general. He is a most stimulating writer and potentially a great artist, frustrated, however, by the overriding force of his reflection. He was so extremely rich in his thought that he felt the urge to express himself through the mouth of many persons; but whereas in the case of a great dramatist, such as Shakespeare, these persons assume real life, here they remain pseudonyms, mere masks without a distinct existence of their own. He is brilliant in the analysis of his and (by implication) our time, and also in his description of psychological and psychopathological possibilities. He overstressed, however, the morbid aspect of human life, being himself a psychopathological case, regarded by some as schizophrenic, by others as of the maniac-depressive type. He certainly inaugurated new trends of thought in philosophy and theology, and formulated questions of such importance that they are still with us. His is the category of the individual which he stressed and overstressed. Nevertheless, he is right in saying that the fatal levelling process of our time can only be stopped by the courage and dauntlessness of persons accepting an absolute responsibility in the face of God.

IV. THE LONELINESS OF THE TRANSCENDENTAL EGO

I

WHY is it necessary to include Husserl in a book on Existentialism although he was by no means an existentialist, but on the contrary rejected Heidegger and could be fittingly called an "essentialist"? It is inevitable, because neither the German nor the French school can be understood without him. Heidegger was his pupil. Jaspers accepted the phenomenological method for psychopathology, but transformed it in such a manner that it has not much in common with Husserl's original intentions.[1] In France, Sartre and Merleau-Ponty are profoundly influenced by him. Sartre's *chef-d'œuvre*, *L'Être et le Néant* bears the sub-title, *essai d'ontologie phénoménologique*. He not only starts with *l'idée de phénomène*, but accepts the phenomenological method as the method of his ontology; he interprets it in an arbitrary manner, mixing up Husserl's and Heidegger's very different interpretations, and declares the phenomenon to be the relative-absolute, *i.e.* relative to someone, to whom it appears, but absolute, in so far as it appears as it is. He discusses and rejects Husserl's theory of the knowledge of other persons, and is in his own psychology dependent on Husserl, Heidegger and Freud. Merleau-Ponty in his *Phénoménologie de la Perception* applies Husserl's phenomenology to the theory of perception. He is so much interested in his thought that he has consulted some of the unpublished manuscripts of the Husserl Archives at Louvain. He too combines phenomenology and existentialism. Perception is to him a specific mode of being, in which the perceptual fields are organized by the *engaged* perceiving subject, and

---

[1] *Cf.* my book, *Neue Wege der Philosophie*, p. 346; Jaspers's paper, "Die phänomenologische Forschung in der Psychopathologie," and his *Allgemeine Psychopathologie*.

"sensing" that vital communication with the world which reveals to us a familiar scene of our life.

Husserl seems to be the most paradoxical among contemporary philosophers. There are, first, three paradoxes concerning his influence. In a recent Swiss booklet on contemporary European philosophy it is said that he, together with Bergson, made the deepest and most far-reaching impression on present-day thought; in this country, however, nothing is to be noticed of it. In Germany he certainly exercised a considerable influence, partly through his *Logical Studies* (1900) and partly through his teaching. He even founded a school and attracted a large circle of pupils, some of whom were outstanding like Geiger, Scheler and Pfänder. When, however, he published his *Ideen zu einer reinen Phänomenologie*, translated under the title *Ideas*, most of his pupils rejected this work and did not accept its implications. Nevertheless Husserl claimed that here he had merely expounded and clarified the standpoint of the *Logical Studies*. Later he had a similar experience at Freiburg, where his most original pupil, Heidegger, broke away from him. In 1931 he told me that he had taken him most seriously, that he had read his *Sein und Zeit* twice, but that he could not discover anything in it. "Heidegger moves on the level of common sense" (*bewegt sich in der natürlichen Einstellung*)—that was the original sin which could not be forgiven. It is somewhat tragic that in the Preface to the English edition of the *Ideas* he had to draw a sharp line between himself and all those who had further developed his teaching. Generally speaking, his influence was not so much based on his thought as he wanted it to be interpreted, as on what others believed or wished it to be. He was generally understood as advocating a "Back to the objects, back to the phenomena, back to the essences!" but he insisted in later years that "Back to the subject, back to consciousness as the source of our knowledge of objects!" was more important.

There are, secondly, three paradoxes concerning his teaching. Husserl began as a mathematician and as a pupil of Weierstrass, but when he attended Franz

Brentano's lectures in 1884–86 he was won for philosophy. He started with reading Avenarius' *Critique of Pure Experience*, *i.e.* with positivism, and with the study of the æsthetic of Kant's *Critique of Pure Reason*. In his first book, *Philosophy of Arithmetic* (1891), he attempted to give a psychological explanation of mathematics, following the custom of that time, but discovered the impossibility of such a task. He therefore attacked "psychologism" in the first volume of his *Logical Studies*. He understands by "psychologism" the attempt to base logic on psychology. Locke, Berkeley and Hume tacitly assumed this to be possible, whereas J. S. Mill, Spencer, Sigwart and Erdmann explicitly tried to base their logic on psychology. Negatively, Husserl shows that the laws of logic are not psychological laws, that logic does not form part of psychology, and that the rules of logic have nothing to do with the psychological facts of thinking. Positively, he maintains that the laws of logic concern the subject-matter or the meaning of propositions, and that these meanings belong to a sphere *sui generis*, *i.e.* to an ideal sphere. He introduces important semantic distinctions like that between *Ausdruck* (expression) and *Bedeutung* (meaning); *e.g.* the three English, German and French words "triangle, Dreieck and triangle" are three expressions, but they all refer to one and the same identical meaning, and this unity of meaning alone is of logical importance.

Here arises the first paradox of his teaching. On the one hand he rejects psychology as the basis of logic and stresses the autonomous ideal character of logic, on the other hand he holds that the meaning of logical propositions can only be revealed by going back to the subject, *i.e.* to those acts of our consciousness in which this meaning is "constituted". To do this, he stresses, is the task of phenomenology, but not of psychology. But what is the difference between the two? In spite of Husserl's strong anti-psychological bias, his phenomenology often appears to be nothing more than a specific sort of psychology, very similar to Kant's transcendental psychology and to Brentano's "intentional" psychology.

The second volume of his *Logical Studies* contains a profound criticism of Locke's, Berkeley's and Hume's theories of abstraction. This leads to a critique of Berkeley's and Hume's nominalism and of modern nominalism in general. He attempts to show that universals are not mere words, but *allgemeine Gegenstände* (universal objects) or *Bedeutungen* (meanings), and that we become conscious of them in acts essentially different from those directed towards individual objects. Now, a criticism of nominalism may be extremely useful and even necessary at the present juncture. There may be cases in which universals are signs, as in algebra, where x, y and z are mere substitute signs; but even there they are substitutes for something to which they must be referred back at the end of the calculation. In other cases, however, if, *e.g.*, I use the word "rose", this word is more than a mere sign, it refers to a specific class of plants. Here the second paradox of Husserl's teaching arises. *Prima facie* he seems to replace modern nominalism by a sort of mediæval realism, *i.e.* by the doctrine that universals are essences or ideal species, and a metaphysics of essences seems to become the basis of his reasoning. This, however, is apparently out of tune with the development of modern logic and science which he himself wished to promote.

Lastly, his attitude to science is somewhat paradoxical. On the one hand he is opposed to science. He rejects the method of science as the method of philosophy; science, he says, preserves the common-sense point of view; it accepts the world as it is. "Philosophy, however, lies in a totally different dimension. It needs a completely different starting-point and a completely new method." He tries to rediscover a specific autonomous region for philosophy. He formulates the antithesis to Positivism, namely that philosophy should be completely independent of science and disregard its results and methods, instead of being completely dependent on it. Nevertheless he wishes to found a philosophy not only as a new science, but as *the* universal and, in a radical sense, exact (*strenge*) science. Now, philosophy is either *the* exact science, then it would seem to follow that its method cannot be opposed to that of science, or it is totally different from science; in this case it is difficult to understand how it can be called a science in the strict sense of the word. Husserl would like to escape this contradiction by transforming philosophy into an eidetic science or a science of essences (*Wesens-wissenschaft*), *i.e.* a science not founded on experience, independent of all empirical science, and nevertheless its basis. He believed, *e.g.*, in eidetic psychology as a basis of empirical psychology; this eidetic psychology is claimed as an *a priori* science, based on an alleged eidetic intuition (*Wesensschau*). All this is pure fancy; there is neither an eidetic intuition nor does it furnish *a priori* foundations of empirical science. Husserl postulates for every empirical science an *a priori* eidetic intuition as a basis and corresponding "regional ontologies"; this is a return to pre-Kantian ontology, like rational psychology, in a modified form. This postulate, however, cannot be and has not been fulfilled.[1] Nevertheless, this experiment is not without interest in spite of, or because of, its failure. It demonstrates that philosophy can be neither completely independent of science, nor can it be an exact science. It stands in a relation of interdependence to science. Husserl offers the most interesting example of a first-rate philosopher who, through a complete lack of common sense, gets into opposition to the "natural" standpoint in and outside science and whose standpoint and "eidetic" science thereby becomes "unnatural".

2

If we wish to resolve this double series of paradoxes we have to go back to his existence. I have met Husserl three times: first in Göttingen about 1912 I heard him lecturing on Descartes; it was quite interesting, but not exciting; then at Freiburg in the 'twenties; and finally at Frankfurt in 1931. The last meeting was the most interesting. He was then seventy-two years old, but most

---

[1] *Cf.* A. Kastil, "Franz Brentano und die Phänomenologie," in *Zeitschrift für Philosophische Forschung*, vol. iii, pp. 402 ff.

impressive and inexhaustible in his lectures on Phenomenology and Anthropology, a real thinker, totally devoted
to the pursuit of truth and to the elaboration of his
philosophy. He was enormously alive, but alive as a
mind and devoted to problems far removed from life.
One day I met him in a patrician house, at the Unter-
mainquai, in an enormous hall in which we walked
constantly up and down for half an hour or so. He told
me that he had worked for nearly thirty years (a slight
overstatement!) so intensely that he had not published
anything, and that he had consequently remained *Privat-
dozent* at Halle for fourteen years. After the publication
of his *Logical Studies* in 1900 he visited Dilthey in 1905, who
told him that this book represented the first fundamentally
new departure in Philosophy since the days of Mill and
Comte, and that he, Dilthey, regarded the fifth and the
sixth essays, *On Intentional Experiences (Erlebnisse) and their
"Contents"*, and *Elements of a Phenomenological Elucidation of
Knowledge, i.e.* the return to the subject and its inner experiences, as most fruitful. This, combined with the fact
that Dilthey was holding a *Seminar* on that book, made a
deep impression on him. I do not say that Dilthey was
the cause for Husserl's subsequent turn to the subject, but
he confirmed his conviction that this way was worth going.

I was struck by the fact that a man who claimed
intuition in the form of eidetic intuition to be the basis of
philosophy, did not rely on it in his life, but was an arduous
worker, perhaps the most industrious scholar among the
philosophers of his generation. His publications are in
fact reports on work done. "I am a sceptic," he said;
"I always believe others more than myself." He was
very critical towards himself; the notes and alterations
added to the new German edition of his *Ideas* prove this.
Nevertheless he was convinced that his starting-point was
the only right one, and that he had discovered the
Absolute in the sphere of consciousness. Then he said a
word which gives the clue to his existence and his philosophy: "One becomes a philosopher through loneliness"
(*Durch Vereinsamung wird der Mensch Philosoph*). "Philosophy arises in the lonely responsible thought of the man

who is philosophizing." There is some truth in that. Nietzsche said: "To go his way in loneliness is the essence of a philosopher", and he spoke of himself as one of the most lonely among the lonely. Husserl's loneliness, however, is of a specific kind. It passed through two stages. It was first human loneliness, arising from the bracketing of the world, in a manner similar to Descartes' doubt, but not identical with it. But he could not stop there. If he doubted the existence of the world with its mountains and rivers, trees, plants and animals, how could he help doubting his own existence in this specific body? He therefore went on from human loneliness to transcendental loneliness. "I have become", he said, "the transcendental Ego"; and this was true. He did not talk as his natural Self, but as an anonymous transcendental Ego, as consciousness in general, as *Bewusstsein überhaupt*, in Kant's sense. Here we have reached the central point, *Husserl's philosophy is the philosophy of the lonely transcendental Self*. We have simultaneously reached the point where we can fix Husserl's position in the history of modern self-estrangement.

In the context of this book Husserl's method is of interest to us as an expression of self-estrangement. His method consists of two steps. The first is the so-called phenomenological reduction, or the transition from the "natural standpoint" or the common-sense point of view to the phenomenological standpoint. On the natural level one believes in the reality of the world and in one's being in the world. The phenomenological reduction implies an ἐποχή, a bracketing of this whole world and of the sciences referring to it. As a result of this reduction, as in Descartes' case, the Ego or Consciousness remains. Had he gone no further, he could have moved in the sphere of the concrete Ego, but he was not satisfied with that. The phenomenological reduction had to be supplemented by the transcendental reduction. Estrangement from the world is not enough; there must be self-estrangement, a bracketing of ourselves until we reach the transcendental Ego, the anonymous consciousness which does not belong to anybody, but which claims to contain the foundation and the "constitutive elements" of all our experience and of all sciences. He himself believed that he had discovered an infinite universe instead of the finite world which he had given up, *i.e.* the manifold of possible *cogitationes* and *cogitata*, of perceptions, memories, etc. But is this not an illusion? "We direct", says Husserl, "the glance of apprehension and theoretical inquiry to *pure consciousness in its own absolute Being.* It is this which remains over as the 'phenomenological residuum' we were in quest of: remains over, we say, although we have 'suspended' the whole world with all things, living creatures, men, ourselves included. We have literally lost nothing, but have won the whole of Absolute Being, which, properly understood, conceals in itself all transcendences, 'constituting' them within itself" (*Ideas*, p. 154). But is not this residuum, far from being the Absolute, merely an abstraction?

3

Did Husserl reach a solution of his paradoxes in his own work? He is especially fruitful in his logical studies, and his most important publications are, in my view, those referring to Logic, *i.e.* his *Logical Studies*, his *Formal and Transcendental Logic*, and his *Experience and Judgment*. If one of these had been translated instead of the *Ideas*, his influence in this country would be far greater than it is. "What matters", says Husserl, "is not so much criticism as the amount of work done." The amount of work done is indeed considerable in these books of which perhaps his *Formal and Transcendental Logic* is the ripest and, in my opinion, the most important, because it implies a profound analysis, criticism and transformation of traditional logic. It may serve as an example of his work.

He begins with an analysis of traditional logic, in order to elucidate the meaning of its problems. Formal logic arose as formal *apophantic*, *i.e.* as a theory of the forms of assertions or propositions in the logical sense. This realm of assertions, however, is by no means homogeneous; on the contrary, it implies three different logical disciplines, among them, first, *the theory of the pure forms of judgments*. It was founded by Aristotle. The Greek genius excelled in isolating and analysing forms. This is true of art, sculpture, architecture, literature, grammar and logic. The Greeks saw that it is possible to consider all propositions from the point of view of form, to isolate their form from the subject-matter expressed in them, and therefore to classify them according to formal characteristics. Consequently, Aristotle distinguished simple and complex propositions: among the simple ones, particular and universal propositions; among the complex ones, *i.e.* those composed of two or more propositions, conjunctive, disjunctive, hypothetical and causal judgments (connected by "and", "either-or", "if-then", or "cause-effect" respectively). The theme of this first form of logic as a theory of the pure forms of propositions is "the mere possibility of propositions, without raising the question whether they are true or false, or whether they are, as mere judgments, compatible or contradictory". In a consistent elaboration this discipline would become a purely logical grammar, or a doctrine of the pure forms of meaning (*eine reine Formenlehre der Bedeutungen*).

Traditional logic implies, secondly, *logic as the science of possible forms of true propositions*. Husserl calls it consequence-logic or logic of non-contradiction. The problem is here no longer "possible forms of propositions", but rather "possible forms of true propositions". This logic considers the forms of propositions in so far as they, singly or together, form the condition for the possible truth or untruth of all possible propositions of a similar form. The non-contradiction of propositions is here in question; for the problem is: Given certain premisses, what follows necessarily? This form of logic implies, on the one hand, the whole Aristotelean syllogistic, but also disciplines of mathematical analysis. It should be noted that, at this stage, the problem is not one of the truth of single propositions, but merely of their "compossibility" and compatibility. If one asks, however, what are the formal laws or rules that make the formulation of true propositions possible, one reaches the third stage, the *logic of truths*. One, but only one, of the conditions of this logic is the law of contradiction. A proposition cannot be true if it is self-contradictory.

So much for the analysis of traditional logic which Husserl pursues much further. It leads at once to the second step, the criticism and transformation of traditional logic. Husserl holds that objective forms of logic cannot be understood if one does not go back to the subjective forms in which they are constituted or founded. This implies a transition to transcendental logic, in a Kantian or rather neo-Kantian sense. Husserl believes that logical forms and their objects have their ground in our mind, *i.e.* in specific subjective forms, in which the objects of our judgments are constituted. Kant would say that they are constituted in acts of synthesis of our mind, and in specific *a priori* forms of this synthesis, *i.e.* in space and time, in the categories and in the ideas, as the forms of synthesis of our intuition, our understanding, and our reason respectively. Husserl, however, interprets the acts of our mind, in Brentano's manner, as being "intentional", *i.e.* they are directed towards something; they are acts of seeing *of*, or hearing *of*, something, and this something is their intentional object. He holds that all objects of our knowledge are constituted in these intentional acts. Logic is not to be based on psychology, but on transcendental phenomenology. He rejects a psychological explanation, because logic and mathematics have meaning and validity transcending the psychological acts directed towards them. He accepts a phenomenological foundation, because he believes with Kant that the objects of our knowledge are constituted in the transcendental subject. This is likewise true of the objects of logic. We are invited to go back to acts in which we have something general (*Etwas überhaupt*) in mind, in the case of the consequence logic; and to acts in which we experience the world of individuals, in the case of the logic of truth. Every proposition, it is said, is in the last resort related to something individual and stands therefore in relation to a real universe; this should apply even to mathematical propositions, in so far as they also have to be applied to reality. Truth is here based on evidence. "The hierarchy of propositions and their meanings are dependent on the hierarchy of evidences, and the first truths and evidences must be the individual ones." Husserl holds that every proposition, whether a truth of reason or a truth of fact, must be based on "pre-predicative evidence". He therefore gives in his book *Erfahrung und Urteil* a most subtle and rich analysis of pre-predicative experience. Here he is most interesting and, in principle, right. There exists, *e.g.*, certainly a prelogical or pre-predicative negation, but whether it arises from a frustration of expectation is another matter. That every logical truth implies former stages of our experience and that our analysis has to reveal its genealogy in the preceding acts of our consciousness, this is a thesis deserving of serious consideration.

What is the importance of these logical studies in the context of the problems of this book? *Prima facie* they seem to have nothing to do with Kierkegaard's thesis that truth is subjectivity. If, however, one goes deeper into the matter, one finds that Husserl says: "Truth is evidently the correlate of the perfect rationality of the original belief, of the certainty of belief" (*Wahrheit ist offenbar das Korrelat des vollkommenen Vernunftcharakters der Urdoxa, der Glaubensgewissheit*).[1] In other words, truth is based on right belief, or on subjectivity. This is not an antithesis to, but a correlate to Kierkegaard's thesis, based on a completely different interpretation of subjectivity which stresses its rational character. All those who attempt the formulation of an existentialist logic should keep this in mind. An existentialist logic, which takes Kierkegaard as its foundation, seems to be impossible, whereas Husserl's way appears to be promising. Generally speaking, his logical studies represent a healthy reaction to a development of logic, in which this discipline became more and more abstract and sometimes a mere play with symbols. In opposition to this they stress the

---

[1] *Ideen* (1st ed.), p. 290. W. R. Boyce Gibson translates: "Truth is manifestly the correlate of the perfect rational character of the protodoxy, the believing certainty."

interdependence of logic and experience. The emphasis is right, though one need not accept Husserl's specific interpretation.

He is most fruitful in the analysis of special problems, logical, semantical and epistemological. He is stimulating in his call "back to the problems, to the objects, to the phenomena as we experience them". His phenomenological method is fruitful, but may be understood and has been understood in very different manners.

He failed, however, as soon as he tried to become the Descartes-Kant of the present generation. He is the last representative of a philosophy of consciousness, *i.e.* of the attempt to base our whole knowledge of the world, of ourselves and of other persons on pure consciousness. This attempt broke down completely in his theory of other selves, on which he worked, as he told me, for ten years. He further failed in his attitude to common sense; its complete rejection does not make sense, for after all a philosopher talks to ordinary people who are unable to exchange their "natural standpoint" for an "unnatural" one. It is therefore understandable that his French audience was surprised and puzzled (*dérouté*) about his *Méditations cartésiennes*, especially about the transformation of Descartes' concrete *moi-même* into an abstract Kantian transcendental *Ego*. For the same reason the existentialists replace his consciousness by existence, re-install the natural standpoint, and liberate the phenomenological method from its unnatural and rationalist elements.

V. THE PHILOSOPHY OF DETACHMENT

I

First place among the philosophers of existence is due to Karl Jaspers, the originator of the movement. Born in 1883, he began by reading Law, went over to Medicine after three terms, became assistant at the Psychiatric Clinic in Heidelberg, Lecturer in Psychology in 1913, Professor of Philosophy in 1921, and is now teaching at the University of Bâle. His first important publication was his *General Psychopathology* (1913), which exercised a considerable influence. Jaspers is the great Psychopathologist-Philosopher of our age. He excels in the description of abnormal personalities, as individuals and as types, of Strindberg, van Gogh, Swedenborg and Hölderlin, as well as of psychasthenics and schizophrenics in general. Applying a distinction, introduced into Psychology by Dilthey, he distinguishes Comprehending and Explaining Psychopathology (*Verstehende und Erklärende Psychopathologie*); the first attempts to understand the interrelations between certain phenomena, which may be either psychological or material, the second applies causal explanation. In either case he finds that something incomprehensible remains within the personality. "What is essential in the concrete decisions of personal fate, remains hidden." This sentence occurs in the Preface to his second great work *Psychology of World-Views* (*Psychologie der Weltanschauungen*, 1919), in spite of the fact that he is chiefly interested in, and attempts to understand, "what fundamental attitudes the soul is able to adopt, and by which forces it is moved". The direct way of philosophizing is here replaced by an indirect one. Instead of constructing a philosophy of his own, Jaspers attempts to penetrate the realm of possible world-views, and to understand their emergence from certain psychological types and from forces which he calls "ideas". All this is undertaken for the sake of clarification, as a means for

59

self-reflection (*Selbstbesinnung*) and as an appeal to the free decision of the individual.

Here he reveals a deep understanding, not only for the situation of persons, but for the human condition, and discovers certain situations, connected with the finite human existence as such, which he calls "limit-situations". They arise because in this world which we experience as object, in distinction from the subject, there is nothing stable, nothing absolute, but everything in constant change, finite and split into opposites. The Whole, the Absolute, and the Essential cannot be found in it. Instead, we experience a shattering of our existence in situations of absolute chance, conflict, suffering, guilt and death. They either throw us into despair, or they awake us to an authentic choice of ourselves and of our destiny. They remind us that there must be something transcending our finite world.

Then he went on to an analysis of the present condition of man and gave a penetrating diagnosis of our time in his booklet *Die geistige Situation der Zeit* (1931), translated under the somewhat misleading title *Man in the Modern World*. He saw the problem which is still our problem, and described the present form of alienation as "provision for the masses in planned production with the help of technical devices". He is concerned about the fate of the person who is in danger of becoming a mere cog within the enormous machine of the modern welfare state and who loses his substance, self, and his spiritual centre. He believes it to be *the* great problem of our time, whether in face of this development the independent person working out his own destiny is able to survive. He wants to show the way from the unauthentic existence of mass-man to the authentic existence of the self. Or rather, he wishes to remind us what it means to be a self and to preserve one's freedom in a world of pressure-groups. The philosophy of the psychopathologist-philosopher becomes essentially *therapeutic*. He wants to appeal to every individual to take care of his historical substance *qua* self. He knows that the enormous variety of cases does not allow the prescription of one and the same cure for all, and that the

philosopher cannot do more than study ideal possibilities
in their relevance to specific cases.

But paradoxically, in spite of this attitude and of his
knowledge that he can only formulate questions and give
no answers, he made the principle of existence the basis
of a philosophy of existence. The term *existence* became
the means of reflective thought and embedded in the
ambiguities and even dialectical contradictions of an
endless reflection. These contradictions arose because
Jaspers tried to combine irreconcilable elements, viz.
Kierkegaard's principle of existence and Max Weber's
critical or sceptical attitude, especially his postulate of
Wertfreiheit der Wissenschaft, which attempted to exclude
valuations from the sphere of objective science and which
recommended the study of possibilities as a condition
for understanding reality. Kierkegaard's imperative,
"Choose yourself at every moment with absolute responsibility before God", and Weber's advice, "Refrain
from any kind of judgment of value and from any decision
in your teaching", seem to be opposed to each other when
applied simultaneously in the act of philosophizing. The
result was that Jaspers became on the one hand *un fidèle
manqué*, and on the other *un sceptique manqué*. Paradoxically Weber determines the *reality* and Kierkegaard
merely the *possibility* of the philosopher Jaspers. For as a
philosopher he follows the principle of moving in nothing
but possibilities. He wishes to remain free for all
possibilities, including the absolute *yes* of irrational faith
and the absolute *no* of nihilism, without ever making a
final decision. As a consequence everything is inverted.
What should be a reality, the choice of the individual,
becomes a mere possibility, and what should remain a
possibility parades as a reality. Thus Jaspers becomes
the gliding philosopher (*der schwebende Philosoph*). He
enjoys this floating, "floating in his situation", "floating
in relation to any determined form of existence" and
Aufstieg zum schwebenden Innesein. "I am conscious of
Being", he says, "by having never accepted a determinate
form, by having never run aground." [1] Here we touch a

[1] *Von der Wahrheit*, p. 1046.

central characteristic of Jaspers's thought. At first it seemed to me to be based on a fear of decision, but now I see that there is more to it. Its positive element is the vitality of a philosopher who enjoys the uncertain flutterings from every form of possible or actual being to another.[1]

Since it is impossible never to make a decision for a determinate form, there are in fact decisions implied: *e.g.* it has been decided, on the one hand, "that authentic being is shapeless" and "that shapelessness represents the highest value", and on the other "that shapeless Being is all-comprehensive", because it is the origin of every form. Consequently his reflection oscillates between the poles of shapelessness and the unobjectified (*Ungegenständliche*) on the one hand, and the all-Comprehensive or all possible objects on the other. It is an attitude which wants to embrace everything in History and Nature and in the Realm of Possibility without making a definite decision for anything; paradoxically combined with the complementary appeal to everyone to make his own choice on the basis of an unconditional imperative.

2

The challenge to which Jaspers responds is evident. But what are the problems he attempts to solve? Without knowing them we cannot understand his statements which are supposed to be their solution. In a charming autobiographical sketch [2] Jaspers tells us that, searching for truth in the sciences, he was disappointed by the often dogmatic and contradictory statements of different scientists. Longing for communication with other persons, he felt frustrated and was thrown back into loneliness. Consulting the great thinkers of the past, he found that Kant had best formulated the fundamental philosophical questions, viz.: What can I know? What shall I do? What may I hope for? What is man? On the basis

---

[1] *Way to Wisdom*, p. 130.
[2] "Über meine Philosophie," in *Rechenschaft und Ausblick*, (Piper, München, 1951), pp. 333 ff.

of his personal experience, with Kierkegaard's contribution in mind, he reformulated them as: (1) What is science? (2) How is communication possible? (3) What is truth? (4) What is man? (5) What is transcendence?

Only the problem of communication is new. It leads to the central thesis that the individual for himself cannot become man; cut off from others he sinks into neurotic despair; only in communication with them can he become himself. But what kinds of communication are possible? How do they belong together? In what sense is the ability to be lonely a source of communication? These topical questions should be compared with the thesis of J. Z. Young's Reith Lectures on *Doubt and Certainty in Science*, that man as the communicating animal owes his pre-eminence to the fact that he developed the power of communication far beyond other animals. Young's biological and Kierkegaard's and Jaspers's existential communication refer to the same problem on profoundly different levels.

What kind of problems then are Jaspers's questions? Linguistic, logical, epistemological or moral? No, they are metaphysical, based on the view that Science, Self, and World have to be transcended. Although Jaspers is often misinterpreted as a moralist, the moral problem does not figure among them. Kant's moral problem is replaced, or rather supplemented, by that of communication. Kant's categorical imperative is accepted, but regarded as insufficient. In so far as ethics plays a rôle in Jaspers's thought, it has a metaphysical function; it allows us to encounter the unconditional in the form of the unconditional imperative. His problems are at the same time existential in that they arise from the self and return to it.

Jaspers's sketch is still more interesting in what it leaves out. The overriding problem, which arises immediately from the challenge of our time, is not mentioned at all, namely how to transform unauthentic being into authentic being. On the contrary, in the end it is overshadowed by the other one, "how the One is in the many, what it is, and how I can be sure of it". Consequently neither unauthentic nor authentic being is really analysed, and the reader has difficulty in assessing the precise meaning of these terms. Jaspers could perhaps reply that the two problems are one and the same, looked at from opposite directions. He could say with the Hindus: "My true self is not the individual soul, but the supreme Self, the One; and therefore I reach my authentic being in identifying myself with the One." This is a possibility considered by him, but not chosen univocally.

We must know further what kind of answers he intends to give. Are they always straightforward and sometimes of absolute certainty? Is he really, as we are told, the Descartes of the moral consciousness who "shatters all doubt" by the "unconditional affirmation of the self in decisions and choice?" [1] Or is this a misinterpretation? Jaspers discounts direct dogmatic answers concerning existence, communication, man, and the transcendent; all of them are indefinable, to be clarified only by indirect answers. Indirect communication is his own mode of existence, appropriate to his rejection of a specific standpoint and his acceptance of the principle of the "universal movability of the standpoint" (*Universale Standpunktsbeweglichkeit*). His Philosophy of the Comprehensive wants to understand and to embrace all standpoints without choosing any one of them. This principle is most interesting, but based on a tragic mistake, it frustrates Jaspers's self-realisation. Theoretically I may stand at any point of the terrestrial or intellectual globe, but practically only at one specific spot at this moment. The *gliding* philosopher cannot do more than utter some calls and, without communicating his own truth, appeal to everyone to awaken to his authentic being.

Jaspers univocally rejects unauthentic being. We are unauthentic as members of mass-society, being lived by society and by the state; as members of the empirical world, dominated by impulses and natural desires; as mere *Dasein* (being-there); and as not being true to ourselves. He is likewise sure that one should go on from "being-there" to "being-oneself" (existence); that exist-

---

[1] H. I. Blackham, *Six Existentialist Thinkers* (Routledge, London, 1952), p. 49.

ence is only real as freedom; that in the ensuing act of choice, I recognize myself as the true self; that choosing, I am; and that this choice, though arising in a concrete historical situation, must be unconditioned by external circumstances. This freedom is not licence, but rather the autonomy, not of a universal self (Kant) or of a general will (Rousseau), but of a concrete individual determining itself in its further choices. The self is called upon to make an unconditional decision, based either on a personal imperative, or on a categorical imperative, or on the ten commandments. Man should choose himself according to his conscience, which is the voice of God in him, and he should therefore regard his self as a gift from God. Always, however, my choice remains a risk. I can never be quite sure that I was right. "*Selbst in der Gewissheit des Entschlusses muss, soweit er in der Welt erscheint, eine Schwebe bleiben.*" "Even in the certainty of my decision, in so far as it is manifest in this world, there must remain a floating (*i.e.* an uncertainty)." [1] Self-security is not granted to us. My conscience may have been in error. I may have been mistaken. Our choice is therefore neither absolute nor necessary.

3

Jaspers is in search of Being, *i.e.* of the Absolute, but is convinced with Kant and the Idealists of East and West that it cannot be found within the world as experienced by us, *i.e.* as an object in contradistinction from the subject. As long as we move within the subject-object-split the world is merely phenomenal, a construction of our mind. As Kant taught us, we order the chaos of our sensations with the help of the synthesis of our intuition (space and time) and of our understanding (categories). "All being must be objectified for us in such forms, it becomes phenomenon for us, it is for us as we know it, and not as it is in itself. Being is neither the object that confronts us, whether we perceive it or think it, nor is it the subject." [2] Only if we succeed in overcoming the split into subject

---

[1] *Der Philosophische Glaube* (München, 1948), p. 58; *The Perennial Scope of Philosophy* (N.Y., 1949), p. 72 (unsatisfactory translation).
[2] *The Perennial Scope of Philosophy*, p. 14. (American ed., p. 8.)

and object and in transcending the phenomenal world have we a chance of reaching authentic being and of becoming free. In other words, Jaspers believes with Kant that we are citizens of two worlds, one material and one spiritual, and that the latter represents true reality. Kant denied the possibility of theoretical knowledge of things-in-themselves and of the *noumenal* world, but he held that *qua* moral beings we belong to that world and that ethics offers a key to metaphysical knowledge. Where Kant was certain, Jaspers is doubtful. Kant was certain of the objectivity of the phenomenal world, of the necessity of the causal laws governing Nature, and of the binding character of the moral law. Jaspers, on the contrary, is opposed to "objectivities", because they seem to curtail the freedom of the individual. He rejects the authority of State and Church, objective metaphysics and ontological knowledge, for by apparently granting the individual "final security in selfless objectivities", they in fact restrict his freedom of communication with other beings.

He attempts to overcome the split between subject and object, because it cuts us off from reality. With Schelling he holds that we are able to transcend to the unity of the subject-object. But again, where Schelling was certain, Jaspers is doubtful. Schelling claimed to grasp, with the help of an intellectual intuition, the unity of subject-object as that of mind and matter, and to possess a knowledge of the identities contained in it. Jaspers rejects this claim, and is satisfied with introducing a new name by calling the unity of subject-object the Comprehensive, *das Umgreifende*, and claiming that "although it cannot be an adequate object, it is of this, and with this in mind, that we speak when we philosophize ".[1] He assumes that this Comprehensive manifests itself in the duality of subject and object, and that it forms the object of Philosophical Faith. "Faith is an experience of the Comprehensive." Philosophical Faith, without *credo* and dogma, is purely contingent potential faith in continuous movement, which never comes to rest in a specific body of truths, but has to be reformulated by everyone on the basis of his own experience. It remains a *venture of radical openness*. The wish to remain open for all possibilities is dominant, combined with the desire to be all-comprehensive.

Here Jaspers enters into competition with Hegel. Like Hegel he desires to incorporate, in his *Logic*, all the fruitful principles of the great philosophies of the past, and follows him in writing a *World-History of Philosophy*, in which all philosophies are interpreted as revelations of Being, or of the Comprehensive, in human existence. Like him, and in opposition to him, he has published an all-comprehensive *Philosophy of History* in his *Vom Ursprung und Ziel der Geschichte* (1949), which culminates in a penetrating analysis of our present situation. This book represents a new Philosophy of History for our age of transition from the Christian era to the period of world-unity. Rejecting Hegel's dictum that the appearance of Christ is the "axis of world-history", *i.e.* the aim of the preceding, and the origin of the subsequent centuries, he tries to fix the real *axis* of history empirically at about 500 B.C. Eager to find a common historical origin for East and West, he claims the time from 860 to 200 B.C. as Axial Era. He holds that in these centuries man as we know him to-day, with his religion, art, philosophy and science, emerged in China, India, Persia, Palestine and Greece. This period, and not the birth of Christ, marks the true turning-point of history. He holds that a new Axial Era is approaching, and the analysis of the three tendencies leading to it, *i.e.* of socialism, the movement towards world-unity, and of faith, forms one of the most valuable parts of the book. He formulates the crucial question, whether Europe has still the strength to avoid a relapse into its Asiatic background with its despotism, uniformity and loss of personal liberty. In Jaspers's development this book marks a transition from reflecting upon mere possibilities to a consideration of historical reality. But does he actually reach reality, or rather a *possible* history, as the stage on which man reveals himself in all his potentialities, and which moves from one fictitious Axial Era to another equally fictitious? Here again it could be said, that where Hegel is certain, Jaspers is doubtful. Hegel actually incorporates the principles of the preceding philosophies in his system, Jaspers, however, merely potentially, because he knows that Nietzsche, Marx and Kierkegaard have created a new climate of thought which makes the repetition of Hegel's venture impossible for us.

Jaspers's existentialism is all-comprehensive without accepting anything as final. It would be true and false to call it Platonic, neo-Platonic, Kantian, Schellingian or Hegelian, for it incorporates elements of these systems, but rejects each system as such. It could be called dogmatic, critical or sceptical: dogmatic, because it accepts the all-Comprehensive, without asking whether there is such a thing; critical, because it rejects dogmatic attitudes wherever they occur either in pseudo-science or in theology; and sceptical, because no finite statement of existence is accepted as definitive. At different stages certain of these elements prevail. The standpoint of his great work, *Philosophie* (1932), could rightly be character-ized as transcendental existentialism, because in it the Kantian act of transcending prevails. "Philosophy of existence", says Jaspers, "is a way of thinking which uses and transcends all material knowledge, in order that man may again become himself." The articulation of this system is based on three acts of transcending, namely first, a transcending to the Universal in the realm of objects, *e.g.* to the idea of the unity of science (*Weltorientierung*); secondly, a transcending of the empirical data, given in our knowledge, to an elucidation of our authentic being (*Existenzerhellung*); and lastly, the attempt to reach the Absolute in metaphysics. The latter is, however, not based on *a priori* cognition, but on the interpretation of our concrete historical experience as a symbol in which Trans-cendence communicates with us. But although each of the finite objects which we encounter is a revelation of the Absolute, not one of them can be identified with it.

4

Here his non-committal attitude comes to the fore. Thought liberates us from the particularity of objects, and "from the fetters of determinate thinking, not by re-linquishing it, but by carrying it to the extreme". Reversing our direction it forces us back from the impasse of solidification (*Verfestigung*). By freeing us from the bondage of finite existence it exercises a quasi-religious function of conversion. In opposition to the Philosophy of Finiteness, as formulated by Heidegger, it turns us to the Infinite. Whereas Heidegger asserts that human existence is essentially finite, Jaspers replies that all authentic being, whether of God or of Man, is indefinite or infinite. "For those who found support in the absoluteness of things and in a theory of knowledge confined to objects, the loss of them is nihilism. Exclusive reality and truth cannot be claimed for that which discourse and objective thinking have made determinate and hence finite." [1] In fact, however, it is not nihilism, but a liberation for authentic being, which is called a "philosophical rebirth". "The fall from established positions (*Festigkeiten*) which, after all, were delusive, becomes an ability of floating. What seemed an abyss, becomes space for freedom; apparent Nothingness is transformed into that from which authentic being speaks to us." [1]

All this is most interesting. It formulates the experience of our age and of all ages, *i.e.* that the "solidity" and security of established positions, human institutions, and of all finite beings are illusory. On this earth everything is transitory and subject to dissolution. An experience, which is *prima facie* merely negative, is here turned to positive account. Jaspers is quite right: if we do not want to fall into the abyss of Nothingness, we have to learn gliding or floating. But if all this has been said, it cannot be denied that reflection and negation prevail in this attitude. Negation of finiteness by itself does not produce a positive result, but merely a movement *qua* movement, dominated by the feeling of the insecurity of finite existence.

A *philosophy of evanescence* emerges. "The reality of the World has an evanescent existence between God and existence." God remains invisible, inconceivable and unthinkable. "No symbol or metaphor can describe

[1] *Way to Wisdom*, pp. 37–38.

Him and none may take His place. All metaphorical representations of God without exceptions are myths, meaningful as such when understood to be mere hints and parallels, but they become superstitions when taken for the reality of God Himself." [1]   Man likewise remains a non-object to himself which cannot be exhausted by knowledge, it can only be experienced.   But although God, the World and Man are essentially non-objective, they nevertheless remain the objects of our attention, to be elucidated again and again.

It is a sort of inverted Hegelianism.   Whereas for Hegel the Absolute was result, here it is non-result, frustration or *Scheitern*.   As soon as something gets its definite shape it is finished for Jaspers.   He is therefore the most elusive of philosophers, and even declines to choose a specific definition of philosophy. *His philosophy of elusiveness* is a game of hide-and-seek going on indefinitely.   It does not offer specific solutions, but it raises questions, awakens men from their dogmatic slumber, and reveals the precariousness of their position.   Traditional forms of philosophizing are fundamentally transformed by it.

It is at the same time potential, though not actual, mysticism.   The elements are there out of which a genuine mystical philosophy could arise; the evanescence of the world and of man has been stressed by many mystics; but here the mystical experience and the belief in the reality of the object of this experience are missing. No mystic could endorse Jaspers's confession, "I do not know whether I believe."   Therefore those who claim him for Huxley's *Perennial Philosophy* should be careful. He simultaneously accepts and rejects it, and consequently remains a *mystique manqué*.

5

Jaspers had the misfortune that his *Philosophie* appeared in 1932, *i.e.* immediately before the advent of the Nazis. He was at once out of favour with the new régime, his wife being a Jewess, and he lost his professorship at

[1] *Way to Wisdom*, p. 48.

Heidelberg in 1937. In the years of his retirement, which lasted until the end of the Second World War in 1945, he went on with his work. This limit-situation which he himself had to experience and to suffer gave him not only time to study the prophet Jeremiah, but brought about a change in his attitude which allows us to speak of a second period. Paradoxically this change finds its expression in a bulky volume of some 1100 pages, *Philosophische Logik*, vol. I, *Von der Wahrheit*. It is paradoxical for two reasons. First, because it still suffers from the contradiction that the principle of existence is strictly personal, fluid and impossible of systematization, and that nevertheless an attempt at systematization is made, this time in an existentialist logic. Secondly, because in the end it turns out to be something completely different from logic. This *Philosophical Logic* or *Of Truth*, which is commonly regarded as the most important German philosophical post-war publication, could best be described as "Variations on a Kierkegaardian Theme", namely the theme that "Subjectivity is Truth". This means that what matters is not objective truth of science which abstracts from the existing subject, but subjective truth in which the existing subject remains the centre of interest and truth becomes the same as "true being" (*Wahrsein*). Jaspers's subject-matter is "the clarification of man as a knowing being" (*Erhellung des erkennenden Menschseins*). "The purpose of Logic, the clarification of our knowledge-of-truth as it occurs in historical time, is to determine the limits and origin of the meaning of truth." In short, Jaspers attempts to create an existentialist logic. In fact, however, he describes in unending reflections his search for true being or for the Transcendent. It should lead him from a state of unreality and untruthfulness, through an indefinite number of finite possible realizations (*Gestalten*) of truth, to the true reality which should redeem him, but which he does not reach. Details of this reflective search (based on a new metaphysics, the *Philosophie des Umgreifenden*) are most interesting, *e.g.* the analysis of different forms of knowing, of language, of the category of "exception", etc., but cannot be discussed here.

The general questions raised by this original enterprise are more important to us, and we shall have to return to them later. But although the book, as we shall see, fails as logic proper, it marks nevertheless an important step in Jaspers's development. It describes his way from untruth to truth, from appearance to reality. The philosophy of existence becomes here a kind of *Ersatz*-religion of the lonely individual. Whereas in his *Philosophie* he proclaimed a conflict between philosophy on the one hand and religion and theology on the other, the Kierkegaardian terms now regain their religious flavour. This does not imply a return to Christianity or to any sort of revealed or dogmatic religion, but to a kind of natural theology. Philosophy is transformed in a manner similar to that occurring in the philosophy of the Stoics and the neo-Platonists in the Hellenistic period. The philosopher now looks for liberation, salvation, peace, and for the perfection of authentic being. "True philosophizing, it is said, is based on an act of concentration, in which reason (*Vernunft*) provides space and movement, love, fulfilment, and symbol (*Chiffer*), the content (*Gehalt*) of the consciousness of being" (p. 962). The philosopher seems to become an initiator into the mysteries of being, and in exceptional moments to partake in the secrets of creation. Jaspers seems to feel himself as a sort of spiritual teacher turned philosopher of existence. He is the mediator, and the methodical form of his philosophizing is mediation (*Zwischensein, das Mittlere*), based on loving knowledge or knowing love, a sort of Spinozistic *amor intellectualis Dei*. But not only the philosopher, but also the world, as interpreted by us, becomes a mediator. "Our possible perfection", he says, "lies in mediation. The way to God leads through the world of appearances. The transformation of the world into a mediation between us and the one God is a transformation of the world into a symbolic being (*Chiffersein*)." Reality itself is experienced as the one God. It is an attempt to overcome the alienation of the world by interpreting its phenomena as symbolic expressions of a transcendent reality. This is Jaspers's way to God, as such very personal, not very clear, but beyond discussion.

What then is dead in Jaspers's Philosophy of Existence? First, the attempt to move through mere possibilities. This is incompatible with the principle of existence. Therefore the ensuing philosophy is non-existential. Kierkegaard would say: "X has thought out all possibilities, and nevertheless he has not existed." "It is a fundamental confusion of modern science that it mistakes the abstract discussion of standpoints for existence, in such a manner that people believe they could exist (gliding indifferently over standpoints), whereas every existing individual as existing has to be more or less one-sided." [1] Secondly, *the endeavour to make the principle of existence the basis of a philosophy, or to produce a philosophy of existence.* Kierkegaard is right, "there cannot be any system of existence".[2] Jaspers knows this, therefore he remains in the attitude of appealing; but, in spite of this, he tries to construct a system; that, however, is a contradiction in terms. In producing a philosophy Jaspers mistakes a part for the whole, an attribute or function of philosophy for its substance.

6

But what is alive in Jaspers's philosophy of existence? This question has to be repeated, seeing that his new publications, *Vom Ursprung der Geschichte* and *Way to Wisdom. An Introduction to Philosophy* (Engl. transl., Gollancz, 1951), show signs of utmost vitality. In attempting to answer it I take the opportunity of replying to objections of a pupil of Jaspers who maintains that neither my exposition nor my criticism of his teacher's philosophy are to the point. I shall, however, restrict myself to those points which concern the fate of existentialism, in which alone I am interested at the moment.

My characterization of Jaspers as "the gliding philosopher" is not rejected; but it is maintained that this gliding has a positive function. "The gliding of his

[1] *Concluding Unscientific Postscript* (German ed.), vol. ii, pp. 302, 337.
[2] *L.c.* (ed. Lowrie), p. 107.

thought has its origin in the fact that the object is not allowed to remain fixed in the act of transcendence, because otherwise the non-objective, the Transcendent, could not be experienced. The gliding does not, however, imply that our thought does not reach any results; on the contrary, it implies that the highest result, the inner experience of Being (*das Innewerden des Seins*), is achieved." This formulation, however, is not quite precise; for a naive reader could object: Is there not perhaps a more direct way for experiencing Being than that which leads through the more than a thousand pages of the *Philosophical Logic*? What Jaspers really aims at is the inner experience of essential Being or of Being in itself. Before entering into a discussion of the problems connected with this attempt, I add the conclusions drawn by my correspondent from these statements, *i.e.* that "gliding" or the act of bringing the problems into the state of gliding (*das In-Schwebe-Bringen*) is something quite different from a "fear of decision". The *Philosophical Logic* says, so he maintains, *expressis verbis*, that what is reached in the second step ought to be put in a state of gliding in order to proceed to the third step, *i.e.* decision (*cf.* pp. 154, 187, 545, etc.).

Two remarks have to be made to these claims, one general and one specific. The first is this, that this gliding is by no means restricted to Jaspers's thought, but that he here expresses something which is characteristic of our age. It is noteworthy that Émile Bréhier in his report on the present state of philosophy in France, *Transformation de la philosophie française* (Paris, 1950), remarks generally, and without any reference to Jaspers, that at the moment the danger to philosophy does not come from without, *e.g.* from science, but from within, *i.e.* from the gliding of problems: "Son véritable péril est interne; il est dans une sorte de *glissement des problèmes* qui les fait évanouir peu à peu et comme se dissiper en des genres de pensée très variés et qui n'ont rien à voir avec la philosophie, dont l'unité et par conséquent l'existence sont ainsi profondément atteintes" (p. 232).

My second point refers to the fact that the decisive

passage is not quoted, although it is contained in a paragraph with the title "The decision how the One is reached (either by a fixation or in a movement which remains open)". It reads: "It is therefore the fundamental philosophical decision, how the One is apprehended. Either I grasp the One in one of the knowing, fixing, curtailing manners, or in a way for which all philosophical thoughts are merely preparations and possibilities, *i.e.* in a movement which is embracing, discursive, losing and regaining itself, and which leads from origin back to origin. This essential movement towards the One, since it cannot be seen from outside, cannot be known in its totality and therefore not be willed in the strict sense of the word. Therefore no advice is possible, how the way could be found and how an itinerary could be planned in a universally valid and identical manner. Nevertheless, the movement, arising from the source of Being and leading from the One to the One, must be able to guide all our knowing and willing. In this case our knowing and willing remain open-minded, from the start directed towards the One, without running into blind alleys, and free from the danger of fixation. Although any precise statements about the way and about the One may be premature and lead us astray, nevertheless it is not impossible to characterize the movement with reference to the whole process of philosophizing, positively, through the illumination of horizons and possibilities, and negatively, through the elimination of misleading pathways" (p. 706).

This quotation confirms, in a surprising manner, everything I have said. For here the fixation (*Verfestigung*) is rejected as a fixing, curtailing manner of thinking, as a loss of essential being, *i.e.* as a misleading movement. This implies a decision against Parmenides and against logic. Psychologically it is extremely interesting that Jaspers believes that he is able to make a decision for a movement which is and remains open. But what is a decision which cannot really be willed? Is it not in fact a decision to make no decision? Let us imagine Nature to be directed by a Jasperian world-mind. What would be the result? No cell, no leaf, no violet, no oak, no kitten, no rose, in short, no form would emerge because endowed with the sin of fixation and curtailment. In other words, Jaspers's alternative is unnatural and unreal. The two possibilities do not exclude, but include, each other in the realms of Nature and Mind, in so far as these are creative. It is the secret of Nature that she has made a decision for both simultaneously, *i.e.* for a fixation within a movement which, nevertheless, remains open, and for an open movement passing through fixations. Nothing is to be said against Jaspers's personal decision. If, however, it is advertised as "the only possible form of philosophizing which is methodically justifiable", philosophy cannot acknowledge this claim. As a matter of fact, this way leads merely to the possibility of Nature, Mind and God, but not to their reality.

This brings me to my central thesis, namely that *the philosophy of existence reaches a state of perfection, fails and is transcended in Jaspers's last writings.* It reaches a state of perfection or it finds its fulfilment, because once more it turns full cycle. The religious motives of its origin are again coming to the fore. It is a return to Kierkegaard, to Biblical religion and to a quasi-mediæval system of axioms. All this, however, happens, not in a straightforward, but in a broken manner. It is said: "The Bible and Biblical religion form the foundation of our philosophizing, provide as such a lasting scheme of reference and are the source of irreplaceable conceptions. Western philosophizing— whether we admit it or not—is always with the Bible, even when it struggles against it." [1] But at the same time the claim to exclusive validity, by which this religion dominated mediæval philosophy, is rejected. Jaspers reaches, in his development, the stage of philosophical faith. He even formulates five philosophical principles of faith, *i.e.* God is; there is an absolute imperative (*Forderung*); man is finite and cannot reach the stage of perfection (*er ist unvollendbar*); man can live guided by God; and, the reality of the world has an evanescent being (*verschwindendes Dasein*) between God and human existence.

[1] *Der Philosophische Glaube*, p. 75 (*The Perennial Scope of Philosophy*, p. 97).

The last thesis is shared by some existentialists, like Kierkegaard and Berdyaev who, however, would like to reject this world altogether. During the Middle Ages these propositions would have been pronounced as dogmas. But in Jaspers's philosophy they have merely the function of appealing and communicating, and their antitheses are being discussed. The philosophy of existence here reaches the stage of perfection, because the aim of existence is fulfilled. From the beginning its intention was to hold open the way to the Transcendent and to God. Nevertheless, Jaspers remains a *fidèle manqué* and a frustrated Christian philosopher.

In fulfilling itself, this existentialism fails. This does by no means imply that Jaspers *qua* philosopher fails, but merely that his philosophy of existence suffers shipwreck. Existentialism fails because it proves unable to provide a basis for either logic or ethics. To have proved this may be counted among the negative merits of Jaspers's *Von der Wahrheit*, the considerable positive merits of which book do not form the subject of my present inquiry. The Philosophical Logic which here emerges is a *mixtum compositum* of metaphysics, logic, epistemology, psychology and ethics. It is extremely interesting and rich in details, but it is not logic. Is it possible to write a logic nowadays, without taking into account the work of those leading logicians, whose names are not even mentioned, *i.e.* Boole, Brentano, Frege, Husserl, Keynes, Lewis, Langford, Lukasiewicz, Morgan, Natorp, Poincaré, Peirce, Royce, Bertrand Russell (whose mere name once appears), Scholz, Schröder, Tarski and Whitehead? It is true, Aristotle forgot to give a definition of logic, and it is not easy to phrase it in such a manner that it is sufficient and comprehensive at the same time. Nevertheless, logic is and remains the science of the rules of correct reasoning. It is our duty to be uncompromising on this point and to avoid concessions which are out of place. For we are faced, in all countries which either are, or have been, under the sway of dictators, with generations of young people who have lost the faculty of thinking for themselves and for whom a serious study of logic, devoted solely to the objective data of this science, is an indispensable medicine. I have never understood why it is the ambition of nearly every German professor of philosophy to produce his own personal logic, instead of devoting his forces to the much more useful task of contributing to the development of the science of logic, as it is a matter of course for any scientist within his field. In fact, human life is too short for this pastime, just as it would be impossible for every individual to construct his own personal language. Nevertheless we have to be most grateful to Jaspers for his original attempt, which forces us to raise the following questions. Is it at all possible to combine the subjective principle of existence with logic and to construct an existentialist logic? Shall we have to acknowledge Jaspers's book as a possible new form of logic, comparable to Hegel's *Logic*, but based on a much tamer form of dialectic and replacing Hegel's all-devouring reason by Kant's finite understanding in its unending search for the Infinite? [1] Or shall we say, in order to avoid possible confusion, that this attempt has nothing to do with logic proper in the traditional and strict sense of the word? And shall we add that the conception of an existentialist logic is based on a misunderstanding because it tries to reconcile irreconcilables? But even if the book were a failure as a whole, we could neglect the rich harvest of its particular analyses only to our own loss. We should say with Goethe: "I love him who desires the Impossible."

This philosophy of existence further fails because it is unable to serve as a basis for ethics. It may not be without interest to note that Frenchmen regard it as a criterion for the success of a philosophy whether or not it is able to construct an ethics. It could be objected that Jaspers talks of "absolute actions" in a most beautiful and edifying manner. That is true and most enjoyable. "The unconditional imperative challenges me as the imperative of my own essential self addressed to my empirical existence. I am becoming conscious of myself as the being that I am, because I should be like this. This inner experience (*Innewerden*) is obscure in the beginning,

[1] *Cf*. pp. 80 ff.

but lucid at the end of my unconditional action." [1]   Is that, I wonder, a sufficient basis for ethics?   Could not a criminal, like Hitler, justify his most cruel actions with exactly the same words?   "The Unconditional as a basis of our action is a matter, not of knowledge, but of faith." Is that satisfactory, so long as the faith, which is supposed to serve as a basis, remains undefined?   Or is it the intention to find a quasi-theological foundation of ethics, seeing that the unconditional imperative figures among the axioms of Philosophical Faith?   In any case, so far it has not been proved that an ethics can be based on Jaspers's principle of existence.   He himself would probably agree with this, for he now rejects the mere "existence" of existentialism.

However that may be, it cannot be denied that the philosophy of existence is now transcended by a metaphysics of the Comprehensive, the outlines of which we have sketched.   It seems as if at this stage of Jaspers's development the philosophy of existence were in a state of dissolution, and as if the metaphysics of the all-comprehensive represented what is alive in it.   The question, what is alive in his philosophy of existence? could therefore be answered by an apparent paradox: "What is alive in it, is that the philosophy of existence reaches a stage of perfection, fails and withers away.   In so doing it fulfils its original function of keeping open the way to the Transcendent and of becoming the jumping-off ground for a new metaphysics which is in fact the old idealistic metaphysics of East and West expressed in a novel language." [2]   The principle of existence as appeal, *i.e.* as a regulative idea in Kant's sense, remains as alive as ever it was. [3]

---

[1] *Way to Wisdom*, p. 55 (my translation).

[2] He himself is aware of this fact.   In an apparent antithesis to Heidegger, who attempts to reject the whole metaphysics of the past in order to replace it by something completely new, Jaspers rejects any such claim.   "My basic idea in its ramifications is only apparently new.   It cannot be really new because I have spent my life conscious of rediscovering ancient wisdom" (*Von der Wahrheit*, p. 192).

[3] *Cf.* pp. 202 ff.

7

In 1950 Jaspers himself (like Marcel, but for very different reasons) gave up the title "philosopher of existence" and now wishes to be a "philosopher of reason" instead. He writes:

> Some twenty years ago I spoke of philosophy of existence. I added that it was not a new and specific philosophy of its own, but the one eternal philosophy in which, at a time when it had lost itself in objectivity, all stress had to be laid on Kierkegaard's basic conception [*i.e.* of truth as subjectivity].
>
> To-day I should prefer to call [my] philosophy "philosophy of reason", because now it seems to be urgent to stress this original characteristic of philosophy. Once reason gets lost, everything is lost. From the very beginning its task has been, and still remains, to acquire reason, to restore itself as reason, albeit as reason proper. This reason submits to the logical necessities of the understanding and appropriates its methods and results without succumbing to its limitations.[1]

What is this reason? It is neither the French *raison*, nor the English *reason*. Following Kant, and T. S. Coleridge for that matter, Jaspers distinguishes reason (*Vernunft*) from the understanding, but neither in the same manner nor with the same precision. The *understanding* is to him "objectifying conceiving (*Verstehen*) with the help of isolating comprehending (*Begreifen*)", whereas the *reason* is unobjectifying understanding which views everything in its relation to the comprehensive whole. It remains inseparable from the thought of the understanding and bound up with it at any moment. "*Vernunft*", says Jaspers, "is *Vernehmen* (apperception) in response to any creature and to any possibility, to Being as well as to Nothing." Described in very personal terms, it remains elusive. Only its functions become apparent. It is the driving power of our thought, the bond between all spheres of our experience and of the Comprehensive (*Dasein, Bewusstsein überhaupt, Geist,*

[1] *Vernunft und Widervernunft in unserer Zeit* (München, 1950), p. 49. *Reason and Anti-Reason in our Time* (C.S.M., London, 1952), p. 63.

Existenz), and between the oppositions and contradictions pervading them. It attempts to combine them all
in a comprehensive unity.

> All this is comprehended by reason and acknowledged in
> its proper place. Reason adds the infinite dialectic, which
> is not exhausted, neither by alternatives nor by the *not only-
> but also*, nor by the *either-or*, neither by mediation nor
> by a breach. It accepts all this, goes over it step by step,
> and, nevertheless, penetrates further, restless in its rest.[1]

It is reason in the process of infinite dialectic, the heir of
Hegel's and Kierkegaard's dialectic. Jaspers accepts
as well as rejects the Hegelian dialectic of alternatives and
of the *not only-but also* with the ensuing mediation, and
likewise the Kierkegaardian dialectic of the *either-or* with
its ensuing breach. However, in the attempt at synthesizing the two, he in fact falls back on the Kantian dialectic
of indefinite progress.

Reason does not allow us to be satisfied with *one* specific
form of truth, but forces us to transcend any of these forms
as preliminary and non-final. An adherence to a specific
truth is as impossible as a fixation to a specific finite
being. "Any allegedly perfect truth reveals itself as
untruth and leads to frustration."

> Truth is always on the way in time, always in movement
> and never becomes final, not even in its most wonderful
> crystallizations. It is a condition of true philosophizing
> not to forget this basic situation. . . . Unauthentic existence
> (*das sich versagende Leben*) wants to have the security of
> finiteness, wants to boast with possession and stability.
> Authentic life takes risks. It is a high-level life, accepting
> the unconditional claims made on it, and the greater
> dangers implied in them. Exposed to extreme situations
> existence has to prove its worth in making decisions between
> alternatives which take the form of an *either-or*. Faced by
> them, it must either find its fulfilment or fall into the abyss.[2]

The underlying conception is imposing. It is a high-level
search for truth, a flight to truth. The existentialist logic
is now replaced by a *logic of reason* which may be realizable.
So far, however, it remains a mere possibility. Hegel's

[1] *Von der Wahrheit* (München, 1947), p. 969.
[2] *L.c.*, p. 961.

logic of reason realized itself in his well-defined method of
dialectic, and whatever may be said against him, he took
on the stern endeavour to express himself in concepts,
and his logic gained a definite shape.   So far this cannot
be said of Jaspers's logic.   Compared with Hegel's logic
it has neither shape, nor objective unity, nor a precisely
formulated method, nor conceptual form, but merely
subjective unity.   "The *leitmotif* of our whole Philosophical Logic", he says, "is the thinker who proceeds
undisturbed on his way."

Arresting as this remark may be, it again proves that the
idea of a logic of reason, as distinguished from a logic of
the understanding, remains unrealized, perhaps because
it cannot be realized in an age of catastrophes.   The
predicament of our time is here turned to advantage.
The logic of reason is treated as if its subject-matter were
the endless progress, not of reason, but of the understanding and of intellectual reflection.   In consequence
thereof Jaspers remains entangled in Hegel's *bad infinity*,
i.e. in the limitless progress of a series in which one never
meets the actual Infinite.   Jaspers is right.   Most human
truths are not definite and open to revision.   Nevertheless the Finite and the Infinite, the Temporal and the
Eternal, are not divided by an unbridgeable chasm.
Life would not be worth living if truth could never be
realized in it.   The spheres in which this is possible may
be small; but they exist, *e.g.*, in mathematics and science.
Their truths are not absolute, they depend on certain
presuppositions.   Nevertheless, within certain limits, we
may have knowledge on which we could not improve.   In
any case, the non-finality of human knowledge is no
reason for taking the *way* to truth as absolute.

What is a reason which does not live in *actual* acts of
response and apperception *here and now*, which does not
apperceive something definite, but which proceeds from
something unseizable to something likewise unseizable?
What a composer would he be who perceived merely dim
hummings and to whom never a melody was revealed!
The Infinite is *in* the Finite, the Eternal *in* the Temporal.
Eternity is present, if only we would grasp it.   Jaspers,

however, prefers to remain a *Homo Viator*. He concludes his essay, *My Way to Philosophy*, with these words:

> To find in this world, responding to it, lovingly the way of reason, and to make thought effective, that is the criterion for the truth of philosophy itself.[1]

In this respect he has succeeded. From the entanglements of existence he has found the way back to reason.

[1] *Rechenschaft und Ausblick* (Piper, München, 1951), p. 332.

VI. HEROIC DEFIANCE

I

IT is a matter of surprise to any serious student that the most fundamental concepts in a specific science, which he expects to be the clearest, are in fact often the most obscure. This is the case with the term "thinking" in philosophy. A most interesting discussion of the problem "Thinking and Language" took place at the meeting of the Aristotelean Society at Edinburgh in July 1951. It was introduced by Miss Iris Murdoch with an attempt to describe the activity of private thought, and concluded by Professor G. Ryle with the remark that the concept of *thinking* is polymorphous, and that there is no general answer to the question, "What does thinking consist of?" This symposium marks an important step in the development of the English linguistic school, *i.e.* the rediscovery that thought cannot be reduced to language and represents an activity *sui generis*. Some thirty years ago the psychologists of the Würzburg school discovered that the act of thinking is not reducible to acts of representation or to an association of ideas, a discovery which was greeted with exhilaration and relief by philosophers. To-day the linguistic philosophers are loth to concede that philosophy is more than "talk about talk".

Professor Ryle is right; the acts of thinking are polymorphous. The word *thinking* has many meanings, as any dictionary will reveal, such as "consider", "be of opinion", "intend", "expect", "form conception of", "exercise the mind otherwise than by passive reception of another's ideas" (an amusing entry of the Oxford Dictionary, revealing the difficulty of saying what thinking really consists of). Consequently one finds different interpretations and definitions of thought, such as "immediate apprehension of the Universal" and "talk of the soul with itself" (Plato), "apprehension of the essence of things" (Aristotle), "reasoning is reckoning" (Descartes, Hobbes);

whereas Locke confesses that "we know not wherein thinking consists". There are, in fact, different types of thinkers. These types differ, first, according to personal gifts; the thought may be prevalently visual and intuitive (Plato, Leonardo, Descartes, Berkeley); tactual (Atomists, Materialists); analytic (Descartes, Hume, Russell, Moore); synthetic (Kant); dialectical (Hegel, Marx); or reflective (Kierkegaard, Jaspers, Marcel). They differ, secondly, according to the age in which the thinker lives or, generally speaking, to the "field" in which he moves; early ages produce adventurous types (pre-Socratics, Francis Bacon); later times, systematic or encyclopædic thought (Aristotle, Thomas, Hegel, Comte); in times of crisis philosophies become expressions of the predicament of the age (Existentialists); thinking varies according to the field in which it arises; disturbances in the field are represented by disturbances of thought. The type of thinker varies, thirdly, according to the prevalence of impersonal or personal factors. In scientific philosophy, in mathematical or symbolic logic, impersonal factors, in existentialism personal factors, prevail. In the first case the philosopher may disappear completely behind his work, in the second case he is able to be rather original, but also very arbitrary. This is Heidegger's case. Lastly, new types arise according to the function which thinking has to fulfil in the life of the philosopher. If he needs it as a weapon of self-defence, or for the unification of his chaotic experience, or for the attainment of peace and security, he becomes a critical, systematic or religious philosopher respectively.

Is Heidegger, as some say, an *Umworter aller Worte* (rewording all words), and as the Logical Positivists assume, a mere talker, *i.e.* someone who plays with words? Or is he a real thinker? And in the latter case, what sort of thinker is he? "Building, Dwelling, and Thinking" (*Bauen, Wohnen, Denken*) was the title of a lecture delivered by Heidegger at Darmstadt on August 5, 1951, a report on which I owe to the courtesy of a German student; a very surprising, unexpected and original combination, which connects thinking with building and dwelling. The questions seem abstruse. "What is Dwelling? How far does Building belong to Residing?" His answers too seem abstruse. "To be a man means to dwell. Thought itself belongs to dwelling." It would be easy to ridicule some of his statements, but that would not help us to understand him. Nor would it be fruitful to analyse his untranslatable lecture. Nevertheless, it reveals his type of thought. His thinking is, in fact, the building and constructing of a dwelling-place, in which the philosopher can reside, or of a labyrinth, in which he dominates absolutely because he alone has in his hands Ariadne's thread which will allow him to find his way out. It is a thinking which cannot be placed in any of the just mentioned categories. It is an activity of the will dominated by what the Germans call *Denkwillen*, which is here a will to power, albeit to intellectual power, a will to construct something absolutely new, in opposition to the whole preceding history of philosophy. This will to power was not unsuccessful. In spite of the fact that he has lost his Chair at the University of Freiburg his influence in Germany is still enormous. French and Spanish complete translations of his works are in progress and new English translations are planned. This extraordinary will-power is coupled with the ability to discover unexpected associations and to coin new words which are essentially ambiguous and which therefore withstand critical attacks. Through the medium of a very personal and arbitrary kind of thinking, fired by an unconscious longing for the Holy (*das Heile und Heilige*), he attempts a unification and systematization of the experience of the inter-war generation, and thereby becomes a true expression of his age.—Is Heidegger then an original thinker and as such a spiritual leader of our time, or does he lead astray? Before we attempt to answer this question we have to ask: Is he an existentialist? This question is by no means easy to answer; and here we are faced with a paradoxical phenomenon. To a certain extent Heidegger, *qua* philosopher of existence, is my creation. My book interpreted him as an existentialist and especially as an ontologist of existence; and by

doing so helped in provoking the existentialist trend
of thought which prevailed in Germany about 1930.
Heidegger at once protested privately against this interpretation during the memorable meeting of the *Davoser
Hochschulkurse* in March 1929, which culminated philosophically in a discussion between Ernst Cassirer and
Heidegger about Kant and Metaphysics. He has since
publicly repeated this protest. But all this proved of no
avail. Such is the power of words and concepts and,
generally speaking, of a construction which brought order
into the chaos of our experience, that the impression he
made of apparently being an existentialist was historically
of greater import than his personal wish to be classified
as an ontologist. His influence in Germany as well as in
France is based on his real or alleged existentialism. Not
only all the writers on existentialism but also the compilers
of textbooks register him as an existentialist, or even make
him the leader of the whole movement. How is this to be
explained? Here again the ascendance of form over the
formless becomes apparent. Heidegger's *Sein und Zeit*
appeared in 1927, five years before Jaspers's *Philosophie*.
Moreover the existentialist Jaspers, in spite of his accepting
the title "Philosophy of Existence" and of his publishing
voluminous books, remained almost providentially shapeless. Therefore it happened that the principle of existence,
through the cunning of the idea, took possession of
Heidegger and made him play, contrary to his own will,
the rôle of an existentialist. Because, instead of moving
in mere possibilities like Jaspers, he chose one possibility
and drew, with extraordinary forming power and penetration, pictures of unauthentic and authentic existence
which were a true expression of the inarticulate longings
of the time, he stole the existentialist show from Jaspers,
just as Sartre did with Marcel in France. That he
himself as a person assimilated the principle merely
intellectually and not existentially, has unfortunately been
proved by his utter human failure in the existential trial
of the Third Reich, whereas Jaspers passed this examination with high honours and gained enormously in stature.

All this, however, does not yet solve the "Heidegger"

problem.   There is something apparently contradictory
in this man that has troubled his readers ever since the
publication of his *Sein und Zeit*.   The following incident
may illustrate this fact.   Immediately after the publication of my book, the catholic philosopher Peter Wust [1]
wrote an enthusiastic article about it on June 9, 1929, in
which he accepted my interpretation of Heidegger.
However, on July 9, 1929, I received the following letter
from him.   "To-day there is one question which I have
long wanted to put to you.   It concerns Heidegger.   In
the meantime I have been reading many interpretations of
his philosophy, *i.e.* what S. Marck, M. Beck, Przywara and
yourself have written.   I have further *tried* to read his *Vom
Wesen des Grundes* and his study of *Kant*.   According to his
last two publications *all* critics would have misinterpreted
him.   But now my question arises.   Though I recognize
his approach and starting-point, *i.e.* his wish to penetrate
to a genuine doctrine of being, I cannot rid myself of the
impression that his whole philosophizing is a single great
buffoonery (*Schaumschlägerei*) of which no one can make
head or tail for the simple reason that he himself does not
know what he really wants.   You, for instance, interpret
him in such a manner that he still forms part of modern
subjectivism.   He, however, rejects such interpretation
(in *Das Wesen des Grundes*), and there are passages in his
Kant-book where he says expressly that he wants to stress
the finiteness of man, almost like Pascal; but does he
clarify what he really wants?   I cannot see it.   Perhaps
I do not understand anything of his philosophy.   But then
I must ask, is that not also a bad sign that I, after a most
sincere effort, have to say that I do not understand him?
Dear Mr Heinemann, if you can, please write me on this
point, *i.e.* my spiritual distress (*Geistesnot*) concerning
Heidegger.   So far my impression of him is of a man who,
with a self-willed terminology, almost unconsciously produces a philosophical mystification such that sometimes
I have the impression that all of us have been cheated
(*genarrt*).   Take, *e.g.*, his definition of truth (ἀλήθεια) as

---

[1] Gabriel Marcel devotes a chapter to him in *Being and Having*, A. & C.
Black, London, 1950.

Unverborgenheit or unhiddenness of being. Are 'truth' and
'not being hidden' really the same? Is it not perhaps of
the essence of truth that, in the last instance, part of it
always remains hidden? And does an 'untruth' by the
mere fact of being revealed become a 'truth'? The
problem 'Heidegger', the sphinx 'Heidegger', haunts me.
I do not want to be unjust to him, certainly not. I have
been accustomed to reading philosophy for more than
twenty years, but I have never experienced such a case
that I had simply to state that here I have to give up.
Kant and Hegel certainly raise many problems, but if one
sincerely penetrates their writings, one gets nearer and
nearer to them; but as to Heidegger, my God! I am
confronted with one great riddle; and I am not alone in
this. Up to now, according to what he says in his last
publications, all the critics have misjudged his ultimate
intentions."

This letter strikingly formulates the still unsolved
"Heidegger"-problem which has since been accentuated.
A narrow, but very active circle of pupils hail him as the
philosophical Messiah of our age who has renewed the
quest for being, whereas Carnap and the Logical Positivists ridicule his statements as completely senseless.
Even such a well-meaning critic as Berdyaev writes:
"Heidegger, proceeding though he does from Kierkegaard,
has, ironically enough, rationalized the Kierkegaardian
theme into a rigid and almost scholastic system. He puts
a genuinely existential experience into the strait-jacket of
rational categories, which are really quite unfit for it, and,
in so doing, conjures up a whole inventory of almost
unbearable and incomprehensible terminology, the only
virtue of which is its undoubted originality. The
terminology, however, is more original than the thought.
Still, no one would deny that Heidegger is endowed with
unusual philosophical gifts, and his thought reveals great
intellectual intensity and concentration." [1]

Who then is Heidegger? If his prophets are right, he
seems to be a Messiah without a message, *i.e.* without a
new ontology. If, however, Carnap is right, how is his

[1] *Dream and Reality*, p. 103.

considerable continental influence to be understood? If his existentialism is a "mistake", does not perhaps "being misunderstood" belong essentially to his mission? He seems to be the double-faced Janus, the Jekyll and Hyde of contemporary philosophy. There is the exoteric Heidegger, with his published works, and the esoteric man, with his unpublished lectures on Anaximander, Heraclitus, Plato's *Sophistes*, Aristotle, St Augustine, Descartes, Leibniz, Hegel and Nietzsche. These lectures circulate in a small circle of the initiated and help in creating myth and mystery. His pupils might say that one cannot really understand him without knowledge of his unpublished work. I myself possess two of his unpublished lectures, but I must confess that they do not impress me as a new revelation. There is further the foreground-Heidegger, the interpreter and analyst of *Dasein* or of human existence, and the background-Heidegger, the *pur sang* ontologist who renews the question concerning the meaning of being. The foreground is painted in distinct and clear colours, whereas the background so far remains shapeless and nebulous. It is only the claims made concerning the background problems that are clearly formulated, *i.e.* that the whole European philosophy from Thales to Husserl was based on a mistake; that all has to be changed; and that Heidegger has come to bring about this transformation. But what is the result? "But being —what is being? It is itself. The thought of the future must learn to experience and to say this. (*Doch das Sein— was ist das Sein? Es ist Es selbst. Dies zu erfahren und zu sagen, muss das künftige Denken lernen.*)"[1] If this trivial tautology is the whole outcome of the new ontology, one can only say: *parturiunt montes, nascetur ridiculus mus!*

In the context of this book I need not and shall not discuss his ontology. Nevertheless, it is impossible to cut it out altogether; for there are not only two Heideggers, the *contre-cœur* existentialist and the would-be ontologist, but also a mixture of both, a third Heidegger, who reinterprets the existentialist statements of *Sein und Zeit* as if they had merely ontological significance, and who now

[1] *Platons Lehre von der Wahrheit*, p. 76.

poses as an ek-sistentialist! For these reasons it is difficult, or almost impossible and unrewarding, to write on Heidegger. I shall therefore confine myself to the most essential points of the existentialist *malgré lui* who, after all, is the more interesting and historically the most influential of the three.

Here we have reached the point where the Heidegger-problem is transformed into a unique case. For I do not know a single case in the history of philosophy where a philosopher has himself reinterpreted his chief work at a later stage of his development in such a manner that his new "authentic" interpretation contradicts not only all former interpretations, but also the plain sense of his original text. This, however, is exactly what is happening here. To put it in a nutshell, the original Heidegger was historically effective because of the following points. *First,* he laid stress on human existence; this implied in a specific sense the priority of existence before essence, which I first formulated in my book (p. 376) and which has since been taken over by Sartre in a misleading manner. Sartre interpreted it ontologically, and this does not make sense because ontologically "existence", however interpreted, presupposes "being". Heidegger, however, meant it epistemologically, *i.e.* if one wants to *know* what being is then one has to start with an analysis of human existence, which contains as one of its elements the understanding of being. His thesis was that only the analysis of existence (as a sort of "fundamental ontology") can lay open the way for understanding being (or for the "regional ontologies"). *Secondly,* man received a privileged position as compared with other organic and inorganic beings. He is never a mere instance of a species; his unique and personal being cannot be described by "categories" applicable to things, but merely by "modes of existence" or existentialia (*Existentialien*). This is a fruitful and valuable point, acceptable even to those who reject Heidegger's arbitrary description of human modes of existence. *Thirdly,* "existence" is here understood as "potential being" (*Seinkönnen*), "a possibility of being or not being oneself". It anticipates the future, it "projects"

itself into the world.   As "the possibility of being oneself"
it is authentic existence, as "the possibility of not
being oneself" unauthentic existence.   Here Heidegger
gives an interesting description of self-estrangement.   In
unauthentic existence the self loses itself in the "It"
(*Man*); it behaves as a member of a crowd, like everybody
or nobody, like the average man; it falls a prey to the
temptations of this world and forgets its own mission.   It
"talks" superficially out of curiosity in an ambiguous
manner.   It handles what is "at hand".   Heidegger
claims that "being at hand" (*das Zuhandene*), *i.e.* the
material we use in our practical activities (*das Zeug*), is
ontologically more fundamental than "being there" (*das
Vorhandene*), and that the world is primarily the sphere of
our activities.   *Fourthly*, human existence is "being-in-
the-world".   This thesis is significant as a starting-point,
for it overcomes the artificial isolation and abstraction of
Descartes' "consciousness"; but the elaboration of this
thesis and the analysis of this mode of existence is as
arbitrary as it is clumsy.   If a faithful commentator tells
us that it is "Already-Being-in-the-world, in advance-of-
itself, as the Being-concerned-with-beings-encountered-in
the-world", the ordinary reader will be more bewildered
than enlightened.   *Fifthly*, the close connection between
existence, being, and time is noteworthy.   Existence is
conceived as having an "ecstatic" character, it has the
possibility of "ecstatic transcendence" in different
directions; and in doing so it creates time.   These
dimensions of time offer, at the same time, the horizon for
an interpretation of being.   Traditionally, Heidegger
contends, "being" has been chiefly understood in the
mode of the present as the *Vorhandene*, whereas he stresses
the mode of the future.   Existence is essentially temporal
and historical.   *Lastly*, the rather doubtful combination
of phenomenology, existentialism and ontology must be
mentioned, because it had a profound influence on the
French school.   It is based on a reinterpretation of
phenomenology as "a method which makes phenomena
visible in the mode in which they present themselves".
Since now "phenomenon" is understood as *das sich-an-ihm-*

Zeigen, i.e. as something that presents itself as the being or the meaning of the object in question, it follows that phenomenology becomes identical with ontology. In its application to existence it has therefore to reveal or to interpret the fundamental ontological structures of existence.

Whereas in *Sein und Zeit* existence or *Dasein* forms the starting-point and the "subject" in a specific transformation, with its different modes of existence the centre of interest, Heidegger now in his latest publications, especially in *Plato's Doctrine of Truth*, and in the additions to the fifth edition of *What is Metaphysics?* reverses his standpoint, and maintains that this reversion was already contained in the third unpublished section of the first part of *Sein und Zeit*. He now replaces the epistemological priority of existence before being by the ontological priority of being before existence. His thesis is now that in the beginning was "being" and not the "subject". "Truth" is now said to be *die Lichtung des Seins*, an ambiguous and oracular expression which means something between an "illumination of", or "open space in", being. He now contends that "being-in-the-world" does not refer to a world as existing or as a realm of objects, but merely to "overtness of being". He now reinterprets all the fundamental characters of existence in a strictly objective manner, *i.e.* not from the point of view of man, but from that of "being". He therefore replaces "existence" by "ek-sistence" and defines it as "standing in the overtness of being" or as "ecstatic standing in the truth of being".[1]

2

What does this amount to? Heidegger is the rebel among contemporary philosophers. He is in revolt against all philosophers of the past. His position is similar to, and at the same time diametrically opposed to, that of the Logical Positivists. That is to say, he arrives at similar rejections, but for opposite reasons. The Logical

[1] *Platons Lehre von der Wahrheit*, pp. 66, 69; *cf.* Llambias de Alvezedo ("Der alte und der neue Heidegger," *Philosophisches Jahrbuch* (1950), vol. lx, pp. 161 ff.), who stresses the fundamental ambiguity of this philosophy.

Positivists reject past metaphysics because it is metaphysics, because it contains statements which are neither tautologies nor verifiable by sense experience. Heidegger rejects past metaphysics not because it is metaphysics, but because it is not the right sort of metaphysics, *i.e.* not so as he would like to have it. He rejects traditional metaphysics because it was based on logic, and rejects logic as the basis of philosophy, whereas the Logical Positivists regard it as a central part of philosophy. Some Logical Positivists reject value-judgments because they cannot be reduced to statements of fact and cannot be verified, if this over-simplification of their position is allowed for comparison's sake; Heidegger, on the other hand, rejects all valuations because they are subjective.

Heidegger as a rebel (and he owes his great influence to the fact that he is a rebel) becomes a *Gegendenker* (anti-thinker), *i.e.* a philosopher who formulates his doctrine in opposition to preceding thinkers. The destruction of the history of ontology is his aim. He is not a revolutionary, but a counter-revolutionary, pointing more to the past than to the future. He has devoted a considerable amount of work to the history of philosophy. His historical works, *e.g.* that on *Kant and Metaphysics*, or *Plato's Doctrine of Truth*, are anti-interpretations; they are opposed either to former interpretations of the same subject or to a specific doctrine of the philosopher in question. In his Kant book he attempts to show that all former interpretations of Kant were false, that Kant is concerned neither with epistemology nor with the foundations of science, but merely with metaphysics, and that he was in fact a forerunner of Heidegger, concerned like himself with a metaphysics of *Dasein* as the basis of all metaphysical knowledge. The finiteness of man, revealing itself in the finiteness of the human understanding, is claimed to be the central idea of the *Critique of Pure Reason*. His essay on Plato is anti-Platonic. Plato is accused of having corrupted the original concept of truth as *Unverborgenheit* (overtness) to that of "correspondence to fact". This transformation, if it ever took place in this alleged form, is said to represent the fall of European metaphysics.

Heidegger is a *Gegendenker* (anti-thinker) in metaphysics. He is opposed to what he calls the metaphysics of essences. He holds that Plato, Aristotle, Thomas Aquinas and Kant belong to this school although they are in fact very different. This whole conception of a metaphysics of essences seems to arise in opposition to his teacher Husserl. The concentration on the essential or on essences with the help of eidetic intuition was a central point in Husserl's teaching. Heidegger seems to extend his opposition to his teacher to the whole preceding metaphysics, without distinguishing the metaphysics of essences, originating with Plato's theory of ideas, and the metaphysics of substances founded by Aristotle, who interpreted the Universe as consisting of a hierarchical order of substances. The fact that he does not make this distinction enables him to reject past metaphysics as a *metaphysics of subjectivity*. There seems to be a certain justification in this characterization, for modern metaphysics from Descartes to Hegel was in fact a metaphysics of subjectivity, because it was based on consciousness (Descartes' *Cogito*), on representation (Leibniz), on the transcendental unity of apperception (Kant), on the *Ego* (Fichte), on impressions and ideas (Hume), and on the mind (Hegel). In this sense, Greek metaphysics was by no means subjective, but in another sense the Aristotelean metaphysics of substances is subjective, namely in so far as it is based on the subject-predicate logic; its "substance" is the "subject" which remains identical in time. From this point of view there is a slight justification in calling all those metaphysics which depend on Aristotle, including that of St Thomas, metaphysics of subjectivity. The core of Heidegger's attack is, however, that all these philosophers were subjective in the sense that they declared to be essential in the object what appeared to them to be essential from the point of view of the knowing subject. Heidegger is against "transforming being subjectively into an object" (*die Subjektivierung des Seins zum blossen Objekt*). He wishes to have being without its deformation through the mind, to have it as it is, and to listen to its revelation. He wants an ontology not based on the mind. The tendency is clear, but seems to derive from a misunderstanding. It is like an attempt to jump over one's own shadow. It is quite impossible to escape what he calls subjectivity; and in fact, instead of escaping it, he gets still deeper into it. Therefore, in spite of his enormous effort to the contrary, he belongs to the metaphysics of essences as well as to the history of subjectivism. He wants to have a metaphysics in which "being" is related to its own origin, and not to its origin in the human mind. He thinks he can find this origin in an analysis of *Dasein* and of time. He holds that in any talk about being, time is involved, and he interprets the modes of time, past, present and future, as ecstatic modes of *Dasein*. All this comes back again to human existence, and therefore to subjectivity.

Heidegger, the *Gegendenker* (anti-thinker), is, further, opposed to logic. He assumes that logic interprets "thinking as representation of being as being, coupled with the generality of concepts", whereas in fact it does nothing of the sort and is the science of correct reasoning. He believes that logic is based on a specific interpretation of *logos*, and that Aristotle's concept of *logos* is derived from a misinterpretation of the original meaning of *logos* prevailing amongst the pre-Socratics. Therefore it should be our endeavour to go back to the original meaning of *logos*. All this unfortunately is based on a misuse of etymology. Although it is true that the word "logic" is derived from *logos*, it does not follow that this etymology is of any relevance whatever to the meaning of logic. Heidegger is quite right in defending himself against the slander that he wanted to install irrationalism instead of rational thought. Nevertheless this attack against logic is somewhat overbearing. It would have made sense to attack the traditional subject-predicate logic as insufficient, and to show that it is based on arbitrary assumptions, that it has to be replaced by the broader assumptions of the logic of relations and by symbolic logic, and that consequently the metaphysics of substances has to make place for a metaphysics of relations. But it does not seem to make sense to go back to a more primitive concept of thought as the revelation of the truth of being.

This whole argumentation is based on an overvaluation of the word *logos*, which does not enter at all into the subject-matter of logic. One can apply the rules of correct reasoning without having ever heard of the word *logos*. He talks against logic, but varying one of his utterances one could say: "By the naughty gesture which accompanies his talk against logic, he attempts to create the impression that he is on the side of thought whereas he is against it." Here again he attempts to jump over his own shadow. One cannot escape logic. If there is to be a metaphysics at all, it cannot be without logical foundations. On this point, the Logical Positivists are infinitely superior to Heidegger. They uphold the key-position of logic, and they go on to a new form of logic.

Heidegger's attack on logic cannot be defended by saying that he only rejects specific forms of logic. No, he attacks logic as such, and this extremism is as provocative as it is futile; it is, moreover, mixed up with his transformation of metaphysics. Here again he is an anti-thinker. However, it would not be quite fair to say that because past metaphysics was the science of being as being, his famous lecture, "What is Metaphysics?" declares "nothing" to form its sole subject-matter. In fact, centring around the concept of nothingness, this lecture rejects logical negation as the source of "not-being", and attempts, on this basis, the dissolution of logic. Its theses are:

(1) "'Not' does not arise through an act of negation, but negation is based on the 'not', which, on its part, arises through the activity of nothingness (*Nichten des Nichts*)."

(2) "'Nothing' is the source of negation, and not the other way round."

(3) "Nothing is neither an object nor anything that *is* at all. Nothing occurs neither by itself nor apart from what-is, as a sort of adjunct. Nothing is that which makes the revelation of what-is, as such possible for our human existence. Nothing not merely provides the conceptual opposite of what-is but is also an original part of essence (*Wesen*). It is in the Being (*Sein*) of what-is that the 'nothing-ing of nothing' (*das Nichten des Nichts*) occurs." [1]

---

[1] *Existence and Being*, p. 370.

(4) Negation is only one way in which negative behaviour expresses itself. Others are "acting in opposition", "detesting", "refusal", "prohibition" and "privation". In other words, negation is explained as a mode of negative behaviour. And negative behaviour again is, ontologically, based on nothingness, or rather on the "nothinging of nothing".

(5) Nothingness is experienced in modes of behaviour rather than as an object. It is revealed to us, not in acts of reasoning, but in the irrational act of anxiety. "Anxiety reveals nothingness."

(6) This result is opposed to logic, therefore the concept of logic is claimed "to be dissolved in the vortex of a more fundamental questioning".

This essay has exercised a considerable influence, especially on Sartre, and is important, not in what it denies, but in what it asserts. As an attack on logic it breaks down completely, for the simple reason that *logical negation and ontological not-being represent two problems on different levels.* This must be clearly understood. Heidegger is quite right, the ontological problem of not-being cannot be reduced to a merely linguistic or logical problem. It may be possible to get rid of such propositions as "Pegasus is not" with the help of Russell's theory of descriptions,[1] but the hard fact of death remains and cannot be eliminated by the most sophisticated linguistic analysis. At any moment we are faced with the possibility of not-being. When I wrote my paper on "The Meaning of Negation" in the *Proceedings of the Aristotelean Society*, 1943–44, I was of the opinion that the theses which I then formulated were sufficient for refuting Heidegger's theses concerning not-being and nothing. But now I see that this is not the case. On the other hand, it must be categorically stated that Heidegger's ontological theses concerning not-being and nothingness are completely unable to destroy the logical function of negation and logic itself. Heidegger here commits the mistake which Aristotle calls μετάβασις εἰς ἄλλο γένος. But although this attack fails, it raises

---

[1] W. V. Quine, "On What There Is," *Proc. Arist. Soc.*, suppl. vol. xxv.

important problems, namely (1) that of negation, (2) the ontological problem of not-being and nothingness, (3) the problem of their interrrelation, and (4) the relation of (*a*) logical negation and (*b*) ontological not-being to experience. We cannot discuss here these difficult problems which are not clearly distinguished by Heidegger.

He maintains that we experience nothingness in anxiety. "Anxiety makes us glide because it makes being in totality, *i.e.* all particular beings, slip away from us." [1] This again is the gliding over an abyss experienced by Jaspers. It is quite true that the object of anxiety is indefinite, whereas that of fear is definite, and that we often worry about nothing; but the conclusion that "Nothing itself, Nothing as such was there", [2] is completely unfounded, for the simple reason that "Nothing itself, Nothing as such", does not exist. But here again a purely logical analysis cannot eliminate the ontological problem. Expressing the mood of our time, Heidegger reveals the human condition as "being exposed to nothingness" (*Hineingehaltensein in das Nichts*). On this point he is right, we are exposed to nothingness. If we become aware of this fact in anxiety, we transcend, says Heidegger, the totality of being, but not in the direction of God, but in that of Nothingness. This experience of nothingness brings the problems of being and of existence to our attention. Thus the ontological problem of not-being is rediscovered.

The *Gegendenker* thinks further, as he says, against values. He is opposed to the philosophy of value of his teacher Rickert and of the Windelband-Rickert-Münsterberg school. This school and their followers, like Hartmann, believed in logical, moral, æsthetic and religious values as having absolute validity, though not existence, in a transcendent realm of values, independent of consciousness. In his violent reaction against the philosophy of value of this school he goes to the extreme of rejecting any theory of value. He does not, however, protest against the doctrine of his teachers, as one would

[1] *Existence and Being*, p. 366.
[2] *L.c.*, p. 367.

expect, from the point of view of the existing subject which finds its existence bereft of values. He does not argue that these transcendent values, separated from the reality of the living subject, are empty and foreign to human existence; no, he opposes them in the name of "Being" (*Sein*). He would reject this realm of values as a bad "metaphysics of essences" which bars the way to a true metaphysics. He jumps to the conclusion that all search for values arises from the desire to find a sub-stitute for the loss of Being. Value, he maintains, is a creation of human subjectivity, *i.e.* of an activity called "valuing". This evaluation merely objectifies human wants (*Bedürfnisziele*); nevertheless this objectified value parades as possessing independent existence, and the result of this objectification is that it hides true Being and deprives it of its dignity. "It is high time", he writes, "to understand that through the characterization as 'value' the valued object is deprived of its dignity. This means that through the evaluation of something as value, the value is merely admitted as an object of human valuation. But whatever is, is not exhausted *qua* being in its being an object, especially not if this objectivity has the character of value. Every act of valuing . . . is subjective (*Subjektivierung*). It does not allow being to *be*, but valuing allows being merely to *be valid* as the object of this activity. The curious attempt to prove the objec-tivity of values does not know what it does. If, to crown all, one proclaims God to be the 'highest value', this implies a deprecation of the essence of God. Thinking in values is here, as always, the greatest possible blasphemy in the face of Being. To think against values does not therefore mean raising one's voice for the worthlessness and nullity of Being, on the contrary it implies, in opposition to the subjective transformation of being into a mere object, bringing the light (*Lichtung*) of the truth of being before our thought." [1] This quotation is most interesting, because it reveals his intention to "think against" values together with the impossibility of doing so. For what is the "dignity" of an object other than a "value"? This

---

[1] *Platons Lehre von der Wahrheit* p. 99.

talk therefore breaks down through its inherent contradiction. It simply does not make sense to reject values and to accept simultaneously the dignity and value of Being. One may negate, wrote Nietzsche, traditional systems of value, but one cannot nullify valuation as such.

Here again Heidegger attempts to jump over his own shadow. It is completely impossible to reject valuation because it is subjective, for the simple reason that in *almost every act of thinking an act of evaluation is implied.*[1] For example if I say, "man is a rational being", it implies that I value "reason" highest amongst the characteristics of man. If I concentrate my attention on anything, it implies an act of selection; I select what I consider important at the moment. Abstraction as well as memory imply acts of valuation. We remember what is of interest to us, *i.e.* what we value. Heidegger himself confirms this by talking of the dignity of being. Here he merely follows tradition. In scholastic ontology "to be (*esse, Sein*) is defined as that perfection through which something becomes a being".[2] In other words one can *talk,* but one cannot *think* against values.

This thinking against values would seem to have catastrophic consequences for ethics. Heidegger's message seems to be that we should listen to the call of Being at this specific moment of history, and that we therefore cannot allow any general maxim to stand in our way. His pupils tell us that he rejects any objective order of values, the Thomistic hierarchical order of values as well as the formal order established by Kant's categorical imperative, and that instead he accepts Fichte's maxim: "Do what you alone are able to do, and what no one else, in your place, could do."[3] If this were true, it would fit very well the picture of the whole man. It would imply that he attaches the highest value to what he, and he alone, is able to do. It would reveal what he desires, *i.e.* to be himself, this specific unique individual.

But you may ask, How do we know what we have to do

---

[1] *Cf.* my paper, "Autonomy or Orthonomy?" in *The Hibbert Journal,* July 1949; D. J. McCracken, *Thinking and Valuing,* London, 1950.
[2] W. Brugger, *Philosophisches Wörterbuch,* Freiburg, 1951.
[3] M. Müller, *Existenzphilosophie,* Heidelberg, 1949.

at this specific moment, if neither our conscience nor
general rules tell us? Heidegger replies that we shall not
"insist" in ourselves, but "ec-sist", *i.e.* the centre of our
being shall not be within, but without us. We shall
ec-sist, we shall transcend in a sort of ecstasis to Being.
Man becomes a *witness of Being*.

3

So it happens that Heidegger, although he rejects
existentialism, has risen again as an "ek-sistentialist";
a transformation, as original as astounding! "The
essence of man", it is now said, "consists in ek-sistence.
It is this that matters essentially, *i.e.* from the point of view
of Being, in so far as Being itself installs man as ek-sistent
as guardian of the truth of being (*insofern das Sein den
Menschen als den ek-sistierenden zur Wächterschaft für die
Wahrheit des Seins in diese selbst ereignet*)." [1] What does that
mean? asks the perplexed reader. Is it a delphic oracle
or intentional concealment? Is perhaps obscurity used
on purpose for producing the semblance of depth? But
has not this author himself exposed concealment as a form
of untruth? Can he therefore be surprised that there are
unbiased and well-meaning readers who regard his
phrasing, and especially the arbitrary and ungrammatical
use of the German verb *ereignen* in a transitive sense, as
unnatural and not as specially attractive? Or is it
perhaps merely an expression of the new poetical ontology
or ontological poetry? "But if Being in its essence (*Sein
in seinem Wesen*)", it is said, "*needs* the essence of man?
If the essence of man consists in the thinking of truth?
Then thought must poetize about the riddle of being.
It brings the primitivity of what is thought about near to
that which ought to be thought (*Es bringt die Frühe des
Gedachten in die Nähe des zu Denkenden*)." This is the final
conclusion of the *Holzwege*.

For almost twenty-five years we have been waiting for
the second volume of *Being and Time*. Instead we now
receive, in a sort of anti-climax, the *Holzwege*, and the

[1] *Platons Lehre von der Wahrheit*, A. Francke (Bern), p. 94.

fifth edition of *What is Metaphysics?* with a new introduction and a reinterpretation of *Sein und Zeit.* Within
our context the question arises: Is the way, which
Heidegger now claims as his own, the *via regia* of contemporary philosophy, or perhaps, as he himself at the
bottom of his heart seems to fear, merely a *Holzweg*, which
may have its attractions but, alas, leads nowhere?

Heidegger maintains that, in the last resort, nobody
ever understood him. He says: "The preface to *Being
and Time* concludes its first page with these propositions:
'The detailed elaboration of the problem of the meaning
of being is the intention of the following dissertation. The
interpretation of time as the possible horizon of any
understanding of being whatsoever, is its preliminary
aim.' There could not be a clearer sign of the power of
that 'forgetfulness of being' (*Seinsvergessenheit*), which is the
fate of all contemporary philosophy and which, nevertheless, was and is a challenge to our thought in *Being and
Time*, than the somnambulist certainty with which the
critics missed this central and unique problem of *Being and
Time*. Therefore it is not a question of the misunderstanding of a book, but rather of our 'loss of being' or of our
'being forsaken by being' (*Seinsverlust*)." [1]

To this I reply with the counter-question: "Is this
claim historically justified?" Two quotations from my
New Pathways in Philosophy may serve as an answer:
"In opposition to traditional ontology Heidegger renews
the question, by which Aristotle had dislodged the old
metaphysics, the question concerning the meaning of
being. This repetition is essential, for so long as this
question remains unanswered, all talk about the renascence
of metaphysics remains empty" (p. 376). "That is the
essentially new point in Heidegger that he installs time as
the principle of interpretation and as the horizon of any
understanding of being, and therefore also of the understanding of man" (p. 374). On the basis of these quotations, which could easily be multiplied, it is hardly possible
to talk of a failure to see the problems of the book. But
the real point of Heidegger's complaint seems to be the

---

[1] *Was ist Metaphysik?* (5th ed.), p. 17.

evaluation of his questions by his contemporaries and the ensuing emphasis put on specific parts of his thought. This, however, arose naturally from the fact that the problem of being remained, and still remains, unanalysed, whereas the interpretation of time was pursued much further. May it not be that his contemporaries did not accept Heidegger's own evaluation of the questions, but accepted what seemed alive to them and rejected what appeared dead? And even if there was a misunderstanding, may not a misunderstanding itself be creative? Paul Natorp maintained that Aristotle never understood Plato. But, if so, was not his "misunderstanding" creative, seeing that it led to a philosophy which dominated centuries? Kant thought it possible to understand an author better than he understood himself.

It is Heidegger's ambition to become the Aristotle of our time, *i.e.* to transcend the old definition of metaphysics as a science of being as being, in this sense to overcome the old metaphysics and to redefine it as the science of "being", or *Sein*, as opposed to *Seiendem*, or of the "truth of being". Since truth is now interpreted as *Unverborgenheit* (ἀλήθεια), *i.e.* as uncovering or unveiling, he is concerned with "paying attention to the revelation of the still uncovered essence of truth as *Unverborgenheit*, as which Being has advertised itself".[1] Having received this information we have to renew the question: "Is the way thus described a *via regia* or a *Holzweg*?" This is not a personal, but an objective question. Every philosopher has the indisputable right to follow his own ways, and the more these ways differ, the better. This path, however, claims to be *the via regia*, and all those who do not choose it are accused of "forgetfulness of being" or of "being forsaken by being". But is this sort of forgetfulness or of being forsaken really *the* disease of our age? Is our generation not rather abandoned by God than by Being? Does our age not suffer from a *loss* of being, *i.e.* of substance? We are searching for being. That is true; but we do it because the human world has lost its substance. We are not searching for it, however, in

[1] *Was ist Metaphysik?* (5th ed.), p. 10.

Heidegger's purely intellectual manner, and a new "fundamental ontology" is unable to satisfy our longing. Is the distinction between *Sein* (to be) and *Seiendem* (being) really of that basic importance which is here attributed to it? Or is it based on a chance-peculiarity of the German language? It cannot properly be translated into English, and only with difficulty into French. This alone makes it suspect as artificial and deceptive. Is it not perhaps based on a naive realism (in the Platonic sense of the word), *i.e.* on a standpoint which on grounds that are linguistically and logically untenable maintains that objects have "being" through participation in *Sein*, or in "being as such" or in the "essence of being"? The concept of being has played a rôle in European metaphysics which stands in no relation whatever to its real importance. "Being" became the Absolute and was as such identified with God. The thesis *Esse est Deus* and not *Deus est esse* became the basic axiom of European metaphysics during the Middle Ages. Nevertheless, it is unable to stand up to a criticism, based on linguistic and logical analysis. It originated from the Aristotelean subject-predicate-logic and from the metaphysics of substances based on it. With the emergence of the logic of relations this metaphysics has lost its ground and this logic its claim to exclusive validity. The dogmatic and uncritical assumptions of *the* being, the essence of being, *the* truth, the essence of truth, the essence of language, "the essential essence of poetry", etc. which, allegedly, may be grasped in an "intuition of essence" (*Wesensschau*) independently of sensory experience, cannot but be rejected by a generation steeped in a thorough analysis of language and logic. Words are here taken for "essences". On the basis of the monomorphic fallacy it is falsely assumed that, because there is the *one* word "truth", there ought to be *one* essence corresponding to it, called the essence of truth. Since the days of Plato this mistake has been repeated over and over again, but it remains a mistake even in the writings of the most sublime mind.

In spite, therefore, of his rejection of the metaphysics of essences he is still dominated by it. What has happened to the *Gegendenker*? In Nietzsche's terminology he has become a *Nebendenker*, a co-thinker, *i.e.* a pupil who uses the methods of his teacher for erecting a new building which is merely an annex. It remains a torso, because its foundations prove to be insufficient. Heidegger's ambition is to go deeper than his teachers Husserl and Rickert and the whole traditional metaphysics, and to be more radical.

Husserl's experiment made sense. His problem was to lay the foundations of our knowledge of being in our consciousness. He moved in the line of Descartes and Kant, with this difference, that he interpreted the acts of our consciousness as intentional. He claimed to discover in our intentional consciousness certain categories which constitute, or are the foundation of, our knowledge of being. Heidegger assumes that he can broaden the basis and at the same time be more fundamental than Husserl. He lives in the illusion that he is able to dispense with consciousness, thought and mind. Therefore he introduces the following alterations. He broadens the range of the objects of his inquiry; they are not merely the objects of our knowledge, but of any mode of behaviour; they imply not only what there is (*das Vorhandene*), but also what is at hand (*das Zuhandene*). Consequently they may be approached through emotions or moods. The subjective foundations are broadened; they remain, however, subjective. Being is therefore not founded in thought or consciousness but in the *existentialia* of *Dasein*. However, through this transformation the terms "being constituted by" and "being founded in" lose their meaning. Different aspects of reality may be revealed in this manner, but the talk about them becomes arbitrary and unconvincing. In other words, Heidegger destroys the basis of the preceding metaphysics without being able to lay the foundation for a new one. What he is talking about is in fact not metaphysics as science, but metaphysics as a natural disposition of man. Ontology without *logos* remains empty talk.

Nevertheless, Heidegger's latest nihilistic ontology is unique and bears witness to the "night of Europe" (A. Camus) which he, following Hölderlin, prefers to call

Weltnacht (world-night). *Weltnacht* designates an age, in which the old gods are dead and the new gods not yet born. God is absent; He withholds Himself; there is no god who visibly and univocally could unite men, fill the world with splendour and give meaning to it. The time is barren, for it does not even notice God's absence. Nothingness has replaced God. "God is dead", Hegel's and Nietzsche's dictum remains dominant and is subjected to a profound analysis.[1] An extreme nihilism emerges: "everything in History as well as in Nature is nothing in every respect"; Hegel's Absolute, his absolute mind, which replaced God and revealed itself at every stage of history, and therewith all its realizations, are now nothing, although every one of them claims to represent true reality. Thus, in the shadow of Hegel, a kind of inverted Hegelianism arises, transformed into an ontological mysticism. Nothingness and, based on it, nihilism now appear as the driving power and even as the law of European history. They pervade, moreover, the whole realm of Being, for this Being is Nothing. "Being conceals itself in its truth", it does not reveal itself. This represents a profoundly pessimistic interpretation of man and universe. Whereas Hegel affirmed every step in the history of thought as a one-sided contribution to truth, Heidegger interprets them as albeit inevitable failures in the revelation of truth.

Yet this extreme nihilism is counterbalanced by positive tendencies. The "deputy of Nothingness" (*Platzhalter des Nichts*) is simultaneously the "shepherd of Being" (*Hirte des Seins*). He knows that only the Christian God, but not God Himself, is dead. Like Nietzsche he remains in search of God, and it is in this search that he turns to poets such as Hölderlin and Rilke, because he holds that the poets name gods and that it is they who discover their traces.[2]

One important question, however, has still to be answered. What is the final solution to the Heidegger

---

[1] In *Holzwege* (Klostermann, Frankfurt, 1950), pp. 193 ff.; cf. *Philosophy*, 1950, p. 342; and H. Kuhn, "Heidegger's *Holzwege*," in *Archiv für Philosophie*, vol. iv, 3 (July 1952), pp. 253 ff.
[2] For a detailed analysis of Heidegger's Hölderlin interpretation, cf. W. Brock, in M. Heidegger, *Existence and Being* (London, 1949), pp. 183 ff.

problem? How is the fact of the two or three Heideggers, and the almost dialectical transition from the *contre-cœur*-existentialist to the ontological ek-sistentialist, to be explained? How is it possible that his ontology is interpreted as ontological realism by his pupil Szilasi, whereas Fink understands it in a subjective, Kantian manner as based on the model of construction and project? [1] Is it perhaps essentially a philosophy of ambiguity? A systematic unity of his published works does not exist; what unifies them is merely a consistent attitude of their author. Heidegger represents a specific form of alienation, *i.e.* the despair of an individual who desperately wants to be himself, inaugurating a new world era of philosophic thought. His attitude, the only one considered adequate to the encounter with Nothingness, is one of *heroic defiance*. He writes in *defiance* of traditional terminology, grammar, thought, metaphysics, logic and ethics; and in so doing he introduces an unbearable jargon and ungrammatical usage of verbs. He bids defiance to the traditional understanding of "truth", to all interpreters of his philosophy and to all existentialists, to humanism, and even to God; for "the It" (*das Es*) or "the Being" is claimed to be higher than God. He defies eternity for the sake of time. It is exactly as Kierkegaard said: "Whereas the weak despairer will not hear about what comfort eternity has for him, so neither will such a despairer hear about it, but for a different reason, namely because this comfort would be the destruction of him as an objection against the whole of existence." This is Heidegger's case, through defiance to absurdity. It did make sense to interpret human existence as "ecstatic transcendence"; but it does not seem to make sense to interpret man as "ecstasis of being" or "being" as "the ecstatic relation to the overtness of Being". Heidegger is the *defiant philosopher* who has exercised a considerable influence through the very existentialism which he now rejects and through the provocative manner in which he questions the foundations of traditional philosophy and thought.

[1] *Cf.* their papers in *Actas del Primer Congresso Nacional de Filosofia*, Mendoza, Argentina, 1949.

VII. THE PHILOSOPHY OF COMMITMENT

I

IF we now turn from the German to the French stage we experience a complete shifting of scene. On the one hand, France and Germany are much more closely connected, though in a *harmonia discors*, than either England and France, or England and Germany. A greater permanent interchange of ideas and a deep interest in what the other country does, produces a sort of continental spirit. On the other hand, profound differences remain. France has a Latin tradition, therefore firm roots in the past and a close connection with Mediterranean civilization. She has, moreover, a democratic tradition which connects her with the Western democracies. The French Revolution marked the end of the *ancien régime* and the rise of a new class, but the ideals of the French Revolution, *liberté, égalité, fraternité*, became the basis of a new tradition. The French regard them as the ideals of humanity, and whoever adheres to them is accepted as a potential Frenchman. Liberty comes first. The French are born individualists and have succeeded in creating the most unstable of democracies. This political instability is, however, balanced by a philosophical stability. French philosophers are Cartesians by tradition.[1] Descartes is *the* French philosopher. He has towered over French philosophers up to the present time, holding under his spell the most diverse personalities and schools, and even his opponents. His ideas have permeated French life and have impressed a specific pattern upon the French mind. His *esprit géométrique* took shape in the wonderfully regular construction of the *Champs Elysées* and of Central Paris, in the geometrical order of the great French parks at Versailles and elsewhere, and in the rational unity and form of Racine's tragedies. His belief in Reason became

[1] *Cf.* my paper, "The Tercentenary of Descartes," in *The Hibbert Journal*, April 1950.

the guiding principle of a most emotional nation and of a large school of French philosophy. French philosophy is much nearer to science than either British or German philosophy. These Latin, democratic and Cartesian traditions are, last but not least, supplemented by a very strong artistic and literary tradition. From Montaigne and Pascal, from La Rochefoucauld, Vauvenargues, Voltaire and Diderot, to Marcel and Sartre, French philosophers have excelled in literary forms, whether in aphorisms, essays, diaries, novels or dramas. But this advantage has to be paid for. In France everything, painting, music, drama and philosophy, is in danger of becoming *literature*. The transformation of the philosopher into an *homme de lettres* may end in the *littérateur*.

The different climate of thought produces different philosophers. Germany, which lacks the Latin, democratic, Cartesian and literary traditions, which prefers Greek antiquity and is predominantly protestant by choice and tradition, is spiritually individualistic. In spite of philosophical schools, Kantian, Hegelian or others, every philosopher tries to start *ab ovo*. He takes philosophy most seriously. Philosophy means work to him to which he is devoted. A diary-entry of Edmund Husserl, dated 25.9.1906, may illustrate this German attitude: [1]

> Pure meditation, pure internal life (*Innenleben*), being absorbed by the problems and devoting myself to them, and to them *only*, that is the hope of my future. If I do not succeed, then I shall have to live a life which is rather death. . . . I have to pursue my way so surely, so firmly, so decidedly, and so in earnest as Dürer's Knight in spite of Death and Devil. . . . And be God with me in spite of the fact that we are all sinners!

This symbol of the knight-errant who pursues his path in spite of Death and Devil and who gives up all the pleasures of life in his search for truth is characteristic of German philosophers, Nietzsche included, but not of Sartre. He is quite the opposite, immersed in life and emerging from it, not introverted, but an extrovert.

He attempts to combine all these traditions, French

[1] *Philosophische Studien* (Berlin, 1951), p. 311.

and German.   Like Descartes he starts with the "truth",
I think, therefore I am, but it has a completely different
meaning for him.   Descartes' *I think* or *cogito* installed
reason as the key for interpreting the Universe as well as
Man in a scientific way.   Sartre maintains that in his
consciousness he is at once aware of the presence of others
and that he is more certain of the others than he is of himself.   He finds himself in a world of intersubjectivity, and
his consciousness starts therefore on a prereflective level.
It is no longer a substance in a well-ordered and meaningful world, but in a world bereft of meaning and purpose it
becomes a striving towards something that it can never
become.   Sartre continues the French literary and artistic
tradition, the line of the moralists as well as that of the
great writers.   He is a successful playwright and novelist.
He likewise continues the democratic tradition.   He is
politically engaged in his *Rassemblement Démocratique
Républicaine*, a political group, which does not want to
be a party, a movement which is anti-Communist, but
which nevertheless wants to liberate the proletariat.   It
defends the elementary concrete liberties of the individual
and especially of the proletarian which, it maintains, are
being sacrificed by the Communists to the interests of a
foreign Power.

On the other hand, he incorporates German sources,
especially Husserl's phenomenological method, which he
applies in his early writings to the study of the imagination
and of the emotions, and Heidegger's metaphysics of
Nothingness.   He is further profoundly influenced by
Hegel, Marx and Freud.   In competition with the latter
he attempts to build up an existentialist psycho-analysis.

Sartre occupies a specific place in the history of Existentialism.   He represents the stage where self-estrangement seems to have reached its highest possible degree,
that is to say, where the pressure of the group has become
so great that the individual is almost forced to live in
self-estrangement as the natural state of affairs.   Almost
providentially he seems to be predestined for his rôle
Born in Paris in 1905, without a firm religious tradition
having a mixed Protestant and Roman Catholic ancestry

losing his parents at an early age, he lived with his grand-
parents at La Rochelle, until he left for the Teachers'
Training College of the University of Paris.   As a research
student in Philosophy he visited Germany and attended
Husserl's lectures.   Returning to Paris he became a
schoolmaster, but had to join the army in 1939.   Taken
prisoner by the Germans in 1940, he was released in 1941
on medical grounds, and used his regained freedom for
teaching philosophy, for leading a group of the Resistance
Movement, and for writing his *chef-d'œuvre*, *L'être et le
néant*.

Sartre lives in an age in which Jaspers's *ultimate situations*
have become situations of extreme self-estrangement.
Jaspers's statements, "I must die, I must suffer, I must
struggle, I involve myself inexorably in guilt", no longer
represent an abstract possibility, but the reality with
which the French people were faced.   Suppressed by a
dictator and invader who, dominated by Satanic, subhuman forces, had sunk to the lowest level of inhumanity,
they experienced "limiting situations" in the sense that
here the limit seemed to have been reached to which
human cruelty and inhumanity can go.   Every single
person was in danger of being crushed at any moment.
Sartre has an unrivalled uncanny appreciation of the
contemporary condition, combined with a gift for analysing, almost brutally, its weakness and the negative and
destructive forces prevalent in human society.

2

His reaction to this situation differs fundamentally from
that of Jaspers.   Jaspers, in a theoretical and contemplative mood, states that we cannot evade or change these
ultimate situations; but Sartre, longing for change and
liberation, experiences his freedom in this same situation.
He asks, and we should listen to this question as if it were
addressed to each one of us: "*À propos de quelle situation
privilégiée avez-vous fait l'expérience de votre liberté?*"   ("In
face of which privileged situation have you made the

experience of your liberty?") The formulation of this question is pertinent. It cuts through the unending, and in most cases fruitless, discussions about the meaning of the word liberty, and about the interrelations between freedom and necessity. The opposition between freedom and necessity is artificial; for "necessity" here means "natural necessity", *i.e.* the unwarranted assumption that Nature, in macrophysics as well as in microphysics, is dominated by causal laws of absolute necessity. Whatever happens is here supposed to be completely determined. This sort of "necessity" and this determinism have been given up as arbitrary assumptions by Modern Physics. The laws of microphysics have to be expressed in terms of probability, and only in some cases this probability does approach certainty and necessity. The true opposite to liberty is not necessity, but compulsion. To be free means, negatively, "not to act under compulsion". It is a paradox of the human condition that in a state of utter compulsion and danger, regarded by them as a "privileged situation", human beings *experience* their freedom in their power of resisting oppression. Sartre's philosophy arises from the new experience of freedom under the dictatorship. In *The Republic of Silence* he gives an unequalled description of this experience.

> We were never more free than during the German occupation. We had lost all our rights, beginning with the right to talk. Every day we were insulted to our faces and had to take it in silence. Under one pretext or another, as workers, Jews, or political prisoners, we were deported *en masse*. Everywhere, on billboards, in the newspapers, on the screen, we encountered the revolting and insipid picture of ourselves that our suppressors wanted us to accept. And because of all this we were free. Because the Nazi venom seeped into our thoughts, every accurate thought was a conquest. Because an all-powerful police tried to force us to hold our tongues, every word took on the value of a declaration of principles. Because we were hunted down, every one of our gestures had the weight of a solemn commitment. The circumstances, atrocious as they often were, finally made it possible for us to live the hectic and impossible existence that is known as the lot of man.
> Exile, captivity, and especially death (which we usually

shrink from facing at all in happier days) became for us the habitual objects of our concern. We learnt that they were neither inevitable accidents, nor even constant and inevitable dangers, but that they must be considered as our lot itself, our destiny, the profound source of our reality as men. At every instant we lived up to the full sense of this commonplace little phrase: "Man is mortal!" And the choice that each of us made of his life was an authentic choice because it was made face to face with death, because it could always have been expressed in these terms: "Rather death than . . ." And here I am not speaking of the élite among us who were real Resistants, but of all Frenchmen who, at every hour of night and day throughout four years, answered *No*. But the very cruelty of the enemy drove us to the extremity of this condition by forcing ourselves to ask ourselves questions that one never considers in time of peace. All those among us . . . who knew any details concerning the Resistance asked themselves anxiously, "If they torture me, shall I be able to keep silent?"

Thus the basic question of liberty was posed, and we were brought to the verge of the deepest knowledge that man can have of himself. For *the secret of man* is not his Œdipus complex or his inferiority complex: *it is the limit of his own liberty, his capacity for resisting torture and death.*

To those who were engaged in underground activities, the conditions of their struggle afforded a new kind of experience. They did not fight openly like soldiers. In all circumstances they were alone. They were hunted down in solitude, arrested in solitude. It was completely forlorn and unbefriended that they held out against torture, alone and naked in the presence of torturers. . . . Alone. Without a friendly word of encouragement. Yet, in the depth of their solitude, it was the others that they were protecting, all the others, all their comrades in the Resistance. *Total responsibility in total solitude—is not this the very definition of liberty?* . . . Thus, in darkness and blood, a Republic was established, the strongest of Republics. Each of its citizens knew that he owed himself to all and that he could count only on himself alone. Each of them, in complete isolation, fulfilled his responsibility and his rôle in history. Each of them, standing against the oppressor, undertook to be himself, freely and irrevocably. And by choosing for himself in liberty, he chose the liberty for all. This Republic without institutions, without an army, without police, was something that at each instant every Frenchman had to win and to affirm against Nazism. No one failed in his duty, and now we are on the threshold of another Republic. May this Republic about to be set up in broad daylight preserve the austere virtues of that other Republic of Silence and of Night.[1]

Goethe once said:

Und wo der Mensch in seiner Qual verstummt,
Gab mir ein Gott zu sagen, was ich leide.

("Where other people become silent in their affliction,
A God gave me the power to express my suffering.")

With a slight variation it may be said of Sartre that, where other people become speechless in their pain, it is given to him to express, not only what a community suffers, but also what each member of the group is gaining in essential experience. What an age in which a society has to be crushed in order to teach its members the true meaning of liberty! No doubt Sartre expresses a genuine experience of a concrete ultimate situation. It is political, as the experience of a political group, moral, as implying a moral choice, and metaphysical, as the experience of the individual who, in face of an ultimate situation, in his utter loneliness remains nevertheless indissolubly connected with, and responsible to, all members of the group and, in the last resort, to all men. As an experience of liberty it rightly stresses its two sides—*i.e.* negatively, the power of resisting oppression, and positively, the genuineness of choice and the responsibility in this choice. If it falsely universalizes an abnormal case and, by overstating the range of responsibility, defines liberty as "total responsibility in total solitude", this is the natural consequence of the exceptional extremeness of the situation.

This is combined with a new experience of reality which is expressed in Sartre's first novel, *La Nausée*. Staring at a root in a public garden, Roquentin experiences the absurdity of inanimate as well as animate beings, his own existence included, and this fills him with the feeling of nausea.

Absurdity was not an idea in my head nor the sound of a voice, it was this long, dead, wooden snake curled up at my

[1] From *The Republic of Silence*, copyright, 1947, by A. J. Liebling. Reprinted by permission of Harcourt, Brace & Co. Inc. The italics are mine.

feet, snake or claw or talon or root, it was all the same. Without formulating anything, I knew that I had found the clue to my existence, to my nausea, to my life. And indeed, everything I have ever grasped since that moment comes back to this fundamental absurdity.[1]

The sentiment of absurdity permeates French atheist existentialism in Camus as well as in Sartre. Friedrich Engels once quoted Eugen Dühring's *dictum:* "The reality of the absurd is the first dogma of the Hegelian unity of logic and 'non-logic' (*Unlogik*)." But that was a critical remark, and Hegel himself would have rejected it as an unfriendly sneer. Sartre, however, does not hesitate to say "*l'absolu ou l'absurde*"; and Camus's *Le Mythe de Sisyphe* begins with the sentence: "The following pages deal with the sentiment of absurdity which prevails in our world." The feeling of absurdity now fills the heart of man and distorts his experience. It cannot be denied that there is a certain absurdity in life. Nature produces an enormous number of living beings, all of which perish either before or after having reached the state of full development. The death of a genius such as Newton, where a mind developed to a stage of perfection seems to be nothing at the next moment, appears as an absurdity if one does not believe in the immortality of the soul. This absurdity, inherent in human life, comes to the fore in our age, because man is in danger of becoming himself absurd. This is what has happened in our time, which is consequently filled with absurdities.

Sartre's philosophy arises from a combination and analysis of these two experiences, *i.e.* of liberty in resistance, and of the apparent absurdity of being and existence, both of which are primarily negative. He experiences his liberty in saying "no" to the oppressor, and he experiences reality in that it says "no" to him, that it is repulsive to him. He discovers himself as *liberté en situation* able to say "no".

---

[1] Translated by M. Harari in Gabriel Marcel's *The Philosophy of Existence*, p. 39.

3

Three fundamental concepts, liberty, situation and negation, must be understood if one wants to understand Sartre; but the remarkable point is that negation is dominant and that it enters the concept of liberty as well as that of situation. The author of *L'Être et le Néant* is the *philosopher of negativity*. His basic experience is the following: "The *no*, as a brusque intuitive discovery, appears to be a consciousness of being, a consciousness of *no*. In one word, if there is being everywhere, it is not merely the Nothing, as Bergson would have it, that is inconceivable: never can one derive negation from being. The necessary condition, which must be fulfilled if it shall be possible to say *no*, is that non-being be a perpetual presence in us as well as outside us, that is to say, that the Nothing haunts Being (*le néant hante l'être*)." [1]

It must be noted that the problem here is: What conditions must be fulfilled in order to enable us to say *no*? This question transcends the merely linguistic aspect of the problem. It is of course possible to restrict one's attention to words. Then, however, one forgets that words are merely means for expressing our feelings, emotions, wishes and thoughts. Even if one treats them in isolation the relation to experience remains; *e.g.* if I say that unicorns do not exist, this statement has (1) a relation to the real universe, for it implies that so far I have never met a unicorn in it; it has (2) a relation to possibilities which transcend the real world; a unicorn may exist in my imagination and in the realm of art. The problem itself is therefore genuine. The formulation of the problem and the solution which it foreshadows are determined by the concrete situation of the moment in which the book was written in the early 'forties. An individual who is faced with the permanent threat of annihilation discovers that non-being is a permanent possibility connected with being, and that the Nothing haunts Being. Out of this experience arises his metaphysics. The metaphysics of nothing-

[1] *L'Être et le Néant*, p. 46 (further quoted as *E.N.*).

ness is no longer, as in Heidegger's case, based on an opposition to logic. Sartre does not think against logic, he expresses the feelings of a world threatened by annihilation.

The mere fact of being an expression of the *Zeitgeist* would, however, not suffice for securing the philosopher of negativity a place in the history of metaphysics. Has he a reasonable claim to such a place? Does he add a new solution of the ontological problem of not-being to those already given? It is most characteristic of our time that the problem of not-being prevails over that of being. Whereas Parmenides, Plato, Aristotle and Descartes were concerned with a redistribution of being, and either excluded not-being or gave it a secondary place, the redistribution and accommodation of not-being seems to be of primary interest to the metaphysicians of our time. In fact, the problem of not-being, *i.e.* how it should be possible that not-being or nothing *is*, has haunted European philosophers since the days of Parmenides.

At least five different solutions seem to be possible.

I. *Being is. Not-being is not.* This is equivalent to saying that *everything is*. Parmenides gave this answer, but by excluding not-being he found himself driven to reject change and diversity also, so that he was left with one all-comprehensive Being. It has been said that the denial of not-being is a fundamental characteristic of rationalism, *e.g.* of Descartes and of Leibniz; but the same could be said of the empiricists. The difference is merely that, while the rationalists tend to identify "everything" with "all", the empiricists identify it with "every particular idea" or "every particular object". *Nihil*, Locke would say, is a negative name which denotes a positive idea, namely being, with a signification of its absence.

II. *Not-being is. Being is not.* This is equivalent to saying that *nothing is*, and it was so formulated, in Gorgias' nihilism, as an antithesis to Parmenides. It is a paradoxical answer of great historical consequence, but does not offer a solution to the problem of being.

III. *Being is* and *not-being is.* This is equivalent to saying that *something is* and *something is not.* This solution allows of many variations, according to the interpretation one gives to the opposition of being and not-being. If one interprets them as contraries, one may say with Democritus that atoms represent full being and empty space not-being, or with Plato that not-being is merely "otherness", or with Aristotle that not-being may be potential being in distinction from actual being, or with the Moderns that, in opposition to "objective being", not-being is merely subjective, perhaps nominal or fictitious. If, however, being and not-being are taken as contradictories, a kind of dialectic ensues, because they cannot any longer be accommodated either on different levels or in different spheres of being, and they therefore clash. The thesis leads to an antithesis, and both have to be reunited in a synthesis (Hegel, Marx). All types of change now seem to become dialectical when in fact they are not. Moreover, the law of contradiction is here partly rejected, because otherwise the antithesis that "not-being is" could not be established, and partly accepted, because without it the transition from the antithesis to the synthesis could not be justified. Or in other words, the apparent success of the dialectic is based on the ambiguity of the term "not-being" or "not-A". As the contradictory to A it is indeterminate; it means "any member of the class which is not-A"; e.g. a colour, which is not-red, may be blue, green, yellow, etc.; as soon as we choose one specific colour we see that "green" as "not-red" is merely the contrary to red. But it may of course be that the class of not-A's is empty; in this case the contradictory is "nothing".

Because these three solutions are unsatisfactory many to-day are prepared to accept a fourth solution, according to which the whole problem is a pseudo-problem. One may argue that "to be" and "not to be" are incomplete symbols, receiving their meaning in particular circumstances, and that all preceding philosophers mistook them for complete symbols. One may ironically nickname the whole problem "Plato's beard", and attempt to get rid of it with the help of Russell's theory of descriptions and with the remark that "something", "everything" and "nothing" are merely variables of quantification.[1] But in spite of this the problem remains, for death cannot be eliminated as a linguistic pseudo-problem. Therefore a fifth solution is attempted by Sartre, according to which nothingness receives a specific place and function within the realm of Being, so that the two propositions, *Everything is* and *Nothing is*, are both valid. He is concerned with a redistribution of not-being rather than of being. Not-being has somehow to be accommodated within the realm of being. His treatment of negation and nothingness offers a key for understanding his ontology.

In formulating the question, What is the origin of negation? he follows Heidegger, and he also accepts his answer that " nothing " is the source of negation and not the other way round; but the manner of his argumentation is original. He asks, What is a question and what does it presuppose? He answers that every question posits the possibility of a negative answer. "In a question one examines a being concerning its being. . . . This manner of being or this being is veiled (*voilé*) : the possibility always remains open that it will reveal itself to be nothing. But from the very fact that an object may always reveal itself as *nothing*, it follows that every question presupposes the faculty of our consciousness to recede in *un recul anéantisant* and to negate the object in question, which thus becomes a simple representation (*présentation*) oscillating between being and nothingness." [2] In other words, he is not satisfied with a merely linguistic or logical explanation for the possibility of a negative answer. He would not deny that in certain cases, *e.g.* when I say that green is not red, the negation is merely logical or conceptual, but he insists that in other cases it is of ontological significance. He holds that a purely logical explanation of negation is impossible, because "there exist an infinite quantity of realities which are not exclusively objects of judgment, but which are experienced, struggled against, dreaded, etc. by men, and which are habitated by negation in their internal structure, as by a necessary condition of their

---

[1] W. V. Quine, "On What There Is", *Review of Metaphysics*, vol. ii, p. 5.
[2] *E.N.*, no. 59. Consciousness is this *recul anéantisant*.

existence. We call them negativities (*negatités*)".[1] Such are absence, distance, alteration, otherness (*altérité*), repulsion, regret and distraction. He has concrete experiences in mind. He visits a *café* expecting to find Peter, but instead he has to experience his absence. The proposition, "Peter is not there", is not at the same level with "Wellington is not there" or "Paul Valéry is not there", because these were not expected to be there. The absence of Peter is experienced as reality, which transforms the whole scene. "The absent Peter haunts the café."[2] One can neither say that these negativities do not form part of our experience, nor can one ban them to a place outside the world. They are dispersed within the world, arise within it and are conditions of reality. Nothingness must therefore be found "not outside being, but in the bosom of being, in its very heart, like a worm (*ver*)".[3]

Whereas Heidegger asked what is the source of negation, and answered "Nothingness", Sartre goes a step further by asking what is the origin of nothingness. Heidegger's "Nothing", he would say, is a transcendent and super-worldly nothing which may explain absolute negation, but it does not take account of inner-worldly negativities which form part of our daily experience, and therefore not of relative negation and relative nothingness. Without denying the transcendence of the absolute Nothing, he attempts to bring nothingness back into this world, and to establish the transcendent Nothing in the very heart of immanence. This fact represents an important and most revealing event in the spiritual history of our time. Whereas former ages, having discovered the transcendent God, were longing to see how He could become immanent in Man and World, our generation, believing that it had discovered transcendent Nothingness, is interested in seeing it descend into the world and into the hearts of men. Or to put it more bluntly, the super-worldly Devil, having lost his transcendent realm, comes down to earth, making a hell of it.

Sartre expresses the experience of a disillusioned

[1] *E.N.*, p. 57.   [2] *Ibid.*, p. 45.   [3] *Ibid.*, p. 57.

generation in which negative experiences, frustration, loss
and pain prevail. It is a generation which is not broken
but fragile, and which experiences this fragility as belonging essentially to its structure. Sartre discovers "being"
as being "fragile". "But what is fragility if not the
probability of non-existence for a specific being in specific
circumstances? A being is fragile if it bears in its being a
definite possibility of not-being." [1] All human beings are
bearing this possibility within themselves; but here we
are faced with a generation in which this chance, very
small in peaceful times, is transformed into a high probability so that anyone may have to die at any moment.
Since it does not make sense to make the world responsible
for this fragility, Sartre concludes that man brings this
fragility into the world. He claims to find the basis of
these negativities in the empirical liberty of man or, as he
puts it, "in the empirical liberty as an act of negating
(*néantisation*) of man on the basis of temporality". This,
however, is merely a sort of secondary negation which must
be based on a primary act of negating. "Evidently", he
says, "one must find the foundation of every negation in an
act of negating exercised at the very bottom of immanence;
i.e. in absolute immanence, in the pure subjectivity of the
instantaneous *cogito*, we have to discover the original act
by which man for himself is his own nothingness." [2] *Man
as a being within the world is his own nothingness, and through
him nothingness comes into the world.* This is Sartre's paradoxical solution. Being and nothingness both exist, but
nothingness has its roots in man, or rather, as we shall see
very soon, in "existence" or in what he calls "*pour-soi*",
"being for himself". In opposition to Heidegger he
transfers nothingness from the realm of the object to that
of the subject, and grafting it on a philosophy of consciousness, he maintains that we, *i.e.* our consciousness, bring
negation and destruction into this world.

This does not imply that negation is again reduced to
logical negation; on the contrary, it receives ontological
status and pervades all acts of the *Ego*, his knowledge as
well as his emotions and actions. Consciousness and

[1] *E.N.*, p. 57. [2] *Ibid.*, p. 83.

liberty turn out to be nothing. Here we have reached a point where his redistribution of nothingness cannot be understood without a reference to his attempted re-distribution of being. Man has a specific prerogative among other beings which are merely there. "Being there" or "being-in-itself" (*être-en-soi*, Hegel's *An-sich-sein*, Heidegger's *Vorhandene* and *Zuhandene*) is a general mode of being. It is just what it is, and therefore merely positive, and "nothingness" cannot have its roots in it. Man alone is "for himself", *l'être-pour-soi* (consciousness, *cogito*, Hegel's *Für-sich-sein*, Heidegger's *Dasein*). "To be conscious" means here "to be present to oneself and to the world", *i.e.* in the latter case to perceive how our body is present in the world, or how our "world comes into being". For although man is essentially "nothing", he is at the same time "everything", the creator of the Universe and of himself, albeit in a paradoxical, absurd and even contradictory manner. We are by no means merely "consciousness", merely *pour-soi*. Our actual experiences, *e.g.* pleasure and pain, are *en-soi*; they are just what they are. But, argues Sartre, as soon as we reflect on them, as we make them the object of conscious interpretation, we are destroying their character and reducing them to nothing. This state of affairs being unsatisfactory and our consciousness becoming essentially "unhappy conscious-ness", we strive to become again what we were before, namely *en-soi*, and to achieve a synthesis, in the true Hegelian manner, of *pour-soi* and *en-soi*. This unity of "being-for-himself" and "being-in-itself" can only be achieved by God, but not by man, because in man the *pour-soi* transcends and negates the *en-soi*. Man is there-fore a *passion inutile*, condemned to failure. "Human reality is pure effort to become God without there being any basis on which to found this effort, and without there being any thing that strives in this way." [1] Man for himself, cut off from God, attempts to become God and falls back into nothingness. He is what he should not be, *en-soi*, and what he should be, i.e. *pour-soi-en-soi*, he is not and even cannot be.

[1] *E.N.*, p. 664.

Man is here conceived as a contradictory being, as an *Ego* depending on the existence of others and including inter-subjectivity as a condition of his existence, but these others depend likewise on him. He is a being in a situation which is biological, economic, political and cultural, and therefore dependent on it, and nevertheless "choosing himself in a situation" and therewith the situation itself. By choosing himself man becomes what he himself makes of himself, *i.e.* his own project, and in so doing he legislates for the whole of mankind. This represents the positive aspect of his liberty; its negative aspect realizes itself in acts of negation.

Thus Sartre arrives at his theses that consciousness is a degradation of being and that it is "nothing". Thereby Heidegger's assertion, that "nothingness" is *Nichtung*, suddenly makes sense, because it becomes an act of the subject. Consciousness, it is claimed, has the power of "reducing to nothing" (*néantir*) or of "nullifying" (*néantiser*). *Néantir* means, in the first instance, something very harmless, namely to "disregard", "paying no attention to", or "putting into brackets". If I perceive, imagine, or remember something, *e.g.* the inkpot on my desk, I disregard everything else that does not interest me at the moment. This is quite true, and not at all new, for it is implied in any act of abstraction. Only the interpretation of these facts is new. Sartre is right; there is always a negative attitude coupled with a positive one. But does this amount to "nullifying"? Sartre may reply that this term means "considering as non-existent for me". Attitudes of this kind exist. Some persons regard it as beneath their dignity to know lower class people. But this is in fact no "nullification", but a refusal to recognize the value of other men. One does not "nullify" the danger of militant Communism by closing one's eyes to it. Sartre, of course, knows this; but he needs the ambiguity of this term, and indeed of most of his terms, in order to build up his system, which is in fact a philosophy of ambiguity. "Disregarding" alone would not do; it must be sometimes "reducing to nothing" or "nullifying".

In any case, human existence is here not only defined by its absurdity and ambiguity, but also by its *negativity*. *L'être humain n'est pas seulement l'être par qui des négativités se dévoilent dans le monde, il est aussi celui qui peut prendre des attitudes négatives vis-à-vis de soi.*[1] ("The human being is not only that being by which negativities are revealed in this world; it is also that being which is able to take negative attitudes to itself.") It brings negativities into the world and it has negative attitudes to itself, and above that, it *is* nothing. Brentano's and Husserl's thesis that consciousness does not exist in isolation, but that it is always consciousness *of* something, *i.e.* contains an "intentional" element, is here misinterpreted in the sense that it is "nothing". On the other hand, the individual, human existence or consciousness, is taken as God or the Absolute. Therefore the paradoxical result is reached, that *Nothing is the Absolute*. *Ce rien est la réalité humaine elle-même, comme la négation radicale par quoi le monde se dévoile* (p. 230). ("This nothingness is the human reality itself, and at the same time, the radical negation through which the world is revealed.") This consequence is fantastic. But there we are, and this is what is alive as well as dead in Sartre's philosophy.

Sartre's world is a world in which the affirmative is transformed into the negative, the normal into the abnormal, good faith into bad faith, and truth into falsehood. The abnormal now parades as the normal, and what is normal in our life appears as abnormal. Existence is freedom, but this freedom is nothing. *La liberté c'est précisément le néant qui est été au cœur de l'homme et qui contraint la réalité-humaine à se faire au lieu d'être* (p. 516). ("Freedom is precisely that Nothingness which has arisen in the heart of man and which forces the human reality to make itself, instead of being itself.") This negativity prevails in the relations of the individual to himself, and also in those to other persons. It leads not only to an inversion, but to a perversion of the natural world of human relationships. The other is not the brother or friend, but the irreconcilable enemy of the individual. A war of all against

[1] *E.N.*, p. 85.

all arises, not in the robust Hobbesian sense, but on a much more subtle and sophisticated level. There is no recognition of the other as a person with inalienable rights; on the contrary, each looks at the other as an object, tries to transform him into an object, to re-ify and to alienate him. Therefore two basic types of human interrelationships are possible: Sadism, which tries to make the other completely dependent on oneself, and Masochism, in which one accepts the liberty of the other person as the basis of one's own liberty. These two attitudes frustrate each other, but the human condition is so absurd that man cannot escape their circle. This may illustrate the new existential psycho-analysis, for these two sexual attitudes are claimed as fundamental. "All the complex behaviours of men towards each other are merely enrichments of these two basic attitudes, and of a third, namely hate" (p. 477). This is, of course, a complete distortion of the normal moral human world. But shall we therefore accuse Sartre of acts of vilification? Unfortunately, his thesis is not the product of a morbid fancy, but it has some truth in it as an ideological reflex of life under dictatorship, of a concentration-camp civilization, or of a world of terror. The grotesque point is that this contingent fact, this temporary disgrace of Eurasia, has here gained the status of metaphysical dignity.

4

It is easy to refute this picture as an absurdity, because it refutes itself. One can point to the contradiction that it does not make sense to establish the abnormal as the norm of the normal, because in this case nothing normal is left. One could argue that a human world without love, sympathy and collaboration could not exist for any considerable length of time. But Sartre could reply: "Look here, the bolshevist dictatorship which is based on exactly these principles has endured for more than thirty years." One could, of course, retort that even there it is merely half the picture, and that the other half is mutual aid and faith in a great revolutionary work. But, nevertheless, the fact remains that the Sartrian hell existed and exists—*e.g.* in concentration camps and in dictatorial states—and the problem is, how to transform people in whom negative attitudes prevail into others who affirm and recognize the dignity of other persons. Negation may predominate at certain times, but it always remains correlative to, and even dependent on, affirmation, and therefore it cannot be the primary fact of human nature.

One could even allocate a place in the history of metaphysics to Sartre by saying that he represents the *reductio ad absurdum* of nihilistic metaphysics. It does not make sense to declare nothingness to be the Absolute in man and in the world. "But", it could be objected, "is not his negativism counterbalanced by a very positive philosophy, an idealism of freedom in Dilthey's sense, and have you not yourself spoken of his substitute-religion of freedom?" It is quite true that liberty plays here a central rôle. But if one prefers to look at him from this angle, one cannot avoid the conclusion that he represents the *reductio ad absurdum* of the idealism of liberty, in particular, and of the modern tendency to autonomy, in general, at least in its emotional and passionate forms.

He desires freedom. Wonderful! But he wants too much. He wishes to be completely and absolutely free in all the spheres of his being, in his emotions and passions as well as in his will. He claims total and infinite liberty. Whereas in fact people are dominated by their emotions and passions, he tries to persuade us that we ourselves have chosen to be jealous or sad; that we have chosen our own being and, in a certain sense, even our coming into this world! Every person is here *un choix absolu, un absolu jouissant d'une date absolue* (p. 640), in other words, a small god. But if we ask what he means by liberty, he answers "a spontaneity which determined itself to be" (p. 517). He mistakes natural, or rather naturalistic, spontaneity for moral liberty, and understands, moreover, this spontaneity as "*spontanéité néantissante*" (p. 518); that is to say, we are again back to nothingness. If we object that he himself has defined man as "*liberté en situation*" and that this situation implies unfreedom and sometimes necessity, he replies that even in prison, in war, or in the hand of a torturer one remains free, because one has chosen to be in this situation. This so-called freedom, which in reality is not freedom at all, is absurd (p. 559).

But is he not right in connecting liberty with responsibility? Does he not make us responsible for our being, our actions, for the world in which we live, for the world war, and for the Universe itself? Yes, he does, and he even reaches the startling conclusion that "man, being condemned to be free, carries the load of the whole world on his shoulders and is responsible for the world and for himself in his specific being" (p. 639). This sounds wonderful, but what does it amount to? "Responsibility" has here a merely naturalistic meaning, namely "consciousness of being the incontestable author of an event or of an object" (*l.c.*). It simply means that *homo-creator*, or rather man the would-be creator, regards himself as the author of all things. In this sense he is "naturally responsible", but he is not "morally responsible"; he is not answerable either to God who does not exist, nor to a moral law or to values which are denied objective validity and depend on the individual as their creator. Sartre maintains that whatever happens is "mine" and that no happening is inhuman. *Les plus atroces situations de la guerre, les pires tortures ne créent d'état de choses inhumain; il n'a pas de situation inhumaine* (p. 639). ("The most atrocious situations in war, the worst tortures do not create an inhuman state of affairs; an inhuman situation does not exist.") This statement reveals the confusion not only of this writer, but of our time. It seems irresponsible, not worthy of a member of the Resistance, because it implies a justification of the most cruel actions of the most inhuman dictators. Torturers are not only inhuman, they are subhuman, they violate the dignity of the human person which is and should be an end in itself, but which is here merely an object of sadistic practice. But Sartre and his followers have lost the moral power of rejecting these atrocities; they don't mind them, provided they themselves are the torturers, as they are in their plays. A society adopting this attitude would be ripe for the rubbish-heap.

What is the reason for these overstatements of an unusually ingenious writer? His secret seems to be that he is a *littérateur engagé* and that consequently his philosophy becomes *littérature engagée*. Sartre is just the opposite to Jaspers, whose dominant attitude is that of detachment, non-commitment and openness for all forms of being. We remarked that Jaspers started with two opposed principles, namely Max Weber's principle of *Wertfreiheit der Wissenschaft* and Kierkegaard's imperative of absolute choice.[1] It is a most interesting spectacle to see that in Jaspers's theoretical philosophy Weber's principle prevails, transformed into the Buddhist attitude of non-identification, whereas Sartre adopts Kierkegaard's imperative, with God left out, deprived of its religious flavour and transformed into the principle of commitment. It is elucidating to compare Jaspers's "Basic Postulates of the Philosophy of the Comprehensive"[2] with Sartre's antitheses.

JASPERS	SARTRE
Keep space open for the Comprehensive!	There is no Comprehensive.
Do not identify yourself with an object of your knowledge!	Commit yourself!
Do not reject any form of the Comprehensive!	Reject all those forms which restrict your liberty!
Do not accept any defamation of existence!	Describe reality in its ugliness, absurdity and obscenity!
Do not allow yourself to be cut off from the Transcendent!	You are cut off from the Transcendent, for it is non-existent.

This opposition reveals that, in contemporary man, two attitudes tend to be separated and developed to extremes which should be co-ordinated within a *via media*.

It is of course quite true that the two principles are

---

[1] *Cf.* p. 61.
[2] *Von der Wahrheit*, p. 188.

known to both of them. Jaspers postulates, as we saw, choice and decision in the realm of action. Theoretically he fully acknowledges its importance. Practically, however, he leaves all the decisions to the reader to whom he appeals, and is careful never to make a decision in the course of his own philosophizing. In fact, therefore, the principle of detachment prevails. He is essentially contemplative, whereas Sartre is prevalently active. Sartre is active, even in his theoretical philosophy. He commits himself whenever he writes. They both fail in harmonizing the two attitudes.

Sartre is the *philosopher as well as the artist of commitment.* The strength and weakness of his philosophy and of his art follow from this fact. What does this commitment amount to? *Le philosophe engagé* presupposes and transcends Kierkegaard's "choice", Hegel's definition of philosophy as an expression of the *Zeitgeist* (*eine Zeit in Gedanken gefasst*), and the Marxist conception of the philosopher as the ideological representative of his class. Committed philosophy does not arise *in vacuo*; it is written for others and in interrelation with others, in a particular historical situation. The writer must be fully conscious of this situation and able to express it. He must accept the responsibilities arising out of it, make his choice, taking into account his obligations to others and act accordingly. His philosophy will be at its best if it rises to the occasion, as it did in *The Republic of Silence.* It will be at its worst when it presses general issues into the strait-jacket of a contingent situation and when it falsely universalizes the latter.

As a result, his philosophy is alive as an expression of the contemporary situation, but dead in so far as the writer commits himself to certain general positions which are untenable. Sartre is enormously alive as writer, essayist, dramatist and psychologist. He has an uncanny gift for diagnosis. He sees phenomena, and is unusually stimulating and provocative in their analysis. On the other hand, he accepts a considerable number of negative commitments. First, he commits himself against God. "God is dead!" was already Nietzsche's cry, but nevertheless he remained in search of Him, because he could not live without Him. If he was an atheist, his chief aim was surely not the propaganda of atheism, but the search for the Unknown God. This is the most terrible self-contradiction from which a human being can suffer. Sartre does not experience these qualms; for him God is definitely dead, and he adds the questionable corollary, that it would not make any difference even if He existed. God's existence is, according to him, neither demonstrable nor possible, for the concept of a being which is by itself (*ens a se*) and its own cause (*causa sui*) is said to be contradictory. The real reason for his atheist existentialism is, however, that he resents the restrictions of his liberty imposed by God as the source of eternal values and of the moral order, which he rejects as well. Secondly, he commits himself against *the* Transcendent as such. *The* Transcendent does not exist, and he would regard a search for it as mistaken. This does not exclude that man is here understood as someone who continually transcends himself in the direction of the future and who is open for all his future possibilities. Thirdly, he commits himself against Providence. "We want", he says, "to drive Providence from our works as we have driven it from our world." Thereby he commits himself against God's creation. "And God saw that it was good." No, replies Sartre, there is neither goodness, nor value, nor even sense in this world, it is bad and absurd. He commits himself against the good will of man, believing in the prevalence of bad faith. He commits himself against the Eternal for the Temporal; against the spirit, for matter, body and sexual pleasures; and against contemplation for social action.

It is by no means just chance that all these commitments imply value judgments. Commitment represents Sartre's specific response to the challenge of his time. It is the response of a man who is at once "within-the-world", "present" to it, and who thinks he is able to transform the situation in which he finds himself into a situation of his own choice. It is a response which implies a valuation. Now unfortunately the situation in which Sartre finds himself is so utterly bad that his first reaction is negative. He therefore commits himself too much to the Negative, Not-being and Nothingness.

This is true of his philosophy as well as of his art. His brilliant essay on *The Imaginary, Phenomenological Psychology of the Imagination*, translated under the somewhat misleading title *The Psychology of Imagination*, may illustrate this point. Following Husserl, he interprets imagination as "imaging", *i.e.* as a specific type of intentional consciousness, in which an object is contemplated by way of quasi-observation. But in opposition to him, he again commits himself at once to negativity by saying that this sort of consciousness posits its object as nothingness, namely either as absent or as having no existence at all. This is a completely unwarranted assumption, but Sartre is committed to it because he has deprived reality of beauty. He maintains that reality is never beautiful, therefore beauty can only be found in the realm of the imaginary, the unreal, and of nothingness. These propositions are evidently false, they contradict our experience of natural beauty. They are, however, most revealing if subjected to an existential psycho-analysis. Sartre's provocative essay on *The Emotions* provides the clue. There he makes the ingenious but debatable attempt to interpret the emotions as a return to the stage of magical existence. "Nous appelerons émotions une chute brusque de la conscience dans la magique. Or, si l'on préfère, il y a émotion quand le monde des ustensiles s'évanant brusquement et que le monde magique apparaît à sa place." The magician Sartre achieves his triumphs in his plays. The psychologist Sartre explains the emotion which constitutes his world in a magical form: "I find it hateful *because* I am angry." It is the world of an angry man.

Uncertain of himself he overstresses his commitments. He goes too far in his negativity. He is entitled to disclaim that we have any knowledge of God and of the Transcendent, but he is unable to prove their non-existence. He is right in distinguishing logical negation and ontological not-being, and in maintaining that man brings *some* negativity into this world, but he is wrong in claiming that he is the source of *all* negativity. He is right in stressing the responsibility for others even in solitary decisions, but he is wrong in making men responsible for actions they did not do and for situations they did not bring about, and for overloading them with total responsibility. He condemns them to infinite liberty which they are unable to bear.

VIII. THE MYSTERIOUS EMPIRICIST

I

MAN makes science, but God creates the metaphysician. One can talk for hours on end about the status of metaphysical propositions, naively assuming that they form a specific class, without having the slightest idea what metaphysics is. The real metaphysician does not talk *about* metaphysics, he talks metaphysics. "Gabri . . e . . e . . l!" I shall never forget Charles Du Bos's exclamation (suggesting that suddenly the archangel Gabriel had come down to earth) at one of the spirited meetings at Gabriel Marcel's home in 1934, in which Berdyaev, Louis Lavelle, René Le Senne, Paul Landsberg and others took part. Marcel is indeed one of the most original among the very few metaphysicians of our time. Convinced of the inexhaustible richness of human experience, he possesses perhaps the greatest adventurous curiosity among contemporary philosophers. A truly European mind, he began with studies of Schelling's influence on Coleridge's metaphysical ideas and of the interrelations between English and German philosophy in general; went through an idealist phase, and liked to compare his critique of Bradley, Bosanquet and Royce with Kierkegaard's critique of Hegel. He is the author of the *Journal Métaphysique*, a metaphysical diary filled with day to day reflections on most profound problems, with "spermatic ideas" *in statu nascenti* and abounding in drafts of prospective philosophical essays. In a certain sense most of his later philosophical publications—at least the most lively among them—are continuations of it. French students complained jokingly that one needed an Ionian diver to trace its pearls, and textbook writers find no other philosophy so difficult to summarize.

Marcel is a complex and polyphonic nature, a successful dramatist and dramatic critic, editor of the collection

Feux croisés, a lover and composer of music, *anima religiosa,* and philosopher. Neither can the dramatist be understood without the philosopher nor the philosopher without the dramatist, nor either without the background from which he emerged. He himself has sketched the latter in his charming autobiographical essay *Regard en arrière,* which he has contributed to the collection of essays written in his honour by Étienne Gilson and others. He was born in 1889 as the only son of a *Conseiller d'État,* who was sometime *Ministre of France* in Stockholm, and later *Directeur aux Beaux-Arts* at the *Bibliothèque Nationale* and at the *Musées Nationaux.* Though privileged, he found himself thrown into a world of tensions and insoluble contradictions: his father was a Catholic agnostic; his mother, of Jewish stock, died when he was four and mysteriously remained with him, overshadowing the influence of her sister, who became his stepmother and later turned Protestant. He suffered from the fact of being the only child, from too much care and attention focused on him, and from the abstract, impersonal, "inhuman" and purely objective training of his school. Here lies the basis not only of his experience, but also of his metaphysics. "A mind is metaphysical", he says, "in so far as its position within reality appears to it essentially unacceptable. . . . It is in a false position. The problem is to correct this or to bring about a *détente.* Metaphysics is just this correction (*redressement*) or this *détente.*" [1] Marcel's dramatic production and his religion rise from the same root. It would even be right to say that he personally found his *redressement* and *détente* when in 1929, following an appeal by François Mauriac, he became a Catholic. In his metaphysics, which is profoundly influenced by his religion, he would hardly claim to have found a corresponding solution.

The difficulty of summarizing Marcel's thought arises from two sources. First, from the range and diffuseness of his *œuvre,* which consists of innumerable articles of all kinds, of more than twenty dramas, and a few philosophical books. Secondly, from the formlessness and non-

[1] *Journal Métaphysique,* p. 279.

finality of the latter. They are either diary notes or collections of lectures. All of them denote stages of a somewhat confused and obscure philosophical itinerary, which follows many side-tracks and often returns to its starting-point. *It* thinks in Marcel, as he himself remarks, more than he thinks. He reflects and has pleasure in pointing out difficulties, and sometimes in making the easy difficult, instead of making the difficult easy. One should have thought that the Gifford Lectures, *The Mystery of Being*, would have offered him an opportunity of giving us his final thought. But no, a course of lectures proved somehow inadequate to his mode of thinking. Even here he remained "in search of" or "groping for". He himself is sadly aware of the fact that his *magnum opus*, which he hoped to prepare in his diaries, will never be written.

2

Nevertheless there is a central point. Marcel is concerned with a transformation of empiricism which is at the same time a transformation of rationalism and of metaphysics. After centuries of rationalistic enlightenment, which tried to explain away what is mysterious in religion, in life and in the Universe, Marcel rediscovers the mysterious within our experience and even the fact that experience itself is a mystery. He is (*sit venia verbo*) a *mysterious empiricist* who fills the old notion of metaphysics as science of being with new life by defining metaphysics as *réflexion braquée sur un mystère*. This implies a complete change of method. Whereas the old rationalist metaphysics started with abstractions, *e.g.* Hegel with the concept of being, and attempted to reach the concrete in the course of their deductions or their dialectical speculations, Marcel starts with an analysis of his own concrete experience. He feels that within the abstractions of science and philosophy the concrete experience and the existing subject have been left out. From the beginning he attempts to give "to existence that metaphysical

priority of which idealism has deprived it".[1] Without
knowing Kierkegaard and without reaching his precision
he opposes "existence", *i.e.* by implication "subjectivity",
to "objectivity". That this is a genuine problem may be
illustrated by the fact that the American philosopher
Otis Lee, in his book *Existence and Enquiry* (1949), likewise
postulates a new method of philosophical inquiry as
analysis or description adequate to deal with the concrete
present which escapes the network of predictive general-
izations established by science. The problem is not
difficult to formulate, but it is extremely difficult to produce a method adequate to its solution. Lee does not
provide it. Did Marcel find it?

It may be illuminating to compare him with Kant.
Like Kant he is opposed to the preceding empiricist as
well as rationalist schools; like him he criticizes both; and
like him he attempts a synthesis of their principles. But
whereas Kant remains within the sphere of "objectivity"
and formulates the critical principle that sense experience
without rational interpretation remains blind, and that
mere concepts without sense experience remain empty—
a principle which allows him to find a solid basis for his
Critique of Pure Reason—Marcel enters the sphere of
subjectivity. His criticism is more personal than objective, and he is less concerned with the form than with the
content of our knowledge. He rejects "experience" as
interpreted by the empiricists—*i.e.* the experience of
sense-data and of daily life—not because it is blind, but
because it seems to him impure and profoundly suspect,
and because it sucks down the spirit without any hope of
its liberation.

Experience, far from being an incoherent chaos of
sensations, volitions and feelings, becomes centred and
focused in the experiencing subject. Becoming multi-
dimensional it gains in breadth; it is no longer restricted
to the "positivist" sphere, to the visible and touchable;
room is left for extra-sensory perception, and we are no
longer allowed to say that something does not exist
because we do not perceive it. Experience gains in depth,

---

[1] *Journal Metaphysique*, p. xi.

for there are different levels of awareness. It is the experience not of an abstract entity "consciousness", but of a human being within-this-world who experiences it in its problematic and mysterious nature and focuses his attention on this as the object of his reflection. Reflection has here not so much the function of illuminating our experience from outside, but of penetrating it from inside. Its method is the Romantic way of *Verinnerlichung*: "L'expérience s'intimise pour ainsi dire, et s'exerce à reconnaître ses implications." In the first place, our experience is no longer one of objects, but of subjects; an experience of persons within the realm of persons with its tensions and its dramatic and often insoluble conflicts. It is based rather on participation in their lives, their joys and sorrows than on external observation. It is, secondly, an experience of objects and, thirdly, an experience of the Transcendent. Marcel argues that "there must exist a possibility of having an experience of the transcendent as such, and unless that possibility exists the word can have no meaning".[1] It is, he maintains, a new mode of experience. In fact, since we respond to external stimuli, the possibility cannot be excluded that we respond to some which transcend the sphere of our sense-perceptions.

3

The corresponding transformation of reason is no less profound. Reason is no longer abstract, formal, deductive and systematic, but concrete, material, intuitive, inductive and unsystematic. It becomes *réflexion*, and Marcel a *reflective existentialist*. It must be noted that French *réflexion* does not denote the same as English "reflection". It is true, there is a sense of *réflexion* which is near to what Locke called *reflection* in opposition to sensation. Whereas to Locke reflection is "the observation employed about the internal operations of the mind", it is to the French "thought or consciousness (*pensée*)

[1] *The Mystery of Being*, vol. i, p. 46.

turning back to itself and concentrating on its spontaneous acts or on a group of them". But it also means "critical suspension of judgment in order to analyse the causes or the reasons of a specific fact". In both these senses it is believed to be the basis of psychology, a sort of introspection coupled with analysis. Marcel uses this psychological reflection for the first stage of his existentialist method. It is what he calls "primary reflection". It is analytic and dissolves the unity of experience. But just as Blondel distinguishes from this *rétrospection analytique* a *prospection synthétique*, which moves forward to its intended goal and final realization, Marcel adds a "secondary reflection" which is synthetic and recuperative and which reconquers the lost unity of experience on a higher level. This is a point where the English term is stretched to breaking-point.[1] It is not difficult to concede that reflection manifests itself at different levels. Marcel, however, wants besides that to vitalize reflection, *i.e.* to transform it into a function of life, as if life, so to speak, were a reflective process. In all those cases where I have been checked and where a certain break in the continuity of my experience has taken place, secondary reflection is said to step in; it allows me to transcend my present situation and to stretch out of myself. Certainly there are integrating and synthesizing forces; Sherrington has shown that the nervous system has essentially an integrative function; but it is difficult to accept "secondary reflection" as this integrative force at the psychological level, especially if one remembers Kant's elaborate analysis of the different forms of synthesis at the levels of intuition, understanding and reason. Reflection seems to remain always what the schoolmen called *intentio secunda*. In spite of all, the retrospective tendency seems to prevail in it. One has first to think, to will, to act, and to produce before one is able to reflect. Reflection can only reveal what was already there in experience, vision and imagination. In so far as reflection is prospective, it is rather *research*. Curiosity is the emotional urge behind the creative philosopher. Philosophy therefore paradoxically

---

[1] *The Mystery of Being*, vol. i, ch. 5.

becomes "research" [1] for the mysteries of existence; and the elucidation of specific human problems and conflicts, chosen at random, is the most valuable function of this philosophy.

At the same time reason becomes *pensée pensante* in opposition to *pensée pensée, thinking thought* and not *thought thought*. This is specifically characteristic of Marcel. Spinoza distinguished *natura naturans* and *natura naturata*. Marcel not only makes a corresponding distinction as to thought, but he thinks himself entitled to reject *pensée pensée* as the fallacious result of reflection, in which the mind has cut itself off from its connection with being and existence. He rejects *Esprit* with a capital E as a depersonalized and dehumanized Mind deprived of all power, presence and existence. This attitude is interesting, but beset with great difficulties. Marcel's strength lies in the process of thinking and experiencing, or in what he calls *expérience en cours*. However, thinking thought is nothing but the way to thought thought, and one cannot always remain on the move. Therefore, though Marcel would like to keep thought at this level, he has continually to transcend it. He cannot help rejecting and accepting "thought thought" at the same time.

The transformation of reason into "incarnate thought" brings out this contradiction. *L'incarnation donnée centrale de la métaphysique*.[2] But what is it? An experience? A principle? A contingent fact? A starting-point? Or what else? Marcel himself is not quite clear about it. Nevertheless the idea of incarnation dominates his thought. He experiences the mind as bound up with its body. He holds that the separation from the body destroys its vitality and its power of knowing reality. He conceives of the body as "absolute mediator" and as "the central criterion to which must be referred all the judgments of existence which I may be led to pronounce". These are opinions which seem to me somewhat odd and indefensible on logical grounds. I do not deny that incarnation points to a real problem. But there seem to

---

[1] *The Mystery of Being*, vol. i, p. 1.
[2] *Être et Avoir*, p. 11.

be two problems, one metaphysical and one epistemological; in traditional terms the one may be called the
soul-body problem, the other the mind-matter problem.
Both are interconnected, but by no means identical. It
is quite true that there would be no knowledge if our soul
were not embodied, for the simple reason that there
would not be any sense-experience on which to build it
up. But the incarnation of thought is a different matter;
it has to embody itself in material of some kind, in sounds,
in colours, or in words and signs. In doing so it becomes
pensée pensée. On the other hand, with the process of
incarnation the counter-process of spiritualization is
indissolubly connected. In fact, we are doing this constantly; and this again implies a translation of *pensée
pensante* into *pensée pensée*.

4

Here we touch a point of great importance, not only
for Marcel, but for any philosophy. The question
whether a philosophy is alive, is intimately connected with
another one, namely whether it is realized, or whether a
philosopher has achieved self-realization. A philosophy
cannot be alive without having realized itself; it can,
however, be realized without being alive, for it can be
stillborn. It is most interesting to ask the question:
What are the criteria according to which one can decide
whether a philosophy is realized or not, and when such a
realization is genuine or spurious? Does a philosopher
merely make great claims which he fails to make good?
Does his thought remain permanently at an embryonic
level or is it fully developed? It would seem that a
philosophical realization is genuine

(1) when it introduces a new mode of thought or a new
method;
(2) when it does not remain vague, indefinite and essentially
ambiguous, but finds a specific shape (*Gestalt*);
(3) when it realizes itself not in images (the way of the poet)
but in concepts; or if in images, there should at
least be a rule for translating these images into
concepts; the philosopher should, in Hegel's words,

die Arbeit des Begriffes auf sich nehmen, *i.e.* he should make a serious effort to express his thought in clear concepts;

(4) his realization should be essential, that is to say, it should represent an essential mode of philosophizing; it should be essential either within the realm of possible philosophies, or within the setting of his own age;

(5) a genuine realization can be repeated in endless variations and is therefore alive, whereas a spurious realization is dead and does not allow of variations;

(6) the realization must not occur in words only, but also in deeds; this is true of any philosophy, but it is especially true of Existentialism; for the chasm between theoretical philosophy and its application in life was, since the days of Kierkegaard, one of the chief targets of existentialist criticism.

It would, however, be a mistake to assume that there is only *one* form of philosophic realization, namely an elaborate system. By no means; there are many ways leading to Rome. But has the realization not always to imply a transition from *thinking thought* to *thought thought*? We cannot therefore avoid asking, whether Marcel's thought is not in such a position that he clearly sees and even experiences the problem of incarnate thought (so to say, as a specific mode of incarnation) and makes it the subject of many penetrating reflections, without achieving in his own thought the transition to *thought thought*. It could be that his rejection of *pensée pensée* made him a prisoner of reflection and hindered him from finding that form of self-realization which would represent the emergence of real shape (*Gestalt*).

5

We now come to his third and most central transformation, which combines the new concept of experience and reflection in his metaphysics as *réflexion braquée sur un mystère*. His problem is very much alive. It is the same which haunted all the existentialists, *i.e.* to overcome the alienation of man. He describes this estrangement in his own terms. He feels very strongly that we are living in a broken world. An increasing socialization of life and the growing powers of the state are invading the privacy of the person and destroying the brotherhood of men and the fertile soil in which creativeness, imagination and reflection can flourish. It is a world in which human beings tend to become *fonctionnaires*, exercising a specific function in human society, reduced to statistical numbers, and are no longer free agents of their own right. In a society dominated by technology everything becomes a "problem" to be solved by reasoning and calculation. "Having" is here more important than "being". Everybody *has* employment, *has* possessions, and *has* certain functions to fulfil. Giving an original analysis of having Marcel distinguishes between "possessing having" (*avoir-possession*), *e.g.* to have a house or a motor-car, and "implicit having" (*avoir-implication*), *e.g.* to have a specific quality, *i.e.* pleasure or pain. "Having" is a source of alienation. Objects which we possess, houses, books, factories, gardens, or ideas and opinions which we regard as our "possessions", in a specific sense "have" us. We are in danger of being imprisoned or devoured by them. People concentrating on having are in danger of becoming captive souls cut off from other persons and not responding to their "presence". They suffer a loss of being or an "ontological deficiency" (*déficience ontologique*). They are, Marcel would say, "absent". They talk and talk what they will do for you, but in an hour of peril they are not there, not "present", *i.e.* not at your disposal. This unavailability (*indisponibilité*), invariably rooted in some sort of estrangement, leads on to denial and betrayal. If you are attacked or in danger they pretend not to know you, they betray you. This world, Marcel says, is the place of betrayal, not only of the *trahison des clercs*, but of everybody by everybody. It is a sombre picture, but not quite as gloomy as that of Sartre, and its formulation already implies a rejection of Sartre's pessimism and despair. For all the terms used point, in spite of their negativity, to their positive supplement.

All the negative terms may be brought down to a loss of participation in the life of others, in "being", and in the Divine life. Possessed by "having", men have lost being and suffer from "ontological deficiency". They feel the urge for being. They are in search of being, they have an "ontological sense" or they feel an "ontological exigence". This urge is the basis of Marcel's ontology. As an urge it is real, and points to a fact and a problem. People who have lost their substance and their centre have a desire for being, *i.e.* for a fullness of life or for self-realization. But how an ontology, *i.e.* a science of being, can be constructed on the basis of this urge or exigence is difficult to see. It would seem that the one contradicts the other. "Ontological exigence" arises from "absence", and "absence" points to "presence". Here Marcel sheds new light on a specific feature in human relationship. There may be persons in the same room with me, and nevertheless they may be absent. On the other hand, a friend in another continent may be "present" to me. "To be present" means "to be in immediate contact with", "to respond to", "to be at the disposal of". If we scrutinize our experience we find to our surprise that among the millions of our contemporaries only a very few are co-present with us in this sense. "Absence" should be replaced by "presence", betrayal by fidelity, denial by faith, and despair by hope. This is Marcel's message and the basis of his Christian philosophy of hope.

The following points would seem to deserve discussion. First, the attempt to transcend the "world of problems" in the sphere of the meta-problematical and of mystery. Marcel introduces the term "ontological mystery" and the distinction between mystery and problem. A problem, he says, is something in front of me, obstructing my path, and therefore in this sense alien to me. I can analyse and tackle it in a detached manner, for it is outside myself. A mystery, however, is something within me, in which I myself am engaged, and which consequently cannot be set in front of me in its entirety. I am somehow engulfed in it. Therefore, if I can make a transition from a problem to a mystery I have overcome the alienation. This happens if I go on to "being", which is said to be meta-problematical and a mystery. In a certain sense Marcel is right. The innermost being of persons cannot be expressed in words, it is ineffable. This is also true of other beings and of being as being. The fact that there is being, that all the enormous varieties of creatures exist, and not "nothing" instead, is a mystery beyond our understanding. Nevertheless the question remains whether the distinction between problem and mystery is precise enough to be made the basis of a new metaphysics. Marcel himself sees that the distinction is merely relative, that there is no mystery which cannot be transformed into a problem, and that if one defined metaphysical thought as "thought concentrated on a mystery" no progress of such a thought is conceivable.[1] Nevertheless, not without contradicting himself, he attempts the construction of a metaphysics. Personally this adventure is most interesting, but it does not provide a basis for a future metaphysics. The problems of metaphysics may be mysterious, but nevertheless they remain problems. Scientific problems are amenable to symbolic expression and finite analysis; in principle they are soluble. Metaphysical problems neither allow of symbolic expression nor of finite analysis; from the point of view of a finite understanding they are insoluble in principle, but this does not imply that they do not allow of elucidation, of discussion and of tentative answers. They seem to be mysterious because they imply something which is either indefinite or infinite. For centuries the attention of men has been focused on form and shape to such a degree that we have quite overlooked the rôle played in our experience by the indefinite, the formless and the shapeless. Problems which imply this element may nevertheless be formulated as precisely as possible, alternative hypotheses for their solution may be posited, their respective merits discussed, and a tentative decision made for one of them.

In this sphere, I am afraid, we shall always be restricted to the hypothetical. Marcel, however, in making the transition from the "problematical" to the "meta-problematical", attempts to find an indubitable basis corresponding to Descartes' allegedly indubitable *Cogito*

[1] *Être et Avoir*, p. 146.

ergo sum, which Marcel rejects.   But how is it possible to make indubitable statements about mysteries which seem to exclude by definition any certainties?   Marcel cuts this Gordian knot by declaring: "To think, or rather to assert, the meta-problematical is to assert it as indubitably real, as something of which I cannot doubt without falling into contradiction.   We are in a sphere where it is no longer possible to dissociate the idea itself from the certainty or degree of certainty which pertains to it." [1] This, however, is no rational solution.   From the point of view of the knowing subject there is nothing indubitable in a mystery; on the contrary, he talks of a mystery because he has no certain knowledge.   In fact, Marcel offers a decision of his will.   He replaces Descartes' *je pense* by *je crois*.   He recognizes faith as the act which makes the mind a living and active reality—a faith not understood as opinion, but as a mode of being and an act of participation in the Divine.   He decides to put indubitable trust in the contents of his faith.

In the end, existence is identified with participation, and *esse* with *co-esse*.   Consequently the lonely isolated individual which formed the basis and starting-point of modern philosophy is replaced by a person standing in vital relations with others, and the *I think* by *we are*. Marcel is concerned with exorcizing the ego-centric spirit, because the latter acts as a barrier between us and others.   My experience arises in communication with that of other persons.   "A complete and concrete know-ledge of oneself cannot be self-centred; however para-doxical it may seem, I should prefer to say that it must be centred in others.   We can understand ourselves by starting from the other, or from others, and only by starting from them. . . . Fundamentally, I have no reason to set any particular store by myself, except in so far as I know that I am loved by other beings who are loved by me." [2]   This is a profound truth worthy of being rediscovered.   It was known to Goethe when he wrote: "One only knows that one exists, if one rediscovers

---

[1] *Position et apprôches concrètes du mystère ontologique* (Vrin, Paris, 1949), p. 62.
[2] *The Mystery of Being*, vol. ii, p. 8.

oneself in others." The transition from the individual to a being-within-the-world (Heidegger), standing in communication with others (Jaspers), or in the I-Thou-relation (Ferdinand Ebner, Martin Buber), or to a person inserted in the collective and in the Universe (Mounier), is by no means particular to Marcel. It reflects a movement in contemporary bourgeois society which, in response to the challenge of collectivism implied in Socialism, Bolshevism and Fascism, attempts to save the person within a society of free persons. Nevertheless, Marcel gives a specific Christian interpretation to this general tendency. "The more my existence takes on the character of including others, the narrower becomes the gap which separates it from being; the more, in other words, I am" [1]—these words not only express the personal truth of a dramatist and could have been uttered by Shakespeare; they have a specifically Christian tinge. Where I would speak of interdependence, Marcel uses the term "intersubjectivity", as if the whole world consisted of persons and as if the overriding relation between them were one of charity.

In this world of intersubjectivity knowledge arises again, as in Antiquity, by participation, but now in a Christian manner "by taking part in the lives of others". "To believe", we are told, is always "to believe in a Thou", and is therefore response to an appeal or to an invocation. The "Thou" is essentially a being which may be invoked by me, and the "I" a person testifying to the reality of the "Thou". The stability of this world is based on fidelity as "continuous testimony" or a "presence actively continued", and its progress on *Fidélité créatrice*. This is apparently destined to replace Bergson's *Évolution créatrice* in a realm of persons; in fact, however, it denotes something very different, namely a fidelity which preserves itself in creativity. Since "being" is here as much as to be in communion with oneself, with the world and with others, fidelity may be either fidelity to oneself, to others or to God. Marcel's profound remarks on fidelity or faithfulness may be regarded as variations of the Kierke-

[1] *L.c.*, vol. ii, p. 33.

gaardian theme that truth is subjectivity; for to be faithful is here identical with being true to oneself, true to
others and true to God.   To be true to God means to have
faith.   Fidelity therefore leads to faith.   "It is on the
ground of Truth", he says, "that we should fight our first
battle for religion."   Faith leads to hope, and hope is the
stuff of which our souls are woven.   Hope liberates us from
the shackles of matter, space and time.   It is trust in the
future, based on trust in an absolute being.   Thus a philosophy of hope replaces a philosophy of despair and anxiety.

Here lies Marcel's importance.   In a country where
Sartre's atheistic existentialism exercises a profound but
deplorable influence on the younger generation, Marcel
shows that a theistic Christian existentialism is possible
as an alternative.   At the same time, this philosophy
represents one specific possibility within the realm of
possible metaphysics.   "Being is a mystery"; this partial
truth is here used as a cornerstone of a new metaphysics.
From this attempt interesting reflections result, which
elucidate certain phenomena of the human scene, but
that a new ontology can be based on it has still to be
proved.   It would not be difficult to point to contradictions implied in this enterprise.   Either there is the "ontological mystery", then no science of ontology is possible;
or there is ontology, then "being" becomes a problem,
and within the precincts of this science the mystery disappears.   But this and other contradictions are unable to
destroy the life of this philosophy, for human beings are
full of contradictions.   In fact, the problems behind this
philosophy are very much alive.   Marcel has a pertinent
feeling of the human situation, of the mortal danger which
surrounds the survival of the person.   He points the way,
but he remains a *homo viator*, a Moses, who himself is not
allowed to enter the promised land.

6

This would be different if the *mysterious empiricist* were
transformed into a *mystical empiricist*.   Such a transformation actually takes place in Guido de Ruggiero's

interpretation of Marcel's philosophy in his small booklet on *Existentialism*.[1] It is as if a Roman eye could only perceive the developed form of the *pensée pensée* and had no gusto for the groping formations of the *pensée pensante*. Ruggiero not only confirms my interpretation, but sketches the perfect form which, like an asymptote, Marcel's philosophy approaches without ever reaching. In this interpretation, to *sense* does not mean to decipher a message, but to participate immediately in the object and to become, in a certain sense, one with it beyond all distinction of subject and object. *Sentir n'est pas recevoir, mais participer immédiatement.*[2] Here the body becomes a primary example of an immediate participation of myself in the other, a sort of incarnation. Existence is precisely incarnation and participation. There is a progressive path of incarnation and participation, from the participation in other things to that in other persons and lastly in God. On this way incarnation and participation are, step by step, transformed into invocation and appeal.

This is a remarkably clear picture of Marcel's thought in ideal prolongation; and, indeed, it is possible to pick up sentences in Marcel's writings which fit perfectly into this picture. But, alas! they appear only at random, so to speak, as possibilities which are discussed together with other alternatives. If one goes deeper into the matter one finds many features which do not square with such a consistent scheme, *e.g.* when the body is called "the mysterious condition of objectivity in general".[3] In short, though Marcel is potentially a mystical empiricist, actually he remains a mysterious empiricist.

7

In 1950 something significant happened which made Marcel reject the title "Christian Existentialist" in the

[1] Secker and Warburg, London, 1946.
[2] *Journal Métaphysique* (Gallimard, Paris, 1927), p. 251.
[3] *Metaphysical Journal* (trans. Bernard Wall) (Rockliff, London, 1952), p. 280.

Preface to the English edition of the *Metaphysical Journal* (Rockliff, London, 1952). This is a remarkable fact, seeing that he himself had published a small collection of his essays under the title *Philosophy of Existence* (Harvill Press, London, 1948), and that he further ungrudgingly accepted the homage paid to him in the book *Existentialisme Chrétien: Gabriel Marcel* (Plon, Paris, 1947), presented to him by Étienne Gilson and some of his friends. He even added his above-mentioned autobiographical sketch to it. Reviewing the first of these books in *The Hibbert Journal* of April 1949 I wrote: "The label 'Christian Existentialist' which has been foisted on him is more of a myth than a reality, but Marcel has accepted it willingly, and fights an amusing duel with Sartre, who has stolen the existentialist show." When I visited Marcel in Paris in September 1949 I found him very pleased with my assessment of his intentions, but there was no sign of a rejection of the label. However, now he abhors it, "because it brought with it the worst of misunderstandings", and wishes to have it repudiated once and for all. This Preface is dated "Autumn 1950", but the rejection is said to have occurred in Milan several months earlier, in the same Italy where this title had first been attached to him.

What is the reason for this sudden volte-face? In the first place, certainly the misunderstandings of the general public, which was unable to distinguish a Christian existentialist from an existentialist *à la* Sartre. In the second place, in all probability the Papal encyclic *Humani generis* of August 12, 1950, which rejects existentialism as an aberration, because of its historicism, irrationalism, individualism, subjectivism and pessimism, because of its neglect of substance and essence, and its degradation of human reason. The papal disfavour is by no means directed against the Christian existentialists; nevertheless, it has put them in an awkward position. The encyclic makes it a duty for Catholic theologians, entrusted with the defence of divine and human wisdom and its infiltration into the hearts of men, to study these "opinions which are more or less deviations from the right path".

"Yes, they shall be acquainted with these doctrines, because diseases cannot be cured, if they are not rightly diagnosed, further because there is often a grain of truth in false opinions, and because they may stimulate a new inquiry into, and an analysis of, certain philosophical and theological truths."

This encyclic is of great importance for understanding the present attitude of the Catholic Church to existentialism. The days of Christian Existentialism seem to have gone, and new catholic books on existentialism are becoming more and more critical. This criticism already begins to be applied to Marcel's philosophy. Joseph Lenz's book, *Der Moderne Deutsche und Französische Existentialismus* (Paulinus-Verlag, Trier, 1951), confirms this. This book appeared first as a series of articles in a journal in 1949–50 and culminated in an appreciative exposition of Marcel's Christian Existentialism. The second edition, however, adding the chief items of the encyclic, remarks in its concluding pages that Marcel, in his opposition to rationalism, was leaning too much towards subjectivism. The crisis and the approaching end of Christian Existentialism are now clearly visible. It is therefore understandable that Marcel himself would now like to be called a neo-Socratic, a title proposed to him by a pupil and, as he thinks, the least inexact title that could be applied to him. In fact, since the days of Kierkegaard, who regarded Socrates as a truly existential thinker, there is a Socratic element in existentialism; but Marcel is far from being a Socratic. A Socratic does not write philosophical diaries, nor does he embrace the Catholic faith as an absolute certainty; he remains groping and searching in his sceptical attitude, talking to ordinary people, asking them unexpected questions, awaking them to the fact of their ignorance, and putting them on the right track. The new label merely reveals Marcel's uneasiness about losing the sanction for his Christian Existentialism.

In his newest publications, especially in *Men Against Humanity* (Harvill Press, London, 1952), he declares "an untiring battle against the spirit of abstraction" in metaphysics as well as in politics to be the *leitmotiv* of his development. He holds that man has a *passion* for abstraction which in politics leads to egalitarianism, fanaticism and mass violence. But is the spirit of abstraction the right target for a philosopher? It may be that some abstractions are abused by fanatics who, however, also abuse concrete religions; but it is likewise certain that language, art, science, philosophy and religion would never have arisen without abstraction. In other words, abstraction as such is neither good nor bad, but may be used for good or evil purposes. Seen from the other side, the struggle against abstractions implies a decision for the concreteness of our experience, and therefore for existence. Consequently it does not lead beyond existentialism. When Marcel adds that his revaluation of words, his attempt to rediscover their original and concrete meaning, denotes a move in the opposite direction, this again leads him into the neighbourhood of Heidegger, whose definition of language as the domicile of being (*Haus des Seins*) is now accepted.[1] We still remain inside existentialism.

I very much doubt that the spirit of abstraction (which, by the way, is itself an abstraction) can be made responsible for political ideologies and for technology. There cannot, however, be any doubt that Marcel responds to the challenge of our time and that he rises to the occasion when he writes:

> To-day, the first and perhaps the only duty of the philosopher is to defend man against himself: to defend man against that extraordinary temptation towards inhumanity to which—almost always without being aware of it—so many human beings to-day have yielded.[2]

This temptation towards inhumanity is especially increased through the possible misuse of technology. And here Marcel makes a valuable contribution to the problems discussed in our second chapter by unmasking what he calls technocracy, *i.e.* the all-pervading power of technology and its nihilistic misuse in society. He has a clear appreciation of the degrading side of technical progress, and attacks the techniques of degradation, *i.e.* "the whole

[1] *Metaphysical Journal*, p. 9.   [2] *Men Against Humanity*, p. 193.

body of methods deliberately put into operation in order to attack and destroy in human persons belonging to some definite class or other their self-respect, and in order to transform them little by little into mere human waste products, conscious of themselves as such, and in the end forced to despair of themselves, not merely at an intellectual level, but in the very depths of their souls." [1] These methods, only too well known from concentration camps, have a tendency to pervade a whole civilization, especially if a propaganda machine makes use of them. Not technology as such is attacked, but the claim of technical knowledge to primacy, the priority of the *know how* before the *know that*, and the concentration on mere technical functioning as opposed to a grasp of reality. Marcel fears that in a technocracy men may become *submen*, more and more reduced to their own specialized function within the state machine. With George Orwell he visualizes a technocratic barbarism which in the hands of a "fanaticized consciousness" may lead man to the edge of the abyss. Here, in his denunciation of inhumanity and of the methods leading to it, Marcel is excellent. He wishes to reawaken in man the feeling that it is an honour to be a man. He regards it as the first ethical commandment to which a philosopher ought to conform, not to sin against the light, but to let the light pass through him. He wants to reinstall the primacy of participation in Being and in Love. "For in the long run all that is not done through Love must invariably end by being done against Love." [2]

In all this, in his attack against the spirit of abstraction, in his defence of the person against the temptations of technocracy and the techniques of degradation, Marcel remains essentially a Christian Existentialist. In all probability, therefore, his protest against this title will be as ineffective as that of Heidegger, because both of them profoundly influenced the existentialist movement. Nevertheless, this protest is most significant: subjectively it illuminates new difficulties in Marcel's self-realization, and objectively it reveals the crisis of Christian Existentialism.

[1] *L.c.*, p. 30.   [2] *L.c.*, p. 55.

IX. THE MYSTICAL ANARCHIST

NICOLAS BERDYAEV, who died at Clamart near Paris on March 23, 1948, at the age of seventy-three, was one of the most human, personally modest, most substantial, catholic, and spiritual philosophers of our age; a philosopher in the original meaning of the word, a lover of wisdom, who was more of a sage and a prophet than a savant; a religious philosopher, whose "conversion" consisted in an act of faith in the power of the spirit. Courageously upholding his belief in the mind and in spiritual realities, he fought for the spiritual integration of Europe and of the world against positivism, materialism and dictatorship of any kind; and was duly imprisoned four times, twice by the old régime in Russia and twice by the new. He was banished by Tzarist Russia to the North; brought to trial and threatened with permanent deportation to Siberia; and finally exiled by the Bolsheviks. Nevertheless, wherever and whenever one met him, whether in Germany, or in his hospitable home at Clamart, or on Broad Street in Oxford, one found him always in good humour, open to all the pressing problems of our age, radiating kindness and creative energy. What was the secret of this man, whose lectures did not seem to be much more than *causeries charmantes*, that made him a spiritual force, conquering first Germany, then France, England and America? Was it that he, the first front-rank Russian philosopher who lived outside Russia, entered into the discussions of Western thinkers, and was able to make good the radical defect of Russian thought, its lack of tradition and of a time-honoured terminology? Or was it that he integrated four or five traditions—that of the great Russian poets and philosophers (like Dostoevsky and Tolstoy whose heroes were of greater importance to him than philosophical and theological schools of thought, and from whom he received his specific brand of Christianity, or the saintly Solovyev who past his last hours in prayer for the Jews and Fyodorov); that of the Slavophils and the Westerners, of Chaadev and Khomyakov, of Herzen and Belinsky, and even of Bakunin and Chernishevsky; that of great European philosophers, of Kant, Schopenhauer, Fichte and Nietzsche; that of great religious thinkers, of Origen, Gregory of Nyssa, St Augustine, Pascal and Kierkegaard; and lastly of the social reformers and socialists, especially of Marx? Or was it that he brought the still unbroken religious and moral substance of the East to a world in which these forces were already in decay?

All these factors combined to produce in Berdyaev the Philo of our age. If Philo, by integrating the traditions. of the Old Testament and of Greece, paved the way for the Middle Ages, Berdyaev, by combining apparently irreconcilable traditions like Theism and Atheism, Personalism and Socialism, Eastern and Western mentality, heralded what he called the New Middle Ages, but which in fact is the coming age of œcumenical civilization and of world unity. His secret was that his creative mind was the meeting-place for many, and potentially for all minds. Suddenly the voices of Alyosha and Ivan Karamazov, Fyodorov, Solovyev, Marx and Nietzsche become alive in his books. His inconsistencies are the expression of the struggle of other spirits within him; they give him, at the same time, his "remarkable insight into the abysmal depths of personality" (C. C. J. Webb). Thus he became a link between East and West, between Christians of different denominations, between Christians and non-Christians, between nations, between past and future, between philosophy and theology, and between the visible and the invisible. He, in his true catholicity, holds the key to a spiritual and religious unity of mankind: "The image of God is in every man. Every man possesses the dignity of a person, even if this person is inhibited or not manifest in him."

Like Philo, and still more like the early Christians, he lived in an age of catastrophe, and shared with them eschatological hopes and fears and an eschatological interpretation of religion. He brought the specifically Russian eschatological interpretation of history to the

West. He is dominated by a violent impetus towards the far, all too far future. Eschatology is to him not what it was to the theologians, a doctrine of the last things, *i.e.* of the end of the world and of humanity, but what it was to the prophets, a visionary anticipation of last things to come. Thus his philosophy becomes prophetic and eschatological in manner and orientation; at the same time it becomes existentialism, because it arises as a response to the catastrophes of our time. If Jaspers and Heidegger respond to the German, Sartre and Marcel to the French tragedies, then Berdyaev responds to the catastrophes of Russia, of Europe, and of Christianity. He thereby becomes of universal significance. A member of the Russian aristocracy and intelligentzia, and always remaining an aristocrat and a dilettante, he witnesses the breakdown and destruction of this class. He bore within him a consciousness of the crisis of historical Christendom, but he still hoped for and awaited a new creative epoch in Christianity. His expulsion from Russia was almost providential, for it made him experience at first hand the very catastrophe of Western civilization predicted long ago by the Slavophils. He did not accept their thesis that this catastrophe was the inevitable outcome of the individualistic atomization of Western life and society, nor did he preach with them that "it is the historical mission of the Orthodox Russians to save their Western brethren from the impending doom by bringing to them the fullness of the Christian truth, life and love, held in the possession of the Orthodox Church and people".[1] He was not, as he has been called, either a representative of the Orthodox Church or a professor. Nevertheless, he came to Europe with a Russian "idea" of a specific kind—he believed in his personal mission to save the West by bringing it the fullness of his personal truth. Thus he became an *eschatological existentialist* of European stature. He universalized the experience of his time. He saw the life of man and of the world torn by contradictions, "which must be faced and maintained in their tension, and which no

---

[1] V. Solovyev, "Lectures on Godmanhood," Introduction (London, 1948), p. 34.

intellectual system of a closed and complete totality, no immanentism or optimism can resolve".[1]

He regarded his philosophy as "existential" because he believed in the priority of the knowing-existing subject over the object, disregarded the knowledge of "objects", dreaded "objectification", preferred intuition to conceptual knowledge, the concrete and particular to the abstract and universal, and existence to essence. "What concerns, absorbs, and haunts me is the destiny of the subject, the microcosm, in which there stirs and throbs the whole universe, and which bears witness to the meaning of its own and the world's existence." [2]

At the same time, this eschatological existentialist reacts violently against any sort of dictatorial régime, be it Tzarist, Bolshevist or Fascist; but he goes much further than Sartre, for he rejects any sort of binding force whatsoever, whether in Society, Civilization or Nature. His individualism becomes thereby a metaphysical nonconformism or anarchism of a very specific kind, *i.e. mystical anarchism*. This again is a specific and rather queer Russian combination, unknown in the West. There have been mystics and anarchists of very different kinds in the West, but never mystical anarchists or anarchical mystics. But this is precisely Berdyaev's case. He is a representative of a group of mystical anarchists which was connected with the revolution of 1905. From Ivan Karamazov's dictum, "I accept God, but I do not accept his world", they derived their slogan "non-acceptance of the world", and combined it with a demand for unconditional and uncompromising freedom of the spirit from all external conditions. Precisely this is Berdyaev's programme and the key to his metaphysical position.

There is something of Lucifer, the eternal rebel, in him. He never concealed his anarchism; but it was not merely a negation of the state, as in the political anarchism of Tolstoy, Bakunin and Kropotkin, but metaphysical anarchism. It represents, objectively, a universal negation of everything that delimits the freedom of the

[1] N. Berdyaev, *Dream and Reality* (London, 1950), p. 93.
[2] *L.c.*, p. 103.

individual, and subjectively, his specific act of negation, or
of nullification (*néantisation*) of whatever obstructs the flow
of his creative imagination.   In spite of his inconsistencies
he was very consistent in his revolutionary attitude.
Revolting against the Russian aristocracy he became a
Marxist; revolting against the Marxist suppression of
freedom and against materialism, he became a revolutionary of the spirit; and scorning the reactionary
attitude of the Russian *émigrés* in Paris, he defended the
October revolution.   He is a moral anarchist, for he
rejects the family, all social institutions and moral laws.
He is a metaphysical anarchist, for he is against any sort
of "objectification".   "My critique of objectification",
he remarks, "denotes an inability to believe in and
rely on the firmness and stability of the 'objective' world,
i.e. the world of our natural and historical environment.
'Objective' things are devoid of ultimate reality; they
are an illusion of our consciousness; they exist only in
proportion to their remoteness from the source of being,
a remoteness which in turn is dependent on a certain state
or orientation of the spirit.   Such remoteness is at any
rate a mark of diminution in reality."   The objectivity
which he attacks is not that of science, but that of things;
he does it on the basis of a world-view which goes back to
Plotinus and Origen, according to which the world is an
emanation from a transcendent source, such that the
remoteness from this source implies a diminution in
reality.   "The objectified world is not the true and real
world", which is the world of the Spirit.   "Only the
subject is ultimately real, 'existential', and only the subject
is capable of knowing reality."   This is an Idealism of
Freedom.   Whereas Being was the highest category from
Aristotle to Jaspers and Heidegger, it is now Freedom.
"Original reality is creative act and freedom, and the
bearer of original reality is the person, the subject, spirit
rather than Being, nature or object.   Objectivity signifies
the enslavement of the spirit to external things: it is
the product of disruption, disunion, estrangement and
enmity." [1]   This is most interesting.   In a certain sense

[1] *L.c.*, p. 286.

it marks a return to Hegel, for here again Nature is in a
state of estrangement in relation to the Creative Mind.
The difference is, that the same idea is here expressed in
the subject-object language. "The world truly exists in
the unobjectified subject." [1] Hegel could not have said
that, and it is characteristic of an age of transition which
rejects the "objectification" of the preceding generation
without having found a new one. The world may exist
potentially, but not actually in the unobjectified subject,
and he, on his part, cannot exist for long without objectification, if he does not want to remain nothing. And is
objectification always enslavement of the spirit? Is this
not an overstatement arising from the violent desire for
the freedom of the spirit?

Seen from this point of view this philosophy is an
inverted Marxism. It rejects matter and materialism as
reactionary; but it does not therefore go back to Hegel's
"mind" and its dialectical movement. Hegel was the
reactionary of the Mind, Berdyaev is the revolutionary
of the Spirit. This Spirit remains transcendent, revealing
itself in isolated flashes to the individual. Like Marx he
wishes to change the world, but rejecting force, he
believes in the creative and transfigurative power of the
Spirit. Having, however, rejected this world, he cannot
but accept an eschatological transformation. "But eschatology is not an invitation to escape into a private
heaven: it is a call to transfigure this evil and stricken
world. It is a witness to the end of this world of ours with
its enslaving objectifications, religious, moral, social and
philosophical alike." [2] This again is completely fantastic.
A revolution of an unreal world at the end of time will not
sound too attractive to a revolutionary who wants a
change of the real world here and now. Berdyaev might
reply that this is a misinterpretation of his intentions, this
transfiguration being anticipated in the "realistic"
creativity of the human mind. "'Realistic' creativity, as
distinct from 'symbolic' creativity, would, in fact, bring
about the transfiguration and the end of this world, and
the emergence of a new heaven and a new earth. The

[1] *L.c.*, p. 286.   [2] *L.c.*, p. 291.

creative act, alike in its power and impotence, is eschatological—a prefiguration of the world to come." [1]   But is
this less fantastic?   Is it more than a dream?   An attempt
to give man that creativity which is being taken away from
God?

This is, in fact, anarchic mysticism.   The *homo mysticus*
prevails in him over the *homo religiosus*.   He believes in a
"universal spirituality", transcending the assumptions of
specific religions, and in a universal mystical experience,
which is likewise a mode of existence and a mode of
knowledge, superior to normal existence and knowledge,
and which establishes a direct and intimate union between
the human spirit and the transcendent spirituality.   As in
Plotinus, Eckhart, Böhme and Angelus Silesius, this
union is achieved by way of ecstasy and by disregarding
all connections with the external world.   His mystical
life is, however, not a continuous evolution, but a series of
isolated flashes, in which alone he really "lives", whereas
he does not like the ordinary life.   It is truly anarchical,
and therefore his literary production in which he incorporates his inspiration and vision is anarchical too.
He creates in acts of rapture, he is being carried away.
His inspiration is flowing so quickly that he cannot follow
in writing, and he leaves blank spaces to be filled in
later on.

This anarchic mysticism is again transformed into a
mystic anarchism in his metaphysics of freedom according
to which freedom precedes being.   It is a mystical theory,
influenced by Böhme, Eckhart and Schelling, the details
of which cannot be discussed here.   In a rather bold
speculation he distinguishes a first freedom, the freedom
of God, originating in the irrational Nothingness which
is hungry for being; a second freedom, experienced by
man participating in the first freedom; and a third
freedom, which is a synthesis of both and which is realized
when God becomes immanent in man. [2]   Freedom, it
would be fair to say, *is* the anarchic mystic's God.

If Jaspers is the gliding philosopher, Berdyaev is the

---

[1] *L.c.*, p. 214.
[2] Cf. *Zeitschrift für Philos. Forschg.*, vol. v, 1, pp. 86 ff.

jumping philosopher, or rather the master-springer who jumps to the end of all things. The impetus for it comes from a vivid experience of the transitoriness of human life "and of the complete lack of solid ground under men's feet", from the expectation and experience of catastrophes, and from the feeling "that the world to-day is tottering to its ruin". Therefore he jumps to an eschatological interpretation of Christianity and of the Universe. "Christianity is the revelation of another world, and to make it conform to this world is to betray it. Eschatological Christianity has and must needs have the effect of a revolution on historical Christianity, because the latter has adapted itself to and fattened itself on the world." [1] Even God has a merely eschatological function. He is neither the creator nor ruler of this world. "He reigns over another Kingdom utterly incommensurable with all the things which this world ascribes to him." "This world is not ruled by God but by the Prince of the World, and his rule is singularly successful." [2] This again is utterly fantastic and arbitrary and amounts to a partial denial and dethronement of God. Psychologically, however, it is not without interest, because it helps us to understand why some of the gnostics and Marcion arrived at a similar world-view.

Berdyaev jumps to the conclusion that the only valid kind of morality is the eschatological one. "Every moral act of love, of mercy and of sacrifice brings to pass the end of the world where hatred, cruelty and selfishness reign supreme. Every creative act entails the end of the kingdom of necessity, servitude and inertia and the promise of a new, an 'other' world, where God's power is revealed in freedom and love." [3] By overcoming the modern schism between religion and ethics he became the *theo-moralist* of our age. Whereas Kant, in his *Moral-theologie*, tried to reduce theology to morals, and God to the giver of the moral law, Berdyaev brought religious life into ethics. Rejecting the autonomy of the human person (in Kant's sense), he does not replace it by theonomy, but by a mystical participation in God's creative activity. He tries to counter Nietzsche's attack against

[1] *L.c.*, p. 291.   [2] *L.c.*, p. 299.   [3] *L.c.*, p. 297.

God by accepting man as co-creator. He wrote the ethics of creativeness which Bergson did not succeed in writing—an ethics which may be described as an activist counterpart to intuitionist ethics. He stressed the particularity of every moral act in its creativeness and understood freedom as creative energy. He believed in the transformation of evil into good, rather than its destruction, and therefore, with Marx, in the transformation, and, with Origen, in the transfiguration of the world. "Not only must all the dead be saved from death and raised to life again, but all must be saved and liberated from hell. Do not build up hell by your will and actions, but do your utmost to destroy it!" What an age, in which Origen's *Apokatastasis panton*, translated into the fantastic language of Russian eschatology, becomes a true expression of our experience! The practical implications of this eschatological ethics are sound and sober. "The practical conclusion derived from this faith turns into an accusation of the age in which I live and into a command to be human in this most inhuman of ages, to guard the image of man, for it is the image of God." [1]

What then is alive and what dead in Berdyaev's philosophy? His personality, his creative impulse, his passion for and his intoxication with freedom, are alive. He is a potential genius, a Boddhisattva who in his next life may become a Buddha. But he is not a real genius because he did not understand that creation calls for industry and work. He did not bother to reduce the vast material to its simplest and most perfect form. He did not see that creation implies the production of form, of structure, and therefore of the Repeatable. He did not grasp the function of repetition and the possibility of perfection within the realm of the Finite. Even the Infinite needs the Finite for its realization. A creative genius like Beethoven experimented with his melodies again and again until they reached the highest possible degree of conciseness and incisiveness, which are both missing in Berdyaev's work. His publications are occasional writings, pamphlets in the great style, rich in

[1] *L.c.*, p. 302.

insights, but no masterpieces. No real development of his thought occurs in them. Together they form a creative chaos, full of inconsistencies and contradictions, but no cosmos or system. He gives *multa*, not *multum*; he is too Russian for the West and too European for the East, but nevertheless a messenger of a new age, in which some sort of synthesis between the spirit of Western Europe and Russia is bound to be attempted.

His anarchical mysticism is dead; it represents a wonderful youthful slogan, but not a ripe and considered standpoint. For, at bottom, anarchism and mysticism are contradictory tendencies. If mysticism means anything it is the union of the human soul with the principle of Life, *i.e.* with Light or with God. Its chief function is to liberate man from the limits or boundaries of his individual existence. In the Infinity of the One the individual loses his identity like a drop in the ocean. What does ecstasis mean but leaving behind body and finite existence? If, however, one desires to be an anarchist at the same time, one cherishes this very same individuality and clings to an extreme individualism. One wants to be oneself and nothing but oneself. One does not want to disappear in the Infinite. That makes a genuine mysticism impossible, and leads to a sort of pseudo-mysticism where God is swallowed by man and not man by God. The individual wishes to be God, he usurps His creative power and relegates God, depriving Him of His power, to the end of all things.

Berdyaev falls a victim to the very chaos of the West which he attempted to overcome. It is all very well to cry for liberty. But freedom in this extreme anarchical form is no liberty at all, in spite of the metaphysical aura by which it is here surrounded; on the contrary, it is just one of the causes of the present chaos. On this point the Slavophils and Solovyev saw much clearer. What Berdyaev exalts, the particular egoistic existence, Solovyev regarded as a "heavy, tortuous and fleeting dream".

The antinomism which follows from his anarchism is likewise dead. It does not make sense to reject the concepts of duty, obligation, oath, contract, vows (like matrimonial vows) as hostile to moral life, and with them all forms of moral rules or laws. And Berdyaev himself, immediately after this rejection, cannot help committing a lovely contradiction by writing: "I considered it a moral duty to defy and to condemn the claims of moralistic and legalistic morality." [1] But if there is one moral duty, does it not imply others as well? In fact, there is no ethics without duty, rules or laws. An eschatological ethics is a mere wish, a pleasant day-dream, but not a possibility which can be realized.

The same must be said of eschatological existentialism. Most interesting as an expression of the desperate crisis of contemporary man, it offers no solution. On the contrary, with its talk of the end of the world it only aggravates the present gloom. The transfiguration of this earth, brought about through the creative act of man, is a mere dream. Is it well dreamt? But what is and should remain alive is the command to be human in this most inhuman of all ages and to guard the image of man, for it is the image of God!

[1] *L.c.*, p. 95.

X. ALIENATION AND BEYOND

I

So far we have considered some existentialist philosophers. We had to discuss them just as they are in their diversity and particularity, and some readers may well have wondered whether they are not so different as human beings, so particular in their language and thought and sometimes so antagonistic to each other that one is unable to see what they have in common. "Even if we agree to call them existentialists", one may object, "we fail to see what that existentialism is on which they agree." We have therefore to return to our starting-point and to repeat the question: What is existentialism? Can this question be answered at all? If it is meant to imply the demand for a real definition, it cannot, for there is no single entity or essence to which this word corresponds. There is not *one* philosophy called existentialism, but several philosophies with profound differences. It is not even possible to make a clear-cut distinction between German philosophers of existence and French existentialists, for Marcel is nearer to Jaspers than to Sartre and therefore rightly calls one of his books *Philosophy of Existence*; Sartre is nearer to Heidegger than to Marcel, and Heidegger would like to form a class of his own as eksistentialist. There is no set of principles common to them all, nor do they share a well-defined method comparable to the dialectic of the Hegelians. Nevertheless they belong together. Children of one and the same age, they are faced with the same challenge to which they have to respond, and are involved in the same predicament. Though their answers are not identical, they move in parallel directions and are, even if opposed to each other, internally related. In other words, the term "existentialism" points to a certain state of mind, to a specific approach or attitude, to a spiritual movement which is of significance in present circumstances and to a specific mode of thought, in any case to something which is alive.

It is a fundamental mistake to assume that what cannot be defined does not exist. On the contrary, anything which is alive cannot be exhausted by definition. I do not deny for a moment that the emphasis on form, *Gestalt*, definition and measurement was of the greatest importance for the development of European science. But we should never forget that life is inexhaustible and that often the formless, which cannot be defined or measured, is the most valuable part of living beings. It is possible to define existentialism in three ways. The first is by ostensive definition, *i.e.* by pointing to existentialists and their books and by saying that what they are doing is existentialism. That we have done. The second is to describe the situation to which they respond and to interpret these philosophies as an expression of the *Zeitgeist*. The third is to change the form of the question and to search for their *function* rather than for their *essence*.

It can hardly be doubted that these philosophies are specific expressions of the *Zeitgeist*, albeit of the first half of the twentieth century. They express something of that which many feel without being able to formulate it. True, it is the feeling of a minority, but of a minority that counts, because it belongs to the intellectual élite. Whilst the majority accepted, voluntarily or forced, the pseudo-philosophies of Marxism, Bolshevism and Fascism, the existentialists defended the rights of the person. It would, however, be incorrect to interpret existentialism as the antithesis to Marxism and Fascism, for on the one hand its battle-front is broader, and on the other, individual existentialists may well be Marxists or Fascists.

The Marxists are therefore not right if they try to explain existentialism away as a last desperate attempt of a declining bourgeoisie, which just before its ultimate submergence clings to an overemphasized individualism as to a life-belt. Existentialism is not the philosophy of a class, and the problems which it discusses transcend the boundaries of a specific group; they are simply human and they reappear within dictatorial states, even in a more pressing, though perhaps insoluble form. Anyone in Russia or her satellite states who wants to be himself in order to live his own life, express his own thought, and practise his own religion, has to experience the agony of existentialist problems. The Bolshevists hate the existentialists as the potential revolutionaries of the future. In fact the existentialists are philosophers of resistance. They attempt to resist the collectivizing trend, bound up with machine production, which seems to lead in any society, whether democratic, fascist or socialist, to a depersonalization of man. This resistance takes various forms. Kierkegaard criticizes the modern tendency towards equality and the levelling brought about by public opinion and the rise of the masses. Jaspers protests against the absorption of man by the machinery of the modern welfare state, Marcel against the increased socialization of life, against the extension of the powers of the State, and against the substitution of the registration card for the person. Most of the French existentialists were members of the Resistance, in deadly opposition to the Nazi oppressors.

The philosophies of existence are philosophies of liberation rather than philosophies of freedom. They attempt to liberate man from the domination of external forces, of society, of the state, and of dictatorial power. They want to set man's authentic self free from the shackles of the unauthentic self. We saw that they experience freedom (Sartre) and that they may formulate a philosophy of freedom (Berdyaev).

Existentialism is in all its forms a philosophy of crisis. It expresses the crisis of man openly and directly, whereas other schools, like that of the Logical Positivists, express it indirectly and unconsciously. For this reason, the fact of estrangement in its enormous complexity and many-sidedness became central with them. To-day it pervades the relations of persons as well as of groups, of classes and races rather than of nations and religious sects. Science and the arts are out of harmony. Science claims to contain the whole of true knowledge. Art, religion and speculative philosophy cannot accept this claim, and contend that wisdom, nurtured by the experience of generations, may be of greater significance than abstract science. Some schools, like those of Gurdieff and Ouspensky, go still further. They reject science as a guide to human action, and build their "Teaching" on esoteric wisdom allegedly coming down to them from primeval times. Hegel's idealistic and Marx's material-istic alienation have led to institutional alienation. Human institutions—the state, the government, the civil service, the party, the factory—have become impersonal and anonymous powers of enormous strength which the individual tries in vain to master. Thence arises the growing sense of frustration, anxiety and despair, which pervades the Western hemisphere. At the back of it all is man's estrangement from Nature, deeply felt by Rousseau and the Romantics; but chiefly that estrangement from God, which is in a certain sense the source of all these troubles and therefore remains a recurrent theme from Kierkegaard to Marcel, and is present, even when not discussed, as in the case of Sartre.

Alienation ends in absurdity, because under its domina-tion the acts of individuals and groups become unco-ordinated. Shall we ridicule or praise Sartre and Camus because of their revelation of *homo absurdus* and of the absurd universe? It is not the universe that is absurd, but man, who projects his absurdity into the world. Nothing is absurd except feelings, thoughts, interpretations, actions or productions of man. Many products of contemporary art and literature are undoubtedly absurd, and in that they are a true mirror of our time. It would, however, be unfair to our age to single it out in this manner. Absurdity is at all times a possibility for human beings though not for animals. It is the price man has to pay for the inexhaustibility and indefiniteness of his nature. If, however, it *actually* dominates him, it points to a *cul-de-sac*, it indicates that a point has been reached where the direction has to be changed. The absurd man needs no refutation, he is his own *reductio ad absurdum*. However, genius and madness, exceptional gifts and absurdity, may co-exist. It would .therefore be a mistake to reject existentialist doctrines as absurdities; for they merely reveal the fact that life on this planet is on the point of becoming absurd. Wherever one looks, whether at the lives of individuals, communities or nations, one cannot help noticing them. The only trouble is, that we fail to see how absurd we ourselves and some of our actions are becoming. Sometimes I cannot help wondering whether Shakespeare's Puck is still about making an ass of many a man who remains quite unaware of his transformation. Are examples really necessary? Everyone knows them: the policy of unconditional surrender followed after a short time by a rearmament of Japan and Germany; the demolition of factories in these countries, which had to be reconstructed after a few months; the United Nations broken up into two hostile camps waging a cold war against each other; and the piling up of arms in both camps for the preservation of peace, but which in very fact enhances the danger of war. "Absurdity of absurdities, all is absurd", seems to be the motto of the contemporary world.

But even if it be granted that existentialism has a representative value by expressing the crisis of our time in its phase of absurdity, the question remains: What then is existentialism? This is the point where we have to change the form of our question. Instead of asking, "What is the essence of existentialism?" we now ask, "What is its function in present circumstances?"

Its first function is to bring about a revaluation of problems and to liberate us from certain traditional problems whether they are material or purely formal and technical. The existentialists maintain that the philosophers of the past overlooked the most pressing problems of man and of human existence. What is the good, they would say, of talking about a transcendent realm of values, if these are not realized here and now in human persons? What alone matters are problems that are lived, directly experienced, suffered and intimately connected with our being; problems in which we are engaged, which form part of ourselves, which we cannot escape. It is a change in the quality of problems, brought about by the climate of the age. The existentialists reject the starting-point of modern philosophers, from

Descartes to the present time, *e.g.* the thesis that nothing but the data of my consciousness are given to me. However these data are interpreted, either with Descartes as "ideas" in their three forms, with Locke as simple ideas, with Hume as impressions, or with Kant as a "chaos of sensations", they are in each case abstractions. Whitehead is right, these philosophers are the victims of the fallacy of misplaced concreteness, they falsely assume that their data are concrete, whereas in fact they are abstract. If these philosophers try to prove or disprove, on the basis of their hypotheses, the existence or non-existence of material objects, of other minds, or of God, they are discussing pseudo-problems. On this point, that is in rejecting certain problems as pseudo-problems, the existentialists are in agreement with the logical positivists. They go, however, much further. They would say that the attempt of the latter to reduce all problems to linguistic problems may again lead to the replacement of real problems by pseudo-problems.

The existentialists have here the function of liberating us from the predominance of analysis. Nobody denies the importance of analysis, but analysis as such is not enough. Analysis is the breaking up of a material or ideal whole into its parts. It can only break down, but not build up. It has been too easily assumed that the model of arithmetical analysis may be applied in psychology and epistemology, *i.e.* that just as all numbers may be broken down into prime numbers, so all our ideas may be analysed into simple ideas. That is what I call the fallacy of simplicity. An analysis into simpler elements is possible, but the so-called simple ideas prove to be very complex, if they are not mere abstractions. Each field of inquiry demands a different form of analysis adequate to its problems. Since in psychology and epistemology the whole is more than its parts, the whole, the totality, the overriding meaning disappears in this sort of analysis. The analysts are inclined to disregard synthesis altogether, in spite of the fact that analysis and synthesis are strictly correlative; or if they acknowledge it, they interpret it in a superficial manner as a "collection of ideas". There is a second sense which may be given to analysis. *Analyser, c'est traduire*, said Hippolyte Taine. In fact, if I am of the opinion that nothing but sense-data are given to me, I have to translate statements about external objects into statements about my sensations. I do not wish to discuss this standpoint here. I can only stress one point. The analysis of ethical statements in the first half of the twentieth century has resulted in greater disagreement than ever before, and we are told that "in some cases disagreement about issues so fundamental arose that certain schools of thought find it unrewarding, if not impossible to communicate with each other".[1] That this should be the case is easily understandable if one notices the arbitrariness of these translations. Stevenson, *e.g.*, would analyse the proposition "this action is right" into: "I approve of it. Do so likewise!" This analysis seems to be completely arbitrary, because the criterion on which the approval is based remains undefined. The danger in all these translations is that they are not equivalent, *i.e.* that they substitute something else foreign to the original meaning. In fact, in both kinds of analysis the negative tendency prevails. In this situation the existentialist would seem to fulfil a useful function by raising the following questions: Is the analysis of ethical statements really the only function of a moral philosopher? Is it not more important to clarify the condition of man, to reveal the danger in which the persons find themselves, to appeal to them to make their own decision and to take the responsibility for their actions, and to discuss the criteria on which the rightness of an action is based? And, generally speaking, is analysis enough? Should we not go on to meta-analysis, *i.e.* to an analysis of analysis on a higher level?[2] Should we not analyse the analysers? Is it not time to see that analysis without the corresponding synthesis is condemned to remain barren and fruitless? Should we not restrict the sphere of influence of analysis

---

[1] *Cf.* R. Firth, "Ethical Absolutism and the Ideal Observer," *Philosophy and Phenomenological Research* (March 1952), vol. xii, p. 317.

[2] Meta-analysis and its function will be precisely defined in a paper earmarked for the *Proceedings* of the XIth International Congress of Philosophy (1953).

within the realm of philosophy and science? The existentialists remind us that there may be some concrete problems of primary importance which are not discussed by analytic science and by analytic philosophy. They concern the existence of human persons.

2

All the existentialists stressed the fact of alienation. Did they succeed in overcoming self-estrangement? The problem of estrangement is, as we saw, multi-dimensional. We have therefore to ask whether there is one solution to it, or whether its different aspects call for diverse remedies. Before attempting an answer, the preliminary somewhat unusual question has to be pondered: Is it at all possible to get rid of this affliction? Will not an element of it always remain because of its having, so to say, metaphysical roots? Is it perhaps our permanent fate to remain foreigners on this earth, in spite of our being at home on it? Is this not even more true of man within the Universe? Though a creature of this world, he nevertheless remains foreign in it. Responding consciously and unconsciously to rays from sun and stars, he does not understand the message they may convey. Cosmic alienation is even greater than earth-alienation. Pantheists and Yogis may believe that they are nearer to the Unity of all beings than to their neighbours and to the earth, but that is a matter of subjective experience and not of verifiable fact. The highest degree of estrangement, *i.e.* a complete break and an unbridgeable gulf, and the lowest degree, where no feeling of difference is left, are seldom realized, but they mark the limits between which the pendulum of our feeling oscillates. There is a limit to our understanding of other persons. In their inner life they all remain, to a certain degree, foreign to us. Is it to be wondered at that this feeling increases if we meet animals, plants, stones or stars?

From this it follows that alienation cannot be completely

eliminated, it can only be reduced to reasonable terms. All we can do is to remove it from the foreground to the background and deprive it of its central position and of its emotional power, but we have to acquiesce in the fact that alienation somehow belongs to our heritage. It brings, moreover, certain advantages with it. It allows us to keep aloof from others in cases where we do not wish to identify ourselves with their doings. In due degree it is to be welcomed so long as it remains less intense than the opposed feeling of togetherness and participation. Normal alienation is healthy, abnormal alienation is morbid, because if dominant it becomes an impediment to creative work, destroying normal relations and transforming trust into mistrust. Therefore all those solutions which assume the possibility of a complete elimination of estrangement seem to be over-simplifications. Neither Hegel's return of the Mind to itself, nor Marx's proletarian revolution, nor Kierkegaard's repetition understood as a restitution of the *status pristinus*, nor Marcel's absolute hope which does not leave room for any sort of despair, offer a definitive solution of the problem, for in spite of them alienation remains. Marcel interprets absolute hope, coupled with absolute faith, as a response of the creature to the infinite Being. Very well; but he adds: "From the moment that I abase myself in some sense before the absolute Thou, who in his infinite condescension has brought me forth out of nothingness, it seems as though I forbid myself ever again to despair, or, more exactly, that I implicitly accept the possibility of despair as an indication of treason, so that I could not give way to it without pronouncing my own condemnation." [1] Indeed, it would be wonderful if man could rid himself of any possibility of despair through a simple act of absolute faith. But is that possible? Does Marcel overlook an unalterable fact of which Kierkegaard was well aware, the inescapable alienation that is bound to arise between any creator and his creation, and therefore between God and His creatures? Having seen the bestial crimes of which some of His creatures are capable, can we

---

[1] *Homo Viator* (trans. by Emma Craufurd) (London, 1951), p. 47

doubt that God's feeling of estrangement towards these creatures must be infinite? And does not God, in spite of all our hopes, wishes and prayers, remain foreign to us? The degree of this alienation may be diminished, but can it be brought down to zero? There may be moments of grace which mystics claim to experience, but in fact it is merely their own mind which is supposed to mirror the Divine: *Es ist der Herren eigner Geist, in dem das Göttliche sich spiegelt*. This fact of man's estrangement from God and from the Universe has nothing to do with the Fall. It follows from the structure of the Universe and from his position in it. Perhaps we are like cuckoos in a nest of swallows. Just as we, living in a foreign country, always remain foreigners, so men would remain foreigners in the Universe even if they were to live hundreds of years. There is a basic incongruity which cannot be eliminated.

Existentialism points here to an urgent problem, or rather to a series of problems, but offers no solution, partly because the problems are so complex and many-sided that no simple solution is possible, and partly because they are, to a certain extent, in principle insoluble.

Shall we reject the whole movement because it has proved unable to solve an insoluble problem? Should we not, on the contrary, repeat the question with which we started: "What is alive and what is dead in Existentialism?" We now see clearly that "existentialist systems", "existentialist logic" and "existentialist ontology" are dead. Existence cannot be systematized; it is a principle of life which escapes all Procrustean systematization. This does not mean that the existentialists are unable to construct philosophies of their own; but if they do, they are bound to transcend the principle of existence. Heidegger, Jaspers, Sartre and Berdyaev illustrate this point. Moreover, reflection, which prevailed over inductive and deductive reasoning in Kierkegaard's, Jaspers's and Marcel's thought, may be a source of an endless dialectical movement, but is hardly the proper basis of a system. In so far as existence can be systematized it ceases to be existence; only if it is not systema-

tized does it remain existence. A "fundamental ontology
of existence" (Heidegger) cannot be constructed, for in
doing so "existence" is taken as a specific kind of being,
i.e. a more fundamental "ontology of being", if the
pleonasm be permitted, is already presupposed. Generally speaking, the German tendency towards an ontological interpretation of existence seems to be misguided.
It is true that man is a being *sui generis,* and that he should
be described with other categories than those applicable to
stones, plants and animals, in spite of the fact that he is a
physico-chemical and organic system and an animal. Let
us also concede that these categories be called "existentialia"; but if we ask what these "existentialia" are
and what the result of this ontological analysis is, we are
told the following. "The structural constituents: (*a*) the
realm of utensils, (*b*) the self as the 'one like many'
. . . in its primarily unauthentic existence, (*c*) the
in-Being with its modes of 'understanding', '*Befind-
lichkeit*', '*Verfallen*', and (*d*) the Being of *Dasein*, Care . . .
—and the unity of the analysed structure may one
day be considered fundamental in a way not altogether dissimilar to Aristotle's doctrine of categories." [1]
Let us assume for brevity's sake that Heidegger's analysis
is correct, and his great success is only to be explained by
the fact that he grasped certain traits characteristic of
contemporary man; but are they traits of man in general
and do they have ontological status? Is understanding a
mode of being? Has care, in its triunity of *Besorgen*
(handling of utensils), *Fürsorge* (care for other persons) and
Selbstsorge (care for one's authentic self), ontological
status? Is it not perhaps merely a mode of behaviour, in
this complexity characteristic of man, but in simpler forms
also to be met with in animals? And does not "care"
imply a judgment of value? I care for something that I
consider worthy of this care. In other words, if one
attempts an ontology of existence one is in danger (1) of
giving ontological status to something which as a mode
of behaviour has no claim to this dignity, (2) of taking

[1] W. Brock, in *Existence and Being,* by Martin Heidegger (London, 1949),
p. 127

something as permanent and universal which is merely temporal and particular, and (3) of confounding judgments of value with statements of fact. The claim to parity with Aristotle's categories is, moreover, unfounded, for the latter were derived from the modes of speech, and therefore neutral to the distinction between object and subject. Aristotle's first category, substance, is applicable to the subject or the self as well as to any object. The possibility of an ontology of existence has still to be demonstrated. Similarly existentialist logic is impossible because logic is the science of correct reasoning, and whatever existence may be, it is certainly not the principle of correct reasoning. In spite of Jaspers's great attempt we have still to wait for the Newton of existentialist logic.

The existentialist philosophers fail because they are unable to find a basis for logic and to give a satisfactory account of science. In so far as they oppose science, reject the objectivity of scientific truth in the name of an alleged existential truth, they are not to be taken seriously. Jaspers experienced the danger implied in this opposition to science during the Nazi régime. He saw that it may lead to the emergence of pseudo-science, to fanatical decisions arrived at in self-willed blindness. "Barriers are erected, man is led into new prisons." He therefore now concludes "that to-day there can be no integrity, reason, or human dignity without a true scientific attitude".[1] In so doing he transcends existentialism proper.

So far the existentialists have failed to provide a new basis for ethics and for a theory of value. Sartre and his friend, Simone de Beauvoir, have seen that an ethics of absurdity does not make sense; but the *Ethics of Ambiguity* which they advertise instead can hardly be accepted as a genuine ethics. If everybody chooses himself as the creator of his own values and rejects all objective values, this absolute freedom seems open to arbitrariness even if qualified by the desire to see others free. If we are told that we have to choose "to will our existence" in its finiteness in such a form that we can pursue it with

[1] *Way to Wisdom* (London, 1951), p. 91.

courage, patience and fidelity, this does not seem to be enough for an ethical choice, for it may be applied to any amoral decision. We still seem to be condemned to wait for an existentialist ethics, while gratefully acknowledging the reality of the concrete problems which are discussed in this school. Does existentialism provide a basis for a new humanism? Sartre claims that it does. But what is this humanism? A humanism of man without God, in which man is his own creator and in which there is no other universe than that of human subjectivity. The only point in which it differs from American materialist humanism is that man is here interpreted as pursuing transcendent aims. Small wonder that Heidegger rejected this sort of humanism but, unfortunately, without caring to substitute a better kind for it.

Nevertheless the existentialists truly reveal the predicament of man at a time when the moral law has lost its Divine sanction and when the individual, unable to fall back on any accepted standard of values, has to make his own solitary decision. The choice of the boy between staying with his mother or joining the Free French Forces, as discussed by Sartre in *Existentialism and Humanism*, represents a real dilemma. In fact, the *problems* of existentialism are alive, for they arise from the *Existenzerschütterung* (shattering of existence) of millions of human beings in Europe and throughout the world. It is by no means a matter of chance that this philosophy arose as a response to national catastrophes, first in Germany after the First World War, then in France after the collapse, and lastly in Italy in similar conditions. The problems of our time have become existential in a manner which differs fundamentally from the way in which questions were asked by the preceding generation. In his autobiography G. E. Moore reports that his philosophical interest was awakened by a discussion between McTaggart and Bertrand Russell. The thesis of the unreality of time gave rise to the question: "What do people mean by saying that time is unreal?" Moore adds that the problems subsequently attracting his attention were always of this type. They were not suggested by "the world or the sciences", but by "things which other philosophers have said about the world or the sciences". For us these apparently secondary, somehow accidental problems are replaced by others which seem to be more central and primary. They arise immediately from our human condition and concern us directly as persons. We are not looking out for problems. The problems choose us. We have to express them. We have to meet their challenge. All of them start from one point and return to it. Because the very existence of man on this earth is menaced, because the annihilation of man, his dehumanization and the destruction of his humanity and of all moral values is a real danger, therefore the meaning of human existence becomes our problem. We have to reinterpret man, his position in the Universe, his relation to his fellow-men and to God. The problems of existentialism are alive in so far as they are, in a narrower sense, expressive of the present crisis of man and, in a broader sense, of the enduring human condition. They are alive first and foremost as *metaphysical problems*. Their importance for the transformation of metaphysics lies in the fact that they are concrete and not abstract, and that they allow us to replace the abstract principle of modern philosophy by a concrete one.[1] Moreover, the existentialist problems have a double function: subjectively, of awakening man from his apathy and of reminding him of his true Self, and objectively, of opening his eyes to a new analysis within the science of man. Indeed the study of Philosophical Anthropology, of Psychology and of Psychopathology, has been stimulated by them. The problems of Phenomenological and Existential Psychology are very much alive, and are actively pursued by Binswanger in Switzerland and by E. Minkowski and his journal, *L'Évolution Psychiatrique*, in France.[2]

The same is true of the moral problems of existentialism. Whatever may be said against Sartre, he forces us to

---

[1] *Cf.* chap. xii.
[2] Besides Sartre's psychological essays, M. Merleau-Ponty's *Phénoménologie de la Perception* and *La Structure du Comportement* are of outstanding importance.

reconsider the formulation of moral problems in the present situation. People are asking for guidance in their moral decisions; one alternative seems to be as good as the other, and it will not do for us to tell them that they should use their own intuition. Intuition may work in a stable society where tradition and accepted standards decide the issue, but not amid the ruins of a shattered world. These are concrete problems concerned with human existence, and not the abstract problems of a hedonic calculus or of the analysis of ethical statements. The man in the street will not understand if we tell him that a philosopher is concerned with nothing but this kind of analysis.

But whatever the attitude of the individual philosopher to these problems may be, even if he should think that they are not his concern, he should still accept the challenge of existentialism. It should help him to overcome the non-existential philosophy of our time. "Non-existential philosophy" is concerned with words or with symbols and their manipulation, with the clarification of scientific propositions or with talk. The linguistic philosophers started with the rejection of metaphysical problems as pseudo-problems, but, alas! they did not foresee that one day they themselves might be enmeshed in linguistic pseudo-problems which they discuss at great length. Linguistic analysis and the distinction of different kinds of symbols are important, but not enough. Words and symbols are only means to an end, and not the end itself. They cannot serve as a final substitute for thinking, not even as the substitute signs of algebra and symbolic logic. A philosopher cannot help asking what they mean. He knows quite well that the word *reality* has different meanings. But even a hard-boiled Logical Positivist can hardly deny that one of these meanings is predominant in the problem of reality when, *e.g.*, a bomb has fallen near him and smashed his leg. He should see that philosophy has something to do with man. It should be an expression of the whole man and not merely of his intellect. It demands a decision of his will as well. His philosophy should be a response to the challenge of his time. He should not try to evade it, and he should not imagine that he could render it non-existent by doing so. Does he perhaps not see what the challenge of our time is? Can he really overlook it? Or does he not wish to see it for the simple reason that he himself is infected with the mortal disease of our age? Whatever formula one may choose, dehumanization of man, annihilation of man, or the question whether man will survive in face of the nihilistic destruction of all human and moral values, the facts are indisputable. Once more the human world resembles the valley full of bones which Ezekiel saw in his vision. And again is the question put to us: "Son of man, can these bones live?" The integration of the diffused and disintegrated parts into a whole, the rehumanization of man, that is the task with which we are confronted. One cannot expect a philosopher to put new breath into dead bones, but one can expect him to remind human beings of what it means to be man. In short, what we need is not Philosophies of Existence, but Existential Philosophers.

XI. WHITHER?

THE reader who has followed us so far may say: "Very well, you have given us an introduction to some existentialists. You have shown us that there are alternatives to linguistic analysis. You have further told us that the existentialists have failed in so far as they attempted to build some sort of system on the principle of existence. This amounts to saying that existentialism as a self-sufficient philosophy is dead. We agree that the problems here discussed are alive, but you have evaded some questions, in particular whether the existentialists are the spiritual leaders of our time, and you have failed to point out *the* alternative way of philosophizing we should choose. Though exploring possible ways, you have not revealed *the* actual way out of the crisis. And that is exactly what we are looking for." I must confess that originally it was not my intention to discuss these points. I do not for a moment pretend that I know the solution. It may even be that *the* solution does not exist. A word of warning must be uttered against those who offer or accept short-cuts which are usually pseudo-solutions. It would be wonderful if the Kingdom of Heaven were just round the corner, but unfortunately it is not the case.

It is somewhat precarious to assess qualities of spiritual leadership in contemporary persons who have never made any such claims. Since, however, the philosophers discussed have played a leading rôle, the problem cannot be evaded. All of them possess traits characteristic of a leader. Heidegger's attitude is so topical that Eduard Herriot, when re-elected President of the French Assembly at the beginning of 1951, adopted it by saying: "You must dispatch the past, ensure the present, and prepare for the future. You are condemned to be heroic." Heroic defiance is necessary in face of deadly danger. But is it possible to base a philosophy on it? I think it is fair to say that Heidegger is essentially the founder of a sect, enormously stimulating through his criticism and exercising a far-reaching influence. But whether he is leading into blind-alleys (*Holzwege*) or into the open, this question is not yet settled. Does it make sense to reject the whole philosophical tradition of the West? One is constantly reminded of Goethe's words:

> Gern wär' ich Überliefrung los
> Und ganz original;
> Doch ist das Unternehmen gross
> Und führt in manche Qual.
> Als Autochthone rechnet' ich
> Es mir zur höchsten Ehre,
> Wenn ich nicht gar zu wunderlich
> Selbst Überliefrung wäre.[1]

"I should like to get rid of tradition and to be completely original; this enterprise is, however, enormous and leads to many sufferings. I would consider it the highest honour to be able to create myself, if I were not, surprisingly, myself the product of tradition."

In fact, if one discounts the originality of terminology, it is the traditional way of ontology which Heidegger regains.

Jaspers is infinitely wiser in rejecting the claim to complete originality, and in reformulating the problems of the *Philosophia Perennis* in a new form. He is the perfect example of the field-exploring or reconnoitring leader. This is a most useful and even indispensable type. However, it should be understood that it may be realized in different modes which, to a certain degree, depend on the historical situation. The discovering type is in search of new facts or of new sciences hitherto undeveloped. Francis Bacon explored the intellectual globe in search of regions not yet cultivated. Descartes, Leibniz and Newton went a step further by creating new sciences. Not so Jaspers. He is exploring too, but more as an historian interested in the forms and the psychological attitudes underlying philosophical systems, as a psychologist studying the variety of normal and abnormal cases, and as a metaphysician penetrating the realm of the possible forms in which truth may be realized. Carrying

---

[1] Sprüche in Reimen, *Sämmtliche Werke*, vol. iii (1840), p. 146.

an overload of historical knowledge his often most elucidating reflection is historically determined; subjectively, in so far as methods and concepts of predecessors creep in, and objectively, in so far as history prevails and nature is sorely neglected. Even in the exploration of possibilities the influence of tradition is enormous. Jaspers transcends the contemporary scene chiefly in order to keep space open for religious faith. This is most useful and a step in the right direction, but not more than a first tentative advance. It would, I think, be fair to say that Jaspers is an actual leader in Psychopathology, and in the Realms of the Past and of the Possible, but that he refrains from showing the way to the future. An actual penetration into the realms of faith and of the unexplored is needed. Even in our days the exploration of the intellectual globe leaves room for discoveries.

Sartre's influence is enormous, but devastating. He is doubtless a leading figure who has an incredible hold on the younger generation in France. He was in all probability an excellent leader of the Resistance, and there his negativity stood him in good stead. But in spite of his enormous gifts, his feel for the needs of his age, his magical power of "appropriating" and mixing all the elements he needs, and in spite of the high entertainment value of his dramas and novels, he does not reach the height of an intellectual leader. He does not believe in the spirit. Instead, he inserts *scènes amoureuses* in his metaphysical tract, a scandal in the history of metaphysics, but most helpful for the sale of the book. Is he perhaps a situation-exploiting pseudo-leader who cashes in on the bewilderment of a generation living in an age of anxiety? It seems as if we had still to wait for a real spiritual leader who, defiant in the face of danger and pretence, combines commitment with detachment, and boldly advances in the direction in which we can follow.

To say that the existentialists are not the true spiritual leaders of our time and to state that existentialism as a system is dead, are only two aspects of one and the same fact. Let us review the position from a higher standpoint, namely from that of the history of man as a spiritual being. *Man for himself;* this seems to be a rather good characterization of contemporary man. He is *man without God,* the heir of Enlightenment and Positivism, of Schopenhauer, Marx, Feuerbach and Nietzsche. He wants to live without God, to be completely free in his choice, his life, his work and his thought. Is existentialism the philosophy of man for himself? At first sight it would seem so. Do not Heidegger's heroic defiance, Sartre's *pour-soi* and his absolute liberty, point to this fact? But if one looks deeper it becomes evident that this forms only the point of departure, and one of the ingredients of existentialism. There is at once the feeling that man is, with others, in a sphere of inter-subjectivity, within the world, in need of communication, and that the possibility of communicating with everyone and everything should be preserved. The uneasiness, created by man's separation from God, is the driving power which animates Kierkegaard and Jaspers as well as Heidegger and Sartre. The will to overcome this separation either from God or from others and from the world is there, but it is felt at once that a contradiction arises between being for oneself and communication with others. "He desires", says Kierkegaard, "at one and the same time to have his thinking in the inwardness of his subjective existence, and yet also to put himself into communication with others. This contradiction cannot possibly (except for thoughtlessness, for which indeed all things are possible) find expression in a direct form." [1] It therefore leads to a dialectic of communication. The will to communication finds itself somehow frustrated, partly because the gulf between man and God is infinite (Kierkegaard), partly because the attitude of the others seems to be hostile (Sartre), partly because the others represent the unauthentic existence of everybody and nobody and threaten to destroy the authentic existence of the Self (Heidegger), and partly because the will to communication with everything is counterbalanced by the desire for detachment (Jaspers).

The result is that existentialism becomes prevalently, though not exclusively, the philosophy of *Man against*

[1] *Concluding Unscientific Postscript* (ed. Lowrie), p. 68.

himself. It is the philosophy of an age where societies as well as individuals are in conflict with themselves. Need it be proved of Kierkegaard who felt "that the outstanding intellectual gifts of our family were only given to us in order that we should rend each other to pieces", and who professed, "The whole of existence is poisoned in my sight, particularly myself"? [1] Need it be repeated that Heidegger is in conflict with all preceding philosophies, with logic and ethics, and with himself? We found in him, on the one hand, an extreme subjectivism, and, on the other, a still more extreme objectivism. Jaspers attempts to combine a thorough detachment and non-identification in the sphere of knowledge and an unconditional imperative in the realm of action. The result is a tension between opposed tendencies and a disconcerting oscillation of thought. That Sartre stresses the antagonistic tendencies in human interrelationships and that his stage is the world of conflict, who can doubt that? Even Berdyaev confesses that contradictions and inconsistencies are inherent in the very nature of his own philosophy and that they cannot and should not be eliminated.

The same may be said of the movement as a whole. On the one hand, the unobjectified subject is glorified by Kierkegaard, Jaspers and Berdyaev. They struggle against objectivity, either as objective reflection or as objectification. On the other hand, the objectivity of Being, independent of any distortion by the subject, is the *leitmotiv* in Heidegger's last philosophy, and operates also, with a slight variation (Being conceived as the subject-object identity), in Jaspers's thought. It has, I hope, become evident that both extremes represent blind alleys. An unobjectified subject is nothing. He cannot persist without objectifying himself. He remains pure possibility without ever reaching reality. It does make sense to protest against Hegel's "objective mind", but it does not make sense to reject every one of the objectifications of Nature and Mind. It is quite true, *qua* historians or in an act of reflection, we may review any number of objects without identifying ourselves with any one of them. But

[1] R. Bretall, *A Kierkegaard Anthology*, p. 11.

it must be understood that these are only secondary activities, not to be mixed up with the creative activities of our mind. On the other hand, to attempt to grasp being as being, independent of the subject, as it reveals itself by itself to us, is a mere illusion. This is exactly what we cannot achieve. We can talk of an object only in so far as it is given in experience.

This split between the extreme subjectivism of the "unobjectified subject" and the extreme objectivism of the "unsubjectified object" arises because existentialism has failed to bridge the gap between Nature and Mind. The alienation between them remains unabated. Here lies the deepest ground for its failure. Jaspers, Heidegger, Sartre and Marcel have nothing to say about Nature. Jaspers preserves the profound Kantian dualism between Nature and the realm of freedom, and therefore his longing for the unity of subject and object remains unsatisfied. The idealism of freedom is unable to give a satisfactory interpretation of Nature.

Mind arises out of Nature. It would not come into being if not as a response to the stimuli of Nature. This is true of all our sense-organs, which develop in response to specific waves, the range of which can be exactly determined in each case. It is also true of our acts of seeing, hearing, smelling, touching, etc. It is no good to object that they represent merely acts of perceiving and have nothing to do with what we commonly call "mind"; for any act of perceiving cannot be reduced to sensing, it implies an act of interpreting. I "sense" certain notes, but I interpret them as Haydn's Symphony No. 100. In fact, our mind could not develop in a completely chaotic world. It is able to conceive forms, shapes and order, and generally speaking regularity because there is regularity. In a certain sense mind *is* nature of a higher order, able to transcend it and to explore the realms of possibility.

A distinction between *natura naturans*, creative nature, and *natura naturata*, created nature, has been made by Spinoza and others. But it is impossible to understand the first without the second. The existentialists are making the mistake of assuming that the *natura naturans* of the mind could exist without its *natura naturata*. Some of them are afraid of the fixity and solidity of its objects, and are anxious not to fix themselves, because that would imply a loss of possibilities. Of course it would; but they would gain reality. They do not see that by telling us that the objects of *natura naturata* are illusions they are making the unobjectified subject still more illusory. Does it really make sense to reflect continuously on one's own existence on the one hand, and on Being on the other, in order to find out in the end what we knew from the beginning, that both are elusive? Would it not be more useful to go on from the realm of mere possibilities to reality, to accept our situation as it really is, and to attempt a new comprehensive interpretation of our experience, implying redistribution of being, meaning and value?

This is exactly the task of metaphysics. There has been an endless discussion on the status of metaphysical propositions which has been fruitless for the simple reason that a well-defined class of such propositions does not exist. It should be understood that a linguistic approach to metaphysics is inadequate. *Metaphysica more linguistico demonstrata* is a contradiction in terms. Instead, we should approach it by way of its problems. Metaphysical problems are *sui generis*, nevertheless they remain problems, and do not become mysteries in Marcel's sense, although they contain a mysterious element. They transcend the finite understanding. They are, in Kantian terminology, problems of reason, and not of the understanding. Problems of the understanding allow of finite analysis, *i.e.* of a breaking up into simpler problems, and of a technical or symbolic solution. In logic, mathematics and physics they may be expressed in mathematical and symbolic language. Theoretically, though not always practically, the problems tackled by different sciences are soluble in principle. The finality of these solutions varies from science to science: is greatest in mathematics and smallest in history. They depend in all cases on certain assumptions which we are making and remain therefore hypothetical and open to correction. We no longer believe in the infallibility of the human understanding. Metaphysical problems differ from scientific ones. They do not allow of finite analysis because they imply an element of infinity or, at least, of indefiniteness; they are comprehensive, though not necessarily all-comprehensive in Jaspers's sense. They are not amenable to mathematical or symbolic treatment, because they are of a qualitative nature which cannot be removed through ratiocination. They are insoluble in principle, *i.e.* from the point of view of the finite understanding. They cannot be analysed into a finite number of propositions or concepts. But this does not imply that they cannot be discussed at all and that they do not allow of any tentative solution whatever. True metaphysical problems cannot be eliminated. One may try to discard them, but nevertheless they reappear, even within science, *e.g.* the mind-body problem in psychology. The problems of existentialism are alive because they are metaphysical.

It cannot be expected of us, at our journey's end, to sketch a new metaphysics; but to point out the direction in which a fruitful advance may be made may not be useless. What is needed is that the state of affairs characterized by the slogan *Man against himself* should be overcome. This is easy to say, but extremely difficult to achieve, because we are up against a human characteristic which, though prevalent in our age, is recurrent in all ages. "To be against oneself" is a specific human trait, nourished by the virtuosity and all the ingenuity of inner reflection, calculation and technology. It may be impossible to eradicate this attitude altogether; nevertheless the aim should be to go on to the stage of *Man with himself*, *i.e.* of Man *with* Man, Man *with* the World, and Man *with* God. Being *with* the world is not identical with being *in* the world, for I can be in the world and nevertheless be against it, or even reject it. This negative attitude prevailed in existentialism. It is most revealing that Heidegger discusses the mode of "being with others" as a *modus deficiens* of authentic existence, namely as the unauthentic mode of day-to-day co-existence. But it may be the other way round. It may be that we are *in* the world, because we are *with* the world. "Being with" implies, in this context, three elements: namely first, to be of the world, to be a part of it, to be co-natural with it; secondly, to respond to it unconsciously by taking part in it; and thirdly, on the level of consciousness, to accept it without eliminating the freedom of decision in each specific case.[1]

There is no room left for developing the consequences of this assumption, which are far-reaching; *e.g.* knowledge by participation, as opposed to knowledge by construction which prevailed in the Modern Era, becomes again possible in a variety of forms. All we can do is attempt to formulate the starting-point, or rather the first axiom of such a philosophy. This will lead us back to the beginning of our inquiry and, at the same time, allow us to elaborate a hypothesis with which we started.

[1] This is, in fact, a return to a primitive attitude. *Cf.* H. & H. A. Frankfort, *The Intellectual Adventure of Ancient Man* (Chicago, 1946), p. 377: "The Hopi . . . working on the land does not set himself in opposition to it. He works *with* the elements, not against them. . . . He is in harmony with the elements, not in conflict; and he does not set out to conquer an opponent. He depends on the corn, but this is part of a mutual inter-dependence, it is not exploitation."

XII. RESPONDEO, ERGO SUM

THE problem is clear. We have to formulate a first axiom which avoids the Scylla of modern subjectivism, from Descartes' *Cogito* to Berdyaev's "unobjectified subject", and the Charybdis of traditional Objectivism, from Parmenides' Being to Heidegger's "unsubjectified object". But how shall we find it? Let me start with a pertinent example. In 1917 Professor Collingwood wrote a book on Truth and Contradiction which he never published. In it he tried to substitute a logic of question and answer for a logic of propositions. He considered it a mistake of traditional logic to take propositions as absolute. He thought a proposition had meaning only as an answer to a question. If we wish to understand a proposition, he maintained, we must know the question it is intended to answer. The *truth* of a proposition consists in its being the *right* answer to that question. Whether there is such a thing as a logic of question and answer seems to me very doubtful, and I am not convinced by Professor A. D. Ritchie's defence of such a possibility. The point Collingwood makes is relevant to historical research. If I wish to understand the fragments of the pre-Socratics, it is essential to know what sort of questions they attempt to answer; but this is an historical problem. It could at best be called epistemological, because it refers to the origin of a specific piece of knowledge. It does not, however, concern logic proper; and a similar kind of argumentation is not applicable to the propositions of logic and mathematics. Collingwood made use of his new logic in his metaphysics, and it is most interesting to compare the chapter on "Question and Answer" in his *Autobiography* with the chapter "On Presupposing" in his *Essay on Metaphysics*. There he repeats that every statement that anybody ever makes is made in answer to a question; and he adds that there must be absolute presuppositions. "An absolute presupposition is one which stands, relatively to all questions to which it is related, as a presupposition, never as an answer." They are postulated because otherwise the process of questioning could go on *ad infinitum.* He is quite right; we have to start in metaphysics, just as in any other science, with first principles. But to call them *absolute* presuppositions and to mix them up with the question-answer relation would seem to be a trifle awkward. To be sure, in the past certain people have taken them as absolute, a fact of psychological and historical interest. Logically, however, they remain relative, hypothetical, open to question, and replaceable at any moment by other principles. The remark that these "absolute presuppositions" are not propositions is interesting, if interpreted as meaning that they are mere rules for the co-ordination of our experience and as such neither true nor false. But I cannot follow Collingwood when he transforms metaphysics into an historical science which inquires what absolute pre-suppositions have been made by physicists in different periods of human history. An inquiry of this sort may be most rewarding, but it is not metaphysics. The point I wish to make is the following. Collingwood has the key-symbol of question and answer in his hands, but instead of using it for the logic of history and for the interpretation of our metaphysical experience, he uses it as a basis for general logic, where it is insufficient, and for transforming metaphysics into its own history, which is misleading. This proves that he was not really a metaphysician, but rather an historian and a philosopher interested in history and its philosophical implications who has done excellent work in this field.

This diversion has, I hope, cleared the ground for introducing *response* instead of "question and answer" as a key-symbol. Response is more general than answer which is restricted to speech. Response is an answer originally given not in words, but in movements, reactions, feelings, impulses, etc. "To respond" may therefore simply mean "to show sensitiveness to stimulus by change of behaviour". In order to make the connection with, and the difference from, Descartes' starting-point as clear as possible, I formulate the first principle as *Respondeo, ergo sum*. I respond, therefore I am. This principle is not offered as a truth of indubitable certainty from which other likewise indubitable propositions could be derived. Like Descartes' *Cogito, ergo sum*, it is a matter-of-fact truth, and not a truth of reason. It does not intend to formulate more than a key-symbol for the co-ordination of the different spheres of our experience, a key-symbol which reveals to us some of the mysteries of human existence. I am in so far as I respond. I arise on all levels of my being (body, sense-organs, soul and mind) only by responding. Man comes into being by an act of response; his evolution consists of interrelated and complicated acts of response. As long as he is alive he responds; when he is dead he no longer responds. In fact, our sense-organs are formed in response to, and as receptacles of, very specific stimuli. They would never have arisen except as an answer to these stimuli, and would be very different in a world in which other stimuli prevailed. The psycho-physical development is based on the so-called response-mechanism. In mankind and higher animals this includes "the sense-organs as *receptors*, which are organized to receive stimulation and to start processes of excitation in the living individual; the *nervous system*, which is specialized for the propagation of excitation; and the muscles and glands or *effectors*, which are specially developed to make reaction possible. It is largely by means of this highly complex total mechanism that the organism is given a functional and integrated unity, and that in turn the integrated individual responds to those physical energies of the environment which effectively stimulate it".[1] Usually at least five months before normal birth such true responses begin, and their history is said to consist in the development of a greater capacity to respond differentially and adaptively to the physical energies of the external world. With the advancement of differentiation and adaptation, and with the rise of consciousness, the purely mechanical circle is broken. We become conscious as to *how* we are

[1] E. G. Boring, *Psychology* (New York, 1935), p. 9.

reacting or how we should respond. Though determined by the stimuli, we are free in the manner in which we respond, and at liberty not to respond at all beyond the sphere of merely mechanical reaction.

Man could be defined as the responsive animal κατ' ἐξοχήν, *i.e.* as that being in which the responsiveness of organic beings reaches its highest peak and its widest application. He possesses the whole range of responses, from automatic, instinctive, unconscious, involuntary, to conditioned, ideo-motor, voluntary and unit responses. He beats the animals by being able to alter the modes of his response, *i.e.* by learning, by responding to signs, and with their help to absent, imaginary or non-existent objects, and by formulating his conscious responses in answers, *i.e.* by speech.

All these responses are being studied by a circle of psychologists which could be called the Response School. Its importance seems to me to lie in the fact that it offers an alternative to Behaviourism and its purely materialistic interpretation of psychological phenomena. This school itself, it is true, regards the stimulus-response relation fundamentally as a relation of cause and effect. "A movement becomes a response when it is known as the effect of a stimulus; a physical event at a receptor becomes a stimulus when it is known as the cause of a response." [1] This view is, however, too narrow. For the stimulus-response relation establishes at the same time and therefore implies a relation of meaning. An example may clarify this. If I am lying on the beach in the sunshine, I may say that the rays of the sun are the cause of my feeling warm; but I can also say that my getting warmer is a sign of the fact that the sun is shining. In a similar manner all our feelings and all our sensations have sign-function. Nor is that all. Our body does not only select those stimuli to which it responds and rejects others present at the same time, it answers simultaneously either positively or negatively. A stimulus opposed to the activity of the organism calls forth a response of opposition or a negative answer, and a stimulus allied to the organism's activity a

[1] E. G. Boring, *The Physical Dimensions of Consciousness* (New York), p. 223.

response of alliance or a positive answer. This implies that the stimuli are either of a positive or a negative value to the organism. Further, when "a stimulus injects greater activity into an active part of the central nervous system than the activity already going on there, it calls forth a *decrease* in activity of the unit itself, whereas one injecting *weaker* activity than that already present evokes an *increase* in activity".[1] Here again the stimuli are of positive or negative value to the organism, according to their ability to increase or decrease its activity. We may therefore conclude that the stimulus-response relation includes relations of being as well as of meaning and of value.

This is the reason why response is so momentous for the human mind. Our feelings, sensations, perceptions and thoughts are imbued by it. This is a point of capital importance. That nothing but the data of our consciousness is given to us, was the almost universally accepted starting-point of modern philosophers, from Descartes and Locke to the present time. True, the Rationalists and Empiricists differed in their interpretation of these data and in their terminology; but they agreed on the following points: (1) that the realm of consciousness is self-sufficient and can be studied in isolation; (2) that its elements are homogeneous so that all of them may be called by the same term, which is *idea* in Descartes' and Locke's terminology; (3) that analysis can be applied to them and that it leads to simple elements, which Locke calls simple ideas; (4) that out of these simple elements (ideas) all the complex ones (ideas) can be formed; (5) that all our knowledge is based on these elements and on the activities of our mind exercised about them, and that it is therefore essentially a knowledge by construction. All these assumptions have to be challenged. We formulate the antitheses: (1) the realm of consciousness is not self-sufficient and cannot be studied in isolation, because the responses are those of the whole man; they occur on, and may be centred in, different levels, subconscious, conscious, and perhaps even supra-conscious; therefore (2) the elements of our experience are not homogeneous, and it is misleading

[1] W. M. Marston and others, *Integrative Psychology* (London, 1931), p. 31

to label all of them under one term such as *ideas*; discontinuity and intermittency is an essential feature of our inner life; (3) it is quite true that analysis should be applied to psychological data; but Locke's analysis is based on the prototype of mathematical analysis; he assumed that just as all numbers may be broken up into prime numbers, so it must be possible to analyse all complex ideas into simple ones; this, however, is a mistake: a new type of analysis appropriate to this field should be chosen; *e.g.* functional analysis, *i.e.* the breaking up of psychological functions into the simpler partial functions out of which they arose through integration;[1] simple ideas do not exist, except in limiting cases; it can be experimentally proved that many of Locke's simple ideas are complex, being integrations out of subconscious elements; (4) it is not the case that in the development of our mind simple ideas precede the formation of complex ones; the *Gestalt*-psychologists have made it probable that perception itself is a form-selecting and form-creating activity, and that what is originally given to us are complex and not simple elements; (5) not all our knowledge is knowledge by construction; besides this type, which plays a great rôle in mathematics and physics and, generally speaking, in theoretical science, there is the important type of knowledge by participation, *i.e.* knowledge which I have because I form part of a group or because I partake in a specific experience or activity.

Our sensations, being answers to external or internal stimuli and therefore signs referring to them, break at once through the isolation of consciousness. They are multi-dimensional, immanent and transcendent, pointing to changes inside and outside; occurring in the present, they are connected with the past and the future. The simple ray which provokes a sensation of red, effects a change in the whole organism, which again is determined by the history of this organism. The range of human responsiveness increases considerably with the development of memory, imagination, understanding and reason;

---

[1] *Cf.* my paper, "The Analysis of 'Experience'," in *Phil. Review*, November 1941.

with the emergence of language and sign-systems; and with man's ability to establish centres of responses on different levels and to move from one of these centres to the other. On the level of memory he responds to the past; the voices of the dead become more real, more essential, and more convincing than those of the living. The imagination enables him to anticipate the future, to make present what is absent, and to accept the creations of poets and artists as part of his own world. The understanding makes it possible for him to respond to sign-systems, to operate them and to grasp their meaning. Finally, on the level of reason, he responds to stimuli coming from the sphere of the Invisible and Transcendent.

The invention of language and sign-systems opens up new fields for human responsiveness with such far-reaching consequences that they cannot be discussed here. It adds the question-answer relation to the stimulus-response relation. It allows man to transform the stimulus into a challenge, to formulate its applications as a question and to make an attempt at answering it. It enables him to make his inarticulate responses at least partially articulate, *i.e.* to express them in words and propositions, and, on the other hand, to formulate questions. The responsive animal becomes an *answering animal*, which is at the same time a *questioning animal*, in the double meaning of seeking information and calling in question. Man starts a dialogue with man, with the universe, and with God.

So far I have attempted to show that the hypothesis, *Respondeo, ergo sum*, formulates a key-symbol on which to base a theory of man and of mind. It plays a rôle in physiology, psychology, biology, anthropology, history, and in the theory of mind. It is, moreover, a truly metaphysical principle because it opens the way to reality. How do I know that my experiences are not mere dreams, fancies or hallucinations? My sensations are real in so far as they are responses. I reach reality, I am real, I have reality, in so far as I respond, and in so far as my responses become answers. I am real, in so far as I am *with* the world and am partaking in the discussion in the world. The stimulus-response relation makes me participate in the life of the world. I am in danger of losing reality if I live an exclusively self-centred life and remain an unobjectified subject. People become unreal if they respond, in anxiety and despair, to "nothing". Man becomes real when, faced with a specific situation, he finds the *right* answer. The fact that my sensations are real does, however, by no means imply that the objects to which they reply are real. The reality of these objects is a different matter, which has to be decided on the merits of the case. The attitude of *Man with himself* differs from that of *Man against himself*; he will plead for a *prima facie* case of trust, whereas the latter begins with mistrust. The former will acknowledge the possibility of expanding the reach of our mind through extra-sensory experience, whereas the latter is inclined to reject everything that he cannot see with his eyes and grasp with his hands.

2

It is impossible to construct a Philosophy of Response in the narrow space at our disposal. All I can do is to point to the fact that response rather than the elusive term existence provides a key-symbol for the reinterpretation of the different fields of our experience, such as science, art, history, ethics and religion, and that it opens up wide fields for new investigation. Response emerges as a term connecting Nature and History, Matter and Mind, and therefore exercises an important function in bridging the gulfs between these realms. In order to achieve this limited purpose we have to redefine *man as an animal of increased and creative responsiveness, able to respond on different levels to stimuli coming from many dimensions, and to formulate his potentially free answers in a variety of ways*. His position among the animals is unique in that he has the possibility of breaking through the natural stimulus-response circle, and liberating himself from the yoke of chiefly passive and automatic responses. An animal lives in its world, emotionally bound up with, and forming part of, its surroundings. Man alone can transcend this closed circle, he alone has the *freedom* of detachment, of saying "yes" and "no" to his emotions and to the objects he encounters. He alone has the faculty of concentrating on certain aspects of these objects, on their being as being, and this enables him to abstract from everything which is without interest at the moment. His answers are potentially bipolar, in two different senses: first, they are answers which raise new questions; and secondly, they move within the polarity of affirmation and negation. In the beginning the two may not be separated, and therefore we find, as Freud and others have pointed out, primitive words which have likewise affirmative and negative connotation, *e.g.* "with" may mean in certain cases "against".

Already animals respond to signs, but these are bound up with certain situations, like the danger calls of birds or the sex calls of cats. *Response to signs* qua *signs* in isolation and the construction of sign-systems is a human prerogative. Man answers with language on three different levels: *i.e.* with ordinary speech and natural language; with the artificial language of logic, mathematics and science; and with the artistic languages of music, painting, sculpture, architecture, etc., which instead of words use sounds, colours, or any other material in order to build up a world of their own. It is important to notice that these artistic languages are languages too, and that they operate with a wordless symbolism. Terminology is arbitrary. Mrs S. K. Langer distinguishes the wordless symbolism of the arts from the discursive symbolism of language by the fact that it is non-discursive and untranslatable, does not allow of definitions within its own system and cannot directly convey generalities. I should prefer to use the term *sign* with reference to natural and artificial language, and the term *symbol* with reference to presentational symbolism. Then it becomes evident that it is a second human prerogative to respond to symbols *qua* symbols with symbolic actions and the creation of symbolic representations. Both sign-response and symbol-response are bound up with *form-response*. So far as we know, man is the only animal which responds to forms *qua* forms, to shapes, to formal relations and to regularities, with the construction of forms, of formal systems or of shapes. This kind of response prevails in mathematicians as well as in musicians; it forms the basis of science and of art.

That response is a key-symbol for psychology and the science of man may be illustrated by the fact that different persons represent specific types of response. There are, *e.g.*, people with unco-ordinated response-centres, where answers arise in different centres like those of sex, volition or æsthetic pleasure, and lead to wobbling and not to clear-cut action. Other people, endowed with extreme sensibility, suggestibility and power of identification with other persons, are of the echo-type. If Leibniz was right in calling the human mind a creative mirror (*schaffender Spiegel*), the mind of these men excels in exact mirroring. These characters are predestined to preserve, as *the* ideal audience, the words of their master. "I shall live no more than I can record, as one should not have more corn growing than one could get in;" said James Boswell; and Eckermann was happy in recording each one of Goethe's words. "There is something miraculous in the manner in which you are able to impress and to excite me by a quiet word, and how my whole essence becomes an echo of thine," wrote Henriette von Willich to Schleiermacher. This response-transformation, very common in women, is by no means restricted to them. "At dead of night you visited me, and it was as if a new soul took possession of me; since this moment I could not leave you," confessed F. H. Jacobi to Goethe with reference to a night in which Goethe inspired him with enthusiasm for Spinoza (letter of July 24, 1774). Goethe's own response was, on the contrary, autonomous. "Everything which affects us", he said, "is merely stimulation, and we have to thank God if something is touched up and we hear a melody."

It would seem to be an admissible hypothesis endowed with a high degree of probability that a group of people enters history and is counted as a nation, as soon as a specific sort of unit-response emerges which differs from that of other nations and which is rich enough to allow of innumerable variations. The world of history is truly responsive, embracing response-circles of different degrees of complexity, latitude and depth, which are partly co-ordinated and partly superimposed on each other. The stimulus-response relation in its enormous qualitative and quantitative range brings out, in the course of time, all the possibilities inherent in humanity. Arnold J. Toynbee in his monumental work, *A Study of History*, has collected a great amount of material for verifying a similar hypothesis of challenge and response. Oddly enough he introduces it as a "myth" in opposition to naturalistic interpretations of history, whereas in fact it is closely connected with biology. His attempt is most provocative and stimulating, although it may be challenged on many points. It is restricted to the special case in which the stimulus is a stimulus of opposition increasing the activity of individuals. Hard countries, new ground, blows, pressures and penalizations are said to act in this manner. The working of alliance-stimuli seems to be overlooked. It is quite true that obstacles increase human activity, but it must be added that (1) a stimulus opposed to the activity of the group calls forth a response of opposition, whereas a stimulus allied to the group-activity evokes a response of alliance; and (2) that an increase in the stimulus is not met in all cases by an increase in the response, but in certain cases by a decrease in the power of the response. True, the challenge of the German aggressor in the Second World War provoked a mighty opposition in Great Britain, but without the stimuli of alliance, and the following actual alliance with the United States and Russia, this country could hardly have survived. These stimuli of alliance cover the same ground, and partly complement and counterbalance the challenges enumerated by Toynbee. Therefore it would also seem to be more appropriate to use here the neutral terms of stimulus and response, and to add that they primarily concern groups in their interrelation with other groups and not their interaction with their natural environment; they further transcend the present and reach out into the past as well as the future.

Our key-symbol allows us further to find a basis for ethics. Man's position in the Universe is unique in that he, as a responding being, becomes answerable for his actions. This is the moral aspect of his freedom. *Respondeo, ergo sum* now means that I am in so far as I accept responsibility for my actions. It is quite impossible to discuss here the complex problem of responsibility in its legal, moral and religious aspect. I can only stress that without responsiveness there would be no responsibility. The latter may be defined, for brevity's sake, as the condition of a free agent who is conscious of having acted in a certain way and has the ability to account for his motives. Responsibility implies the feeling of being answerable to somebody for something, *i.e.* for a course of action which either does or does not conform to a specific rule. It arises, not as total responsibility in total solitude, but either as limited responsibility in specific circumstances or as an absolute responsibility before God.

Finally, our key-symbol allows us to understand religion. Man is the only being able to respond to stimuli outside the "world" of animals. Man alone responds to God, speaks with God, and prays to God. This fact gives us the clue for understanding religion and the mystics, without forcing us to admit the claim of the mystics to experience ultimate reality. The hypothesis is that religion is based on a specific type of responsiveness of the spiritual centre of man to the Transcendent, *i.e.* to powers transcending the sphere of sense-experience. Religion is not based on a feeling of dependence (Schleiermacher), nor is it "the knowledge of the Absolute in a finite consciousness" (Hegel). It is based on a response to the Absolute which has the power of elevating man above the misery of earthly turmoil and of redeeming him. What matters is the manner in which *we* respond, not whether God answers or not. In fact, we can never be sure of an answer. Moreover the Universe, in which to live is our privilege and fate, is merely potentially responsive, but actually, in many respects, utterly unresponsive.

This is the paradox of the human condition. Living in complete insecurity under the constant menace of annihilation, we experience the unreliability of human institutions and the instability of all finite objects. In our despair we are inclined to doubt everything, even God's existence, of whom we cannot and shall not make an image. But at the height of our suffering, when everything seems to break down, suddenly we find ourselves confronted with an unconditional request which we have to answer. In such moments we experience God, and we learn that it is *we* who have to respond. We have to find *our* affirmation, which as a personal truth becomes objective if in very fact it be the right answer to the transcendent call in this specific situation. It is *we* who have to do those actions without which the eternal Light cannot conquer the forces of darkness.

3 [1]

It would be most tempting to add a considerable amount of interesting material for elaborating a philosophy of response, but I have to restrict myself to a few remarks concerning the relation between "existence" and "response". This appears necessary in order to correct some misunderstandings which have arisen (among well-meaning critics and also those who missed the point) concerning the interrelation of these principles, as well as the alleged death of existentialism. My thesis that existence should be replaced by response, calls for the following elucidations and qualifications.

(1) It follows from all I have said that existence cannot become a basis for a systematic philosophy. The axiom, *Existo, ergo sum*, is empty and fruitless. For, if existence is understood in its traditional meaning, the proposition remains an empty tautology. If, however, it is interpreted in Kierkegaard's sense, it indeed succeeds in opening a new way to God; but this way remains indeterminate as such and receives its specific determination only from a specific religion, namely from Christianity. Finally, if one attempts, with Heidegger, an ontological interpretation of existence, this likewise has proved unable to provide a basis for a new ontology because the latter would rest on the foundations of the old ontology. The *Respondeo, ergo sum* on the other hand is neither empty

---

[1] Added in the Second Edition.

nor fruitless. It has a very strong empirical basis in physics, biology, physiology, neurology, psychology, psychopathology and history. It further offers a key to understanding many phenomena within these sciences and many others beyond them, and it elucidates the function of the mind in its connection with, and its difference from, physical and biological processes. I hope to prove this in another book.

(2) "Response" overcomes Kierkegaard's isolation and overestimation of the individual. It at once establishes the possibility of communication on many different levels. It has further the great advantage of absorbing the I-Thou relations of the so-called Dialogical Philosophy of Martin Buber and others, without excluding the I-It relations.

(3) In spite of all this, it preserves what is essential in Kierkegaard's thesis, namely the relation of the individual with the Transcendent, and also important features of existence itself. In fact, the *respondeo, ergo sum* would be transformed into the *existo, ergo sum* if all my answers were existential. For in this case their sum would reveal my existence. Usually, however, this does not happen because not all my answers are existential. What conditions must then be fulfilled in order that they may be called existential? I respond existentially if I make a decision in spite of uncertainty, determine myself by it and at the same time give an answer appropriate to the circumstances. Thereby I gain self-realization and grasp a new aspect of reality. Such my answer *should* be.

This is the essential conclusion which leads us back to the starting-point of this book. Existence in Kierkegaard's sense is not a descriptive term referring to what there is, as it was traditionally. Nor is it a constitutive idea in Kant's sense, *i.e.* an idea on which objective experience, a science or a system, could be based. The category of causality, for instance, was constitutive in his interpretation, because he thought physics to be impossible without it. Rather is existence a regulative idea (Kant), that is to say, a rule prescribing the direction of our search and research. Kant regarded continuity as such an idea. Thus the proposition, *natura non facit saltus*, is not true as a dogmatic statement, but it may regulate our search for missing links in the evolution of species. Existence is, however, not an objectively-regulative idea, *i.e.* one applied by us to the unification of our knowledge beyond the limits of empirical statements, but a subjectively-regulative idea; for it brings unity into the chaos of our personal experience. As such it is of ethical, religious and metaphysical significance and can, and should, be preserved in a philosophy of response. As a general imperative it says: "Your responses shall be existential!" "Within all spheres of your being you shall act in such a manner that you exist in and through your answers!" Morally it implies: "You shall react in such a manner that you are able to accept responsibility for every one of your answers!" As a religious principle it demands: "Reply with absolute responsibility in the face of God!" In metaphysical language it exhorts us: "Answer so that you mirror the Universe in your specific way from your point of view!"

Existence as appeal is therefore preserved. Its call should be heard privately as well as publicly. It may, for instance, help the physicist, releasing the enormous powers of the atom, in the difficult decisions as to the use he should make of his discoveries. For the principle implies that persons are infinitely more valuable than objects of any kind, and it makes the scientist responsible for the consequences arising from the misuse of his discoveries.

In short, existence as a constitutive principle is dead, but it remains alive as a regulative idea. The existentialists were mistaken when they took it as a basis for constructing existentialist systems. They were right in so far as they understood it as a call or appeal. The postulate to become existential in thought and action concerns everybody. An existential philosopher is one whose thought *is* action. Consequently he exists in his action-responses and in them creates himself and his world. He lives up to Fichte's statement: "Philosophy is a transformation, regeneration and renewal of the spirit in its deepest root: the emergence of a new organ and, with it, of a new world in the flux of time."

THEOLOGIA DIABOLI [1]

I

HUMAN societies are to-day secularized to a degree unheard of in former times. Some of them are indifferent and others hostile to religion, some "humanistic", others openly atheistic. There are millions of people to whom nothing is sacred. But why is it that nations soaked in humanism, which have achieved a high standard of material well-being, are nevertheless unhappy? Can a society which has completely lost the sense of the holy reach a state of relative perfection? Further, is it possible to eliminate the sense of the sacred altogether? Or does it reassert itself, if it is artificially suppressed, and then focus itself on pseudo-objects? Has the void created by the disappearance of the holy not to be filled somehow? Have the sociologists, following Durkheim and Robertson Smith, in their attempt to give a sociological explanation of the sacred, not overlooked the vital rôle which it has played and should play in human society?

The relevance of these problems may be illustrated by two outstanding examples representing opposed points of view. Louis Massignon, the famous French Orientalist, gave a remarkable address to the Seminar on the Gandhian Outlook, convened by the Indian National Commission for Co-operation with Unesco at New Delhi in January 1953.[2] He reported how, some forty-four years ago, his life was saved through *Atithi Dharma*, the right of sanctuary. While doing archæological work in Iraq the Montafiq Arabs wanted to kill him as a spy, but an Arab nobleman intervened: "If you kill Massignon you will be killing one of ourselves. He is our guest and a guest is sacred. He is the guest of God and you must not touch him." Massignon would like to see the sacredness of human lives, of places and cities, restored in the

[1] Reprinted by courtesy of the editor of *The Hibbert Journal*.
[2] *Gandhian Outlook and Techniques*, Ministry of Education, Government of India, 1953.

Western world. "We have lost the sense of sacredness. We have lost the sense of Gandhi who was the last of the saints." Whereas this scholar, representing the best French tradition, has to turn to the Arabs and Indians in order to find the sense of sacredness still alive, Sartre reveals the opposite attitude of humanist France. In his latest publications, in *Saint Genet* and in *Le Diable et le bon Dieu*, translated as *Lucifer and the Lord*, his atheistic humanism is developed to its extreme consequences and therewith to its perfection, but fails at the same time. What happens here is of general interest, because it throws a revealing light on the present stage of the human crisis.

It is significant that in both cases an outcast forms the centre of interest. *Lucifer and the Lord* describes the contradictory emotions and actions of a man who, as a bastard son of a nobleman and of a peasant woman, is rejected by both classes and identifies himself sometimes with the interests of the one class and, at other times, with those of the other. The term "outside" (*dehors*) now acquires the sociological meaning of being *déclassé* or being excluded. "Dehors! Refuse ce monde qui ne veut pas de toi! Fais le Mal: tu verras comme on se sent léger (Outside! Reject the world which does not want you! Do evil: and you will see how that will put you at ease!)". He therefore rejects the same society that has excluded him, commits himself to the devil and finds compensation in evil-doing and in revenge.

Saint Genet pursues this rebellion to its extreme possibilities. For Genet is an outcast, not because he is a bastard, but because of his moral equipment as "a gaoled thief, liar, vagabond, homosexual, traitor, and mischievous man" who has been gaoled for theft and who discovered his poetic mission in prison. This work, *Saint Genet, Comédien et Martyr*,[1] a 600-page introduction to Jean Genet's Collected Works, does not fit into any of the traditional book categories. It may be looked at from different perspectives, and it is interesting in each of them. The literary critic and the student of French will read it as a biographical and psychological study of a poet and his works; the psychologist as an example of an existential psycho-analysis, more hampered than helped by a continuous flow of dialectical reflexions which enter and connect all stages of the analysis. The Freudians and the Marxists will certainly react most violently to the claim that the limitations of their respective interpretations are here

[1] Page-references are to the 5th ed., Paris, 1952.

demonstrated; and that only liberty and the choice a person makes of himself, of his life and of the meaning of the universe, is apt to offer a clue to his whole personality, to his style and composition in their formal characteristics, to the structure of his images, and to the particularity of his taste. "The history of an individual as a detailed account of his liberation" —that sounds indeed more Hegelian than Freudian or Marxist. Philosophically the analysis of alienation is remarkable. The attempt is made to describe the stages in which Genet becomes alienated from himself, and this self-alienation is interpreted as a penetration of the other persons into the Self, as a progressive internal assimilation of the judgments of the others and of his condemnation by them. The young Genet is described as an "inhuman product" whose foremost problem is humanization. "How to bring the others to acknowledge his merits? How to become a man, how to become himself?" These problems are said to be insoluble in Genet's case, because the society apparently needs the evil-doer, but not the good man, for the justification of its own existence.

2

This is a point where the book reaches the level of universal significance. It attempts a justification of the criminal, of crime, of evil, in short of the diabolical. Theologically it could be called *Justificatio Diaboli* (*Diabolo-dicy*, if this neologism were allowed), which takes the place of the traditional *Theodicy*. Sartre's apology for the criminal cannot be pursued into all its details, but may be recommended to friends of pornography. That M. Sartre feels impelled to besmear his philosopher's gown by defending a person who describes in detail the abominable *coitus per anum*, testifies to a degradation of Western-European civilization which, alas, is only too similar to that of the late Roman civilization immediately before its fall. Nevertheless, in spite of the repulsive dirt which is thrown up, the study of an unconditionally bad will, *i.e.* of a will which has as its basic structure the intention of doing evil, is philosophically noteworthy. Up to the end, Evil remains Genet's highest aim. Poetry seems to him to be a means for doing evil and for destroying being. He becomes a poet because he is a mischievous man.

What Kant still considered impossible has now become reality. Kant, it is true, accepted the radically Evil (*das radikal Böse*), *i.e.* an inclination common to all men to deviate *occasionally* from the path of the moral law; but he believed a mischievous reason, an absolutely evil will of a devilish being renouncing the moral law in rebellious mood, to be impossible. That is no longer true in the twentieth century. Here indeed the moral law is rejected in revolutionary defiance, and the categorical imperatives of the evil will are formulated at one stage of Genet's dialectical evolution. They are:

(1) Regard every event, even if, and especially when, it is harmful (*nuisible*), as if it were the product of your un-conditioned will and a gratuitous gift which you have decided to make to yourself.

(2) Your principal motive should be the horror that your future action may inspire in others and in yourself.

(3) Act in such a manner that society treats you always as an object and as a means, and never as an end in itself or as a person.

(4) Act as if the maxim of your action could be regarded as a rule in the thieves' tavern (p. 71).

These are rules of a perverted will, evidently formulated in opposition to Kant's ethics and clearly marked by a flavour of absurdity. They express, in the order of their formulation:

(1) The megalomania of a man who would like to possess the creative power of a negative God, *i.e.* of the Devil;

(2) the sadistic cruelty of a character anxious to dominate others and to equal the dictators;

(3) the masochistic self-abasement of a "have-not" who throws his most valuable possession overboard—his personal integrity—and who allows himself to become a mere object and merely a means to an end; and

(4) the cynical contempt of the realm of persons or of the Kantian realm of ends, and the corresponding exaltation of the thieves' tavern!

The formulation of the third maxim reveals, moreover, a rather superficial knowledge of Kant's ethics. Kant rightly demanded:

So act as to treat humanity, whether in thine own person or in that of any other, in every case as an end withal, never as means only.

Sartre overlooks the important qualification "as means *only*". Thus arises an unbearable moral objectification (*Verding-lichung*) and even an enslavement of man who is now deprived of any possibility of liberation and even of freedom itself.

For how could an object and a means be free? Moreover, this maxim remains empty and therefore meaningless, because it is beyond the power of the individual to determine the actions of his society. Nevertheless, these maxims provide a clue for the psycho-analysis of their author, which is best passed over in silence, and for the interpretation of his plays. *Les Morts sans Sépulture* (*The Unburied Dead*) translated under the rather misleading title *Men without Shadow*, and the sacrilegious scenes in *Lucifer and the Lord* are written with the intention of provoking horror. It is even possible and perhaps probable that this catechism of the criminal owes its origin to the same intention.

Besides that, it represents a *reductio ad absurdum* of the moral autonomy, claimed by modern man from Descartes to Kant and Sartre, when the autonomous individual or collective Self is possessed by an evil will. It confirms that the salient point is not that the moral law be *self-given*, but that it is the *right* one. In other words, the principle of *autonomy* has to be replaced by that of *orthonomy*.[1] Sartre's maxims of the autonomous bad will reveal the moral absurdity of nihilism. For all these rules are reducible to the following one: "If you cannot improve your position, let it deteriorate! The worse, the better!" The hope seems to be that nihilism developed to its extreme possibilities will be dialectically transformed into its antithesis.

3

The apology for the criminal is supplemented by the justification of crime and evil itself. This is coupled with an attack on the "respectable people", the just, the judges, or *les salauds* who condemned the thief. The evil man is explained away as a myth or as a projection of the dishonest impulses of the honest man. Everyone struggles against the evil deeds which he himself is tempted to do; he therefore needs the criminal as a scapegoat in order to saddle him with those acts which he himself would like to commit. One is said to condemn the homosexual because oneself would like to be such. A rather abstruse piece of reasoning! Evil itself is declared to be a myth and a projection. Thence it follows as a last consequence: "The Good is nothing but an illusion; the Evil is a Nothingness that creates itself on the ruins of the

[1] *Cf.* my paper, "Autonomy or Orthonomy", *The Hibbert Journal*, July 1949.

Good." Therewith the distinction between good and evil disappears. Both are illusions, both nothing. *Nihil est.*

Thus the atheistic existentialism reaches its final form or its "perfection", *i.e.* a limit beyond which it cannot be pursued. This fact is dramatically expressed in *Lucifer and the Lord* and confirmed by the author himself:

> I have tried to show that Goetz, a freelance captain of mercenaries and an anarchist of evil, destroys nothing when he believes he is destroying the most. He destroys human lives, but cannot disturb society or social judgments; everything he does ends, to his fury, by benefiting the rulers. When, in time, he tries to perform an act of absolute good, and gives his lands to the peasants, this is equally without significance. Whether he tries the absolute through good or through evil, he succeeds only in destroying human lives.[1]

And these lives have evidently lost any value. The man without centre, who is outside himself, reaches here the climax of this centrifugal tendency. Apparently Goetz has made decisions, first for the absolute Evil and then for the absolute Good, merely in order to fall back, in the end, on the absolute Evil. Since it is, however, impossible to incorporate in one's will the Absolute, either in its affirmative or in its negative form, his decisions were merely pseudo-decisions, not self-decisions, *i.e.* such that the Self itself takes shape in them. One cannot become a Self except by identifying oneself with one's own actions, *i.e.* by accepting responsibility for them. However, neither Goetz nor Genet is prepared to do that. They talk as if their former sins were committed by others.

Therefore they founder, and with them Sartre's atheistic existentialism. The term "failure" is borrowed from Jaspers, who receives as thanks a mischievous and completely unjustified kick. The metaphysical aura of "failure" is used for hiding Genet's abortive attempts at self-realization: "Il veut l'impossible pour être sûr de ne pouvoir le réaliser" (p. 182). But it is not only Genet who founders. Sartre himself suffers shipwreck in attempting to base an ethic on his principles. It is literally true of himself what he wrote to Camus:

> Votre moralité s'est d'abord changée en moralisme. Aujourdhui elle n'est plus que littérature, demain elle sera peut-être immoralité.[2]

---

[1] Flap of the French edition, translated by Philip Toynbee.
[2] *Les Temps Modernes* (1952), p. 353.

His attack on the hypocritical bourgeois morality may be justified; but to identify bourgeois morality with ethics generally, to sink both in the ambiguous concept of traditional morality, and to eliminate thereby the distinction between good and evil, between moral actions and crimes, is senseless. It is sensible to defend, with Antigone, the unwritten laws of the human heart against the contingent rulings of the State, or to attack a class morality on the basis of a universal human ethic. If, however, the criticism of traditional ethics is based on nihilism, the result is a moral perversion. Evil is now adored as if it were the Good.

Sartre's moral débâcle follows necessarily from his own assumptions, which are clearly brought out in Simone de Beauvoir's *Ethics of Ambiguity*. She reveals the fact that Sartre's existentialism is a philosophy of ambiguity. Man, according to him, is in an essentially ambiguous position. He desires to live, but is certain of death, he searches for being, but finds non-being, he is a subject, but inevitably makes others his objects and himself becomes an object for them. In this situation freedom represents the only unambiguous fact. "Every man is originally free, in the sense that he casts himself into the world. . . . Freedom is the source from which significations and all values spring. It is the original condition of all justification of existence." Freedom absorbs all moral values and almost substitutes itself for morality. "To will oneself moral and to will oneself free are one and the same decision". These decisions are made by particular men in particular situations whose particularity is as radical and as irreducible as subjectivity itself.

Unfortunately, however, this glorified freedom becomes itself ambiguous and absurd in a condition of ambiguity and absurdity. Sartre desires too much. He wants to be free not only from external and internal causes, but also from objective values which are not created by himself. Contemptuously he calls people who accept a set of objective values respectable and serious men; they prefer mental security to real human freedom. We should instead make an authentic choice by creating our own values and by bestowing value on our actions.

This is Sartre's πρῶτον ψεῦδος. It is impossible to formulate an ethic and to create poetry in an ambiguous and absurd world, bereft of meaning and value. One cannot breathe in a vacuum. Every choice implies that I prefer action A to action B, C, etc. It therefore presupposes an order of preference and a standard, according to which A is to be preferred to B, C, etc. An individual cannot make particular choices without a standard, and as a matter of fact does not create the standard by every action he makes, but accepts it from the society in which he lives and from tradition. The desire to be free from objective values formulated by others remains therefore completely empty, it simply cannot be fulfilled. The trouble with Sartre and his followers is that they have no standards at all. Consequently he is able to accept theft as a means of liberation and Genet's statement: "Je suis allé vers le vol comme vers une libération", and to add: "vers la lumière" (p. 373). In short, Sartre's freedom is no real liberty, but caprice and licence, and therefore insufficient as a basis of ethics. Real freedom consists in accepting responsibility for one's own actions in relation to others within a moral order, and equally for this order itself. A choice is not authentic because it is made by the Self and of the Self, but because it is the *right* choice, *i.e.* it is the choice of the right moral order and of the right action in these particular circumstances, made on the basis of this moral standard. Human societies cannot exist without moral standards if they do not want to perish. If there are no standards, and if nothing is sacred, then of course the difference between good and evil disappears, then the evil may seem to be the myth of the respectable people. It is quite true, neither *the* good people nor *the* bad people exist, but only people to whom the possibility of good and of bad actions is offered at any moment. But the experience of our century has convinced us that Evil is more than a myth and may, at times, become a reality of devastating power.

4

This moral breakdown is not yet the end of the story. Sartre, more interested in dialectics than in truth, presses on. The dialectic of evil will is what really matters in *Lucifer and the Lord* as well as in *Saint Genet*. The remarkable fact, however, is not the transformation of the evil will into the good will, but the replacement of his atheistic humanism by its antithesis. Sartre himself says of *Lucifer and the Lord*: "The play deals entirely with the relationship between man and God, or if you prefer, with the relationship between man and the Absolute." But how is it possible that an atheistic humanist concentrates his attention on the relationship between man and God, especially when he makes the message of God's alleged death part and parcel of his drama? In fact, Goetz has reached only one real decision, namely, the negative one against God. In his megalomania he thinks there is only one opponent worthy of him, namely God. The atheistic humanist struggles consciously against God, but his sub-consciousness forces him to acknowledge against his will that he cannot live without him, because he cannot become himself without God. What he calls God's death was only a re-pression of the idea of God which now reasserts itself with still greater force. Even in his acts of hate and of blasphemy Goetz confirms the power of the Divine. The same happens in *Saint Genet*, though in a somewhat chaotic and sometimes repulsive manner. It reveals itself in a rather abstruse way in Jean-Paul's strivings for holiness and saintliness, in his sanctification of a thief, in Genet's almost insane self-deification, in his esoteric "religion of the thief", in his alleged mysticism and ontological and theological morality.

One may find much of this repulsive and the transition from the thief to the Saint not convincing. "Quand le Mal était possible à ses yeux Genet faisait le Mal pour être méchant; à présent que le Mal se révèle impossible, Genet fera le Mal pour être Saint." (p. 183). Is not the word "Saint" used here in order to embellish something that does not deserve it? "To betray to the limit of despair and self-renunciation which may be called self-denial, that is to *be* a saint." I wonder. We are accustomed to attribute saintliness to the opposite type, *i.e.* to those who do not betray either themselves or their friends or their principles, but who, in the face of death, stand by them fearlessly. Nevertheless, the fact remains that the atheistic humanist feels compelled to talk the language of religion and to use religious categories, such as "sin", "con-version" and the "holy".

Sartre's development runs parallel to that of psychotherapy from Freud to Jung. Freud's psycho-analysis was atheistic and anti-religious, he declared religion to be a childhood-neurosis. Jung, however, found that most neurotic conflicts of his patients who were over thirty-five were of a religious nature, and, generally speaking, that religious symbols arise unconsciously in the souls of men, and that their interpretation is helpful in the treatment of neuroses. The problem is in fact the same in the sphere of human existence and in psycho-logy, namely that of self-realization and of becoming a Self. Man who has lost his centre seems to be unable to find it except in the Transcendent. Sartre confirms this against his own will.

He bears witness that even in an age which seems to have lost the sense of sacredness, and to have fallen back into barbarism, people are unable to live without it. Though his intellect attacks religion and the Divine without mercy, the suppressed feeling of the holy reasserts itself and focuses on persons and objects unworthy of it. Shall we reject Sartre because of it? Or shall we rather point to the ambiguity of the sacred, revealed by Robertson Smith? According to his interpretation, which Durkheim accepted, the holy has two aspects, positive and negative, clean and unclean, saintly and sacrilegious, divine and diabolical. In fact, it happens quite often in primitive religions that something which is unclean or an evil force becomes, by a mere change of external circumstances, a sacred object or a helpful power. Shall we hope that Sartre's philosophy of ambiguity will enable him to find a better appreciation of the meaning and function of the sacred in human societies in its positive aspect? In the end, Massignon is right. The West needs to recover the true sense of sacredness.

II

WILL-O'-THE-WISP?

CONCERNING my interpretation of Heidegger, it was to be expected that I would be accused of missing the point. If, however, one of our contemporaries adds, "the point being in Heidegger's words", "*die Frage nach dem Sinn von* SEIN" ("the question concerning the meaning of BEING"), I am afraid he comes twenty-five years too late. This very point is discussed *in extenso* in my book, *Neue Wege der Philosophie* (Leipzig, 1929), pp. 376 ff., 384 ff., and I may be permitted to refer my critic to that book. The real point at issue is, however, the just estimate of Heidegger's importance. There is no question that his influence has been, and still is, very great. The point is, whether for good or ill. In order to find this out, the reader may turn first to the *Festschrift*, published on the occasion of his sixtieth birthday, *Martin Heideggers Einfluss auf die Wissenschaften*, (Bern, 1949). There his influence on theology, psychology, psychopathology, history, etc. is discussed by specialists. It will be noticed that his influence was enormously stimulating; for instance, Bultmann's "demythologizing" is its outcome. His influence "on the sciences" is, however, more or less restricted to "German" sciences.

Heidegger is a specific Teutonic phenomenon. His thought is bound up with the German language and is strictly speaking untranslatable. Moreover, only in Germany could someone be held in the highest esteem who continues claiming for about thirty years that he will say something important, and in fact never says it. This point may be illustrated by his recently published *Einführung in die Metaphysik* (Tübingen, 1953), which is in reality a course of lectures delivered in 1935. It may be recommended as a relatively easy introduction to his metaphysics which, however, is not the new one but the old one. It centres in the Greek problem of the essence of being which, in opposition to becoming, semblance, thought and obligation (*Sollen*), is defined as constant presence: $\overset{,}{o}v$ as $o\overset{,}{v}\sigma i\alpha$. In the end we are where we were some two thousand years ago, and the final claim that the formula "Being and Time", replacing the old one of "Being and Thought" opens up new vistas, remains unfulfilled.

In spite of the uncritical adherence of my critic to his master, a revaluation of Heidegger's thought seems to be imperative, in the interests not only of Germany, but of the whole of Europe. He misled the German youth in 1933, and is apt to mislead it again in the future. I am glad to see that one of his former pupils, Karl Löwith, in *Heidegger, ·Denker in dürftiger Zeit* (Frankfurt, 1953), gives a sober, penetrating and balanced account of his thought which in all essentials confirms my interpretation. He says:

> "Heidegger has managed to give new standards to a whole generation of students, to convince them that 'logic' and 'reason' (*Vernunft*) have to be dissolved 'in a whirlwind of a more fundamental kind of questioning', that ethics, civilization and humaneness (*Humanität*) . . . are no serious concern of ours, that man is not the *animal rationale*, but an ecstatic 'shepherd of Being', and that all theoretical imagination and technological construction, on which scientific thought is said to be based, represent the fall of subjectivity which becomes a prey of its corresponding objectivity and of absolute 'objectification' (*Vergegenständlichung*)" (p. 16).

Can such an influence be called other than catastrophic?

What are we to say of a man who calls the earth *Unwelt der Irrnis* and *Irrstern* (*i.e.* "misfigured world of error" and "star of error") in order to find a metaphysical excuse for his previous misjudgment of the Nazi régime and for his present, and possibly future, misjudgment of the Bolshevists? Can we avoid the conclusion that we are faced with an enormously gifted, but potentially misleading and wholly irresponsible *Irrgeist*? A disillusionment about Heidegger would seem to be a prerequisite for a new start of Continental philosophy. It remains, however, true as Goethe said (whom Heidegger subordinates to Hölderlin in his misjudgment):

> *Es irrt der Mensch, solang er strebt* ("Men err, so long as they are striving").

And I shall not be surprised if one day the former Jesuit novice returns as the Prodigal Son to his father's house.

III

FROM EXISTENCE TO ESSENCE?

ROGER TROISFONTAINES' *De l'Existence à l'Être. La Philosophie de Gabriel Marcel* (Louvain, 1953) represents, with its two enormous volumes, the most comprehensive and most penetrating study of this philosopher. In a charming preface Marcel stresses the tentative (*heuristique*) character of his exploratory method, and is nevertheless grateful to his friend and spiritual child for the strictly systematic representation of his ideas. He accepts the interpretation of his thought as leading from Existentialism to Essentialism. A philosophy of participation or *une philosophie de la présence*, similar to Louis Lavelle's conception, is the outcome. "Existence" is now interpreted as an unconscious participation in reality, and "Being" refers to a conscious free participation in which the person as such is constituted. The four forms of participation—in the world, in oneself, in others, and in God—provide the chief structural articulation of the work. A quite new Marcel emerges, whose thought is wonderfully systematized and in strict conformity with the Thomist teaching of the Catholic Church, but it is more a possible Marcel than the real one of the *pensée pensante*. The enormous and valuable bibliography proves, moreover, that the latter still prevails and covers vast realms of literary exploration. I am not here concerned with a criticism of this book, which is a labour of love, devoted to exposition and to pleading and not to judging, and which is of the greatest help in elucidating special topics. I can only mention two points which confirm my interpretation.

First, Marcel is quoted as having said at Madrid in 1950 that philosophical reflexion ought to concentrate on the "essences" in Plato's sense:

> "On ne saurait s'élever trop énergiquement contre un existentialisme caricatural qui prétend dévaluer l'essence et de ne lui accorder qu'un statut subalterne. Ceci ne veut d'ailleurs dire que les essences n'aient pas à être repensées à partir d'une philosophie qui affirme le primat de la subjectivité ou plus exactement d'une intersubjectivité dont la pensée scolastique a le plus souvent méconnu les droits" (I, p. 147).

The "existentialisme caricatural" which is here rejected is of course Sartre's standpoint, but Marcel's rejection goes much further. Since 1948 he always declared, when he met the word existentialism: "As far as I am concerned, this word shall not be pronounced any more". In 1951 he even spoke of "l'affreux vocable existentialisme". It can hardly be called an over-statement if these words of the leading Christian existentialist are taken as a confirmation of the crisis of Christian existentialism. The primacy of subjectivity, or rather intersubjectivity, is, nevertheless, reaffirmed.

Secondly, in this new interpretation quite a few points emerge which make it clear that Marcel is on the way to a philosophy of response. "The question: *Who am I?* now becomes: *What is my vocation?* To which appeal have I to respond with an act of commitment in order to confer an ontological significance on my life?" I would say that here also existence as appeal and call is preserved. Moreover, "response as an act of commitment" can hardly be mistaken for a reaction. Those of my readers who have misinterpreted "response" as "mechanical and biological reaction" may be reminded of the fact that a response may occur without a reaction. The Indian Guru, for instance, remains silent when a pupil asks him a specific question, and the pupil finds his answer in this silence. "Response by silence" certainly transcends the biological sphere. It is by no means unknown in the West, and has played a considerable rôle in the French *Théâtre du Silence* or *Théâtre de l'Inexprimé*.[1] The language of silence may sometimes be even more effective than the spoken word. Whenever you cannot reply with words, you may still respond with silence.

[1] *Cf.* May Daniels, *The French Drama of the Unspoken*, London, 1953.

BIBLIOGRAPHICAL NOTES

There is no necessity for a complete bibliography, because the following bibliographies are already in existence.

A. GENERAL BIBLIOGRAPHIES

Revue Internationale de Philosophie (Juillet 1949), no. 9, pp. 343 ff., includes a bibliography of Italian Existentialism. Addendum in no. 10, pp. 502 ff. (The whole no. 9 is devoted to "L'existentialisme devant l'opinion philosophique.")

YANITELLI, VICTOR R., S.J., "A Bibliographical Introduction to Existentialism," *The Modern Schoolman*, vol. xxvi, no. 4, May 1949.

DOUGLAS, KENNETH, *A Critical Bibliography of Existentialism* (*The Paris School*), Yale French Studies Special Monograph No. 1, New Haven, Conn., 1950. (Most useful.)

JOLIVET, RÉGIS, *Französische Existenzphilosophie*, A. Francke, Bern, 1948 (with useful summaries).

Archivio di Filosofia (Organo del R. Istituto di Studi Filosofici), Roma, anno XV, vols. i e ii, 1946. (Most comprehensive bibliography of Italian Existentialism, supplemented in later volumes.)

BOLLNOW, O. F., *Deutsche Existenzphilosophie*, Bern, 1954.

B. SPECIAL BIBLIOGRAPHIES

JOLIVET, RÉGIS, *Kierkegaard*, A. Francke, Bern, 1948 (with helpful summaries).

ORTMANN NIELSEN, EDITH, and THULSTRUP, NIELS, *Sören Kierkegaard. Contributions towards a Bibliography*, Ejnar Munskgaard, Copenhagen, 1951. (Of interest only to the specialist; only those works and articles are listed which are accessible in Danish libraries.)

WAHL, JEAN, *Études Kierkegaardiennes*, Aubier, Paris (2 éd., 1949). (Is, at the same time, one of the most penetrating studies of Kierkegaard's thought, and discusses his influence on Heidegger and Jaspers.)

PATOCKA, JAN, "Husserl Bibliographie," in *Revue Internationale de Philosophie*, no. 2 (Janvier 1939), pp. 374 ff. (The whole issue is devoted to Husserl.) Supplement in the same *Revue*, no. 14 (October 1950), pp. 469 ff.

FARBER, M., in *Philosophical Essays in Memory of Edmund Husserl*, Harvard University Press, 1940.

For a comprehensive bibliography of Jaspers's publications, cf. *Offener Horizont, Festschrift für Karl Jaspers* (München, 1953), pp. 449 ff.

For Heidegger, *cf.* De Waelhens, Alphonse, *La Philosophie de Martin Heidegger*, Bibliothèque Philosophique de Louvain, Louvain, 1942. (The most comprehensive monograph so far devoted to Heidegger.)

Douglas's above-named bibliography contains a complete bibliography of Sartre's, Simone de Beauvoir's and Maurice Merleau-Ponty's publications and of books and articles referring to them.

New publications are listed in *Bibliographie de la Philosophie*, J. Vrin, Paris, and in *Bulletin Analytique*, *Philosophie*, Centre National de la Recherche Scientifique, Paris.

For Marcel, *cf.* R. Troisfontaines', *De L'Existence à L'Être* (Louvain, 1953), vol. II, pp. 381 ff.

C. INDIVIDUAL AUTHORS

The study of the works in their original language is indispensable for a deeper understanding of most existentialists, because it is almost impossible to translate them adequately. Nevertheless, for the convenience of the reader, only the English translations are quoted, together with the more important secondary sources.

I. KIERKEGAARD

R. BRETALL, *A Kierkegaard Anthology*, Princeton University Press and Oxford University Press, 1946. (Useful for a first orientation.)

The Concluding Unscientific Postscript; The Point of View for my Work as an Author; The Present Age; Repetition; The Sickness unto Death; The Concept of Dread, and other works, translated by D. F. Swenson, W. Lowrie and A. Dru, are published by the Oxford University Press and by the Princeton University Press.

LOWRIE, W., *Kierkegaard*, Oxford and Princeton University Press, 1936. (Excellent biography, with many extracts from his books and journals.)

II. Husserl

"Phenomenology." Article in the *Encyclopædia Britannica*,
    1927 (14th ed.), vol. 17, pp. 699–702.
Ideas: An Introduction to Pure Phenomenology (translation by
    W. R. Boyce Gibson), Allen & Unwin, London, 1931.

His influence in the English-speaking world would probably
have been greater if his *Logische Untersuchungen* had been
translated instead. I understand that this is now being done
in America.

The International Phenomenological Society publishes *Philosophy and Phenomenological Research*, a quarterly journal,
edited by Marvin Farber.

Husserl's literary remains, consisting of more than 40,000
pages in his own shorthand writing, are now in the Husserl-
Archiv in Louvain. Its director is the chief editor of *Husserl-
iana*, of which so far five volumes have appeared, published
by Martinus Nijhoff, The Hague.

III. Jaspers

Man in the Modern Age (translation by E. and C. Paul), Kegan
    Paul & Henry Holt & Co. Revised edition 1952.
The Perennial Scope of Philosophy (translation by R. Manheim),
    Kegan Paul and Philosophical Library, New York, 1950.
The European Spirit (translated, with an Introduction by
    Gregor Smith), S.C.M. Press, 1948.
"Philosophy and Science," in *World Review*, March 1950.
"The Importance of Nietzsche, Marx and Kierkegaard," in
    The Hibbert Journal, April 1951.
Way to Wisdom: An Introduction to Philosophy, Gollancz, 1951.
Reason and Anti-Reason in our Time, S.C.M. Press, 1952.
Rechenschaft und Ausblick. Reden und Aufsätze, Piper, München,
    1951. (With interesting autobiographical sketches.)
The *Psychopathologie* is being translated.
Dufrenne, M., and Ricœur, P., *Karl Jaspers et la philosophie
    de l'existence*, 1947. (Good, but not up-to-date.)
Tragedy is not enough (translation by A. T. Reiche, H. T. Moore
    and K. W. Deutsch), Gollancz, 1953.
The Origin and Goal of History, Routledge, 1953.

IV. Heidegger

Existence and Being, Vision Press, 1949. (A translation of four essays, with a long, penetrating introduction by Werner Brock.)

Comprehensive bibliography in O. F. Bollnow, *Deutsche Existenzphilosophie*, Bern, 1953.

DE WAELHENS, A., *La Philosophie de Martin Heidegger*, Institut supérieur de Philosophie, Louvain, 1942.

LÖWITH, K., *Heidegger. Denker in dürftiger Zeit*. Frankfurt, 1953.

V. Sartre

Existentialism and Humanism (translation and introduction by Philip Mairet), Methuen, 1950.

Baudelaire (translation by Martin Turnell), Horizon, 1949.

Portrait of the Anti-Semite (translation by Erik de Mauny), Secker & Warburg, 1948.

What is Literature? (translation by Bernard Frechtman), Methuen, 1950.

The Psychology of the Imagination, Rider, 1951. (This is a translation of *L'Imaginaire, Psychologie Phénoménologique de l'Imagination*, Paris, 1940, and not of *L'Imagination*, Paris, 1940.)

DE WAELHENS, A., "J. P. Sartre, L'être et le néant," *Erasmus*, vol. i, col. 521 ff. May 1947.

VI. Marcel

The Philosophy of Existence (translation by Manya Harari), The Harvill Press, 1948.

The Mystery of Being. Two volumes. The Harvill Press, 1950–51.

Being and Having (translation by Katharine Farrer), Dacre Press, 1950.

Men Against Humanity (translation by G. S. Fraser), The Harvill Press, 1952.

Metaphysical Journal (translation by Bernard Wall), Rockliff, 1952.

Homo Viator (translation by Emma Craufurd), Gollancz, 1951.

GILSON, ÉT., and others, *Existentialisme Chrétien: Gabriel Marcel*, Plon, Paris, 1947.

WAHL, J., "*Le journal métaphysique de Gabriel Marcel*," in *Revue de Métaphysique et de Morale*, January 1930, reprinted in *Vers le concret*, 1932.

RICŒUR, P., *Gabriel Marcel et Karl Jaspers*, "Écrivains du temps présent," Paris, 1948.

TROISFONTAINES, R., *cf.* under B.

VII. BERDYAEV

There is no better introduction to Berdyaev than his Essay in Autobiography: *Dream and Reality*, Geoffrey Bles, 1950. It is the best guide to his writings, most of which have been translated and are also published by Bles. *The Destiny of Man* is the most important of them.

CLARKE, O. F., *Introduction to Berdyaev*, Geoffrey Bles, 1950. (Based on personal acquaintance.)

VIII. VARIA

LUKACS, GEORGE, *Existentialisme ou Marxisme?* Paris, 1948. (Marxist criticism of Existentialism.)

LENZ, JOSEPH, *Der moderne deutsche und französische Existentialismus*, Paulinus-Verlag, Trier, 1951. (A sober and objective assessment of the movement from the official Catholic point of view.)

GILSON, ÉT., *Being and Some Philosophers*, Pontifical Institute of Mediæval Studies, Toronto, 1949. (A neo-Thomist attempt to incorporate existentialist elements in Thomism, which is interpreted as a synthesis of essence and existence.)

CAMUS, ALBERT, *Le Mythe de Sisyphe* (27th ed.), Gallimard, Paris, 1942. (Interesting as an expression of the *sensibilité absurde*; Camus, though influenced by the existentialists, is not an existentialist.)

DE WAELHENS, A., *Une Philosophie de l'Ambiguité. L'existentialisme de Maurice Merleau-Ponty*, Publications Universitaires de Louvain, 1951.

KNITTERMEYER, H., *Die Philosophie der Existenz*, Humboldt Verlag, Wien, 1952. (With bibliographies of recent German contributions.)

IX. ADDENDA TO 1958 EDITION

For books by Husserl, Heidegger and Jaspers, published after 1954, see my recent Surveys of German Philosophy in the journal *Philosophy*, London, as well as the second German edition of the present book (Kohlhammer, Stuttgart, 1957). This may also be consulted for Sartre, especially for his early phenomenological writings and his study of imagination.

Sartre's *Being and Nothingness* is now available in a translation by Hazel Barnes, Philosophical Library, New York, 1957. *Existentialism from Dostoevsky to Sartre,* edited by Walter Kaufmann, Meridian, New York, 1957, is a rather personal selection of philosophical and literary pieces.

The Jaspers bibliography is brought up-to-date in the *Karl Jaspers* volume of the *Library of Living Philosophers,* edited by P. A. Schilpp. To date only the German edition has appeared (Kohlhammer, Stuttgart). It should be consulted for Jaspers' "Philosophical Autobiography" and his "Postscript" and for the German contributions. See also the Postscript to the third edition of his *Philosophie* (Berlin, 1956), and the Postscript to the second edition of his *Existenzphilosophie* (Berlin, 1956), in which he explains the situation out of which these lectures arose and notes my priority in coining this term.

For "Existentialism and Religion" see H. W. Bartsch, *Kerygma and Myth,* translated by R. H. Fuller, Macmillan, New York, 1953. (The German edition contains a discussion between Rudolf Bultmann and Jaspers in the third volume.)

DAVIS, G. W., *Existentialism and Theology* New York, 1957, refers to Bultmann.

ROBERTS, D. E., *Existentialism and Religious Belief,* Oxford University Press, New York, 1957.

MICHALSON, C., ed., *Christianity and the Existentialists,* Charles Scribner's Sons, New York, 1956.

MACQUARRIE, J., *An Existentialist Theology.* A Comparison of Heidegger and Bultmann. Macmillan, New York, 1956.

For the discussion between Existentialism and Marxism, see M. Merleau-Ponty, *Les Aventures de la Dialectique,* Paris, 1955; Raymond Aron, *The Opium of the Intellectuals,*

London, 1957; A. Duhrssen, "Some French Hegelians" in *The Review of Metaphysics*, VII, 2.

For the Italian "positive existentialism" see Nicola Abbagnano's publications, his "Collezione de Filosofia" and his journal *Rivista di Filosofia*.

For Spain see J. Marias, "Presence and Absence of Existentialism in Spain" in *Philosophy and Phenomenological Research*, XV, 2.

"Existentialism and Psychotherapy": for Jaspers see the relevant papers in *Offener Horizont* and in the Schilpp volume.

Paradoxically, Heidegger's influence is far greater and has given rise to the school of the *Daseinsanalytiker* (Binswanger, Boss, Kuhn). The following works may be recommended: Ludwig Binswanger, *Der Mensch in der Psychiatrie* (Pfullingen, 1957); *Grundformen und Erkenntnis menschlichen Daseins* (Zürich, 1942).

A sober criticism of this school by a leading psychiatrist is contained in Eugen Kahn's "Wieder einmal: die Daseinsanalyse," *Psychiatrica et Neurologica*, Vol. 133, No. 6, 1957 (S. Karger, Basel and New York).

INDEX